CITY OF SCOUNDRELS

CITY OF SCOUNDRELS

The Twelve Days of Disaster That Gave Birth to Modern Chicago

GARY KRIST

WITHDRAWN

CROWN PUBLISHERS
NEW YORK

Copyright © 2012 by Gary Krist

Published in the United States by Crown Publishers, an imprint of the
Crown Publishing Group, a division of Random House, Inc., New York.
www.crownpublishing.com

CROWN and the Crown colophon are registered trademarks
of Random House, Inc.

Library of Congress Cataloging-in-Publication Data
Krist, Gary.
City of scoundrels: the twelve days of disaster that gave birth
to modern Chicago/Gary Krist.—1st ed.
p.   cm.
Includes bibliographical references and index.
1. Chicago (Ill.)—History—20th century.   2. Disasters—Illinois—Chicago—
History—20th century.   3. Chicago (Ill.)—Civilization.   I. Title.
F548.5.K75 2012
977.3'11042—dc22   2011010906

ISBN 978-0-307-45429-4
eISBN 978-0-307-45431-7

Printed in the United States of America

Book design by Leonard W. Henderson
Map designed by Jeffrey L. Ward
Jacket design by Laura Duffy
Jacket illustration: Rob Wood/Wood Ronsaville Harlin, Inc.

1 3 5 7 9 10 8 6 4 2

First Edition

For Anna,

my favorite Chicagoan

AUTHOR'S NOTE

City of Scoundrels is a work of nonfiction, adhering strictly to the historical record and incorporating no invented dialogue or other undocumented re-creations. Unless otherwise attributed, anything between quotation marks is either actual dialogue (as reported by a witness or in a newspaper) or else a citation from a diary, memoir, book, letter, telegram, court transcript, or other document, as cited in the notes. In some quotations I have, for clarity's sake, silently corrected the original spelling, syntax, or punctuation. Since reporters of the day lacked modern recording technology, different newspaper or other reports about the same event occasionally have slightly differing versions of what was said or done; in these cases, I have sometimes combined elements from several different accounts of an event, speech, or conversation to create what I hope is a more complete picture of what actually occurred.

CONTENTS

Great wars have been followed by an unusually large number of killings between private citizens and individuals.

—Clarence Darrow

It came to me then that I had been fighting the wrong war. The Germans weren't the enemy. The enemy was right here at home.

—Harry Haywood

Chicago ain't no Sunday School.

—"Bathhouse John" Coughlin

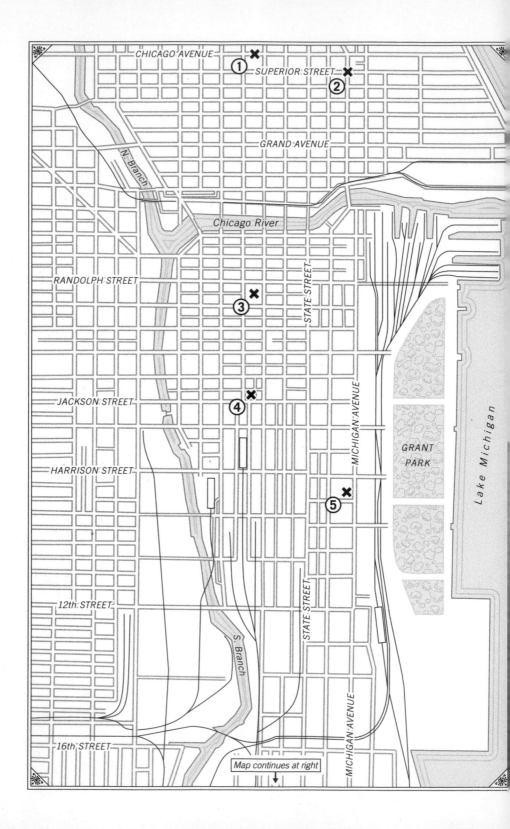

Map continues at right

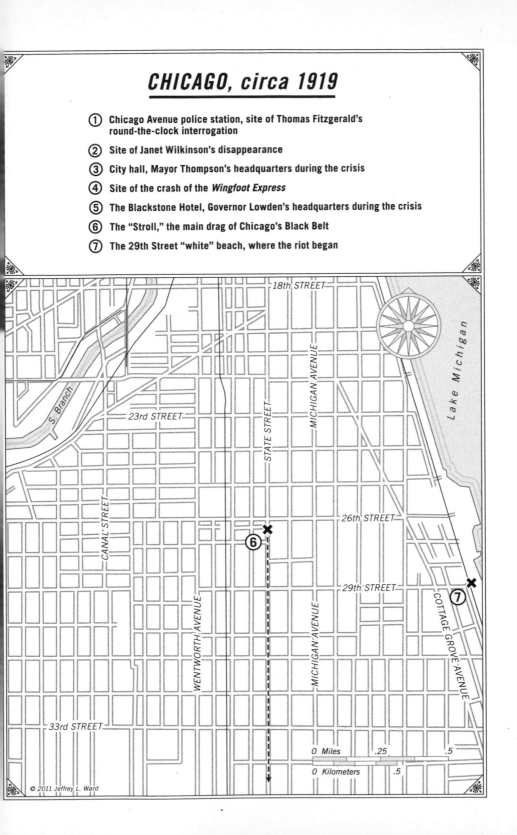

CHICAGO, circa 1919

① Chicago Avenue police station, site of Thomas Fitzgerald's round-the-clock interrogation

② Site of Janet Wilkinson's disappearance

③ City hall, Mayor Thompson's headquarters during the crisis

④ Site of the crash of the *Wingfoot Express*

⑤ The Blackstone Hotel, Governor Lowden's headquarters during the crisis

⑥ The "Stroll," the main drag of Chicago's Black Belt

⑦ The 29th Street "white" beach, where the riot began

18th STREET

Lake Michigan

MICHIGAN AVENUE

STATE STREET

S. Branch

23rd STREET

CANAL STREET

26th STREET

⑥

WENTWORTH AVENUE

MICHIGAN AVENUE

29th STREET

COTTAGE GROVE AVENUE

⑦

33rd STREET

0 Miles .25 .5

0 Kilometers .5

© 2011 Jeffrey L. Ward

PROLOGUE

The Burning Hive

THE SPANISH INFLUENZA had nearly killed Carl Otto that summer, but now the young bank telegrapher, clearly on the mend, was eager to return to work. On the warm, sunny morning of Monday, July 21, therefore, he rose early to prepare for his commute. His wife, Elsie, was concerned about his health and tried to discourage him. Carl was still not well, she insisted, and his extended sick leave didn't officially end until tomorrow. Couldn't he put off work for just one more day?

But Carl was adamant. He truly enjoyed his job at the bank and valued his reputation as a conscientious worker. And although he knew better than to make light of his illness (the recent flu epidemic had already killed more people than the Great War had), he felt he should delay his return no longer. He was, after all, an employee of one of Chicago's premier financial institutions: the Illinois Trust and Savings Bank, located right in the heart of the downtown Loop district. Standing at the foot of the Chicago Board of Trade Building on the corner of LaSalle Street and Jackson Boulevard, the bank was an important conduit for the countless transactions generated each day by the largest and most significant commodities exchange in the world. New York's Wall Street may have been the center for the trading of company shares, but it was in the pits of the Chicago Board of Trade that the fate of real things—of wheat, corn, hogs, lumber, cattle, and oats—was determined. Populations worldwide were dependent on it for the raw fuel of civilization itself.

As telegrapher and "all-around utility man" for the Illinois Trust, Carl Otto was a vital cog in the complex machinery of that market. From his telegraph desk in the bank's central courtyard, right under the building's distinctive two-story skylight, he kept his employers and their clients in close communication with the financial centers of the East Coast. As a translator for the Foreign Department (Carl had been born in Germany and spoke several languages), he also facilitated transactions with companies in the grain-importing countries of Europe and Asia. Besides, Monday was usually the bank's busiest day of the week. Carl felt that he *had* to go back.

The couple discussed the matter over breakfast. In Elsie Otto's opinion, the worldwide commodities market could surely survive without her husband until Tuesday. She argued that their son, Stanley, a six-year-old orphan whom the couple had adopted some time before, would appreciate another day of his father's company. But Carl would not be dissuaded. Determined to be punctual on his first day back, the telegrapher said good-bye to his wife and son, left their little cottage at 4219 North Lincoln Street on the city's far North Side, and headed for the Loop.[1]

* * *

At roughly the same hour about twelve miles south—at 5448 Calumet Avenue, in the city's Washington Park neighborhood—Earl H. Davenport was also just leaving home for his morning commute. After years of working as a sportswriter for various newspapers around town, Davenport had recently switched careers. He had taken on a public relations job representing the White City Amusement Park, South Side Chicago's most popular summer recreation center. Named after the world's fair that had done so much to boost Chicago's image a generation earlier—the 1893 World's Columbian Exposition, also known as the White City—the park was an entertainment extravaganza, a thirteen-acre playground of bowling alleys, shooting galleries, roller coasters, ballrooms, and novelty attractions such as the Midget City and a walk-through diorama depicting the famous Johnstown Flood. Handling the publicity for such a place was Davenport's idea of fun.

This week, though, Earl was working on a special assignment. White City's aerodrome, leased by the navy during the recent war for the construction of B-class dirigibles, was now being used for commercial purposes again. A crew from the Goodyear Tire and Rubber Company in Akron had arrived on the site several weeks earlier to assemble one of their already fabled blimps, an airship called the *Wingfoot Express.* Davenport was using the opportunity to launch a major promotion. Even as the *Wingfoot* was being put together and tested, he was busy urging newspaper photographers and city dignitaries to come down to the White City and take a ride. Just last week, in fact, he had asked Frederick Proctor, a former sportswriting colleague who now worked for the Board of Trade, to issue invitations to the board's president and several of its other members to make a flight as official guests of the amusement park.

Davenport, a plump, balding man of unfailing good nature, planned to go up himself on one of the airship's maiden flights. As he'd written in that week's edition of the *White City News,* he felt just "like a kid with his first pair of red-top boots" anticipating his airborne adventure. Technical problems with the bag's carrier mechanism had postponed the blimp's debut several times, but now, on this bright Monday morning, Davenport was hoping that his luck would change. The weather was good, and the engineers had had the whole weekend to put the *Wingfoot* in top flying condition. Confident that he'd finally be taking to the skies, Davenport pulled on an old pair of tennis shoes—appropriate footwear for a blimp ride, he thought—and set out on his one-mile trip south to the park.[2]

✳ ✳ ✳

Another person hoping to get on the blimp that day was Roger J. Adams, president of the Adams Aerial Transportation Company. Having arrived in Chicago on Sunday via the overnight train from New York, Adams had quickly made arrangements with Goodyear representatives for a demonstration of the *Wingfoot.* His eponymous company, which had recently inaugurated a passenger-carrying hydroplane service between Albany and New York City, was now in negotiations with a consortium of Italian capitalists to start a transatlantic dirigible service. The group was considering buying the

Wingfoot Express or another craft of the same type for this purpose, so Adams was eager to see the blimp in action.

Knowing the value of good publicity for his nascent business, Adams had that morning contacted the *Chicago Daily News* to offer himself as an aviation expert qualified to comment on this exciting new technology. The paper had sent over a reporter to interview him. Dirigibles (the terms "dirigible" and "blimp" were used interchangeably in 1919) had been employed with some success on scouting missions during the war, and now many people hoped that the airships could revolutionize long-distance passenger travel and mail delivery. During his talk with the *Daily News* reporter, Adams waxed eloquent on the unlimited possibilities for Chicago as a center of national and international air services. "Chicago," he opined to the reporter, "will be the Blimpopolis of the Western World!" He predicted that transatlantic flights from London would end in Illinois rather than in New York, which would be merely "a crossroads aerial station" where pilots might make a whistle-stop en route. "There is no reason why passenger blimps cannot go direct from Chicago to London and vice versa," Adams concluded. "The seacoast city as a 'port' will become obsolete in the day of aerial travel."

The *Daily News* reporter had taken all of this down, promising that an article would appear in that afternoon's edition. This was, after all, just the kind of news the local papers loved to print. Always sensitive to their status as residents of the nation's second city, Chicagoans liked to disparage New York and tout their own town as the city of the future, the true American metropolis of the still-young twentieth century. Having an expert like Adams say that Chicago—rather than the old and hidebound cities of the East—would soon be the world's "Blimpopolis" was just what readers wanted to hear.

But now Adams was eager to see the blimp itself. With the time of his afternoon appointment approaching, he found a taxi and headed down to the White City aerodrome. After a short drive, they passed the amusement park at Sixty-third Street and South Parkway, its landmark electric tower, brilliantly illuminated at night by thousands of lights, looming above in the sunshine of a quiet weekday afternoon. As the cab approached the aerodrome at the other end of the park, however, Adams could see that something was wrong. There was no blimp tethered outside the enormous hangar. Could it somehow still be inside, not yet inflated?

Adams got out of the cab and inquired at the hangar. No, he was told, the blimp was already gone. It had left shortly after noon, heading for the airfield in Grant Park, from which point it would make several exhibition flights around the city. Adams mentioned his appointment for a ride that day, but no one seemed to know anything about it.

Frustrated, the entrepreneur got back into his cab and directed the driver to take him north again to Grant Park, on the shore of Lake Michigan just east of the Loop. If he was going to get his blimp ride that day, Roger Adams was apparently going to have to chase the airship down.[3]

* * *

In the meantime, the entire city of Chicago had begun to take notice of the *Wingfoot Express*. Visible from many parts of the city on its flight from White City, the giant silver lozenge was attracting crowds of gawkers on street corners citywide. Chicagoans had seen plenty of aeroplanes during the war, but blimps were still something of a novelty in the city skies. Some people were even telephoning the newspapers, trying to find out exactly what it was and what it was doing.

Around midafternoon, a telephone rang at the Madison Street offices of the *Chicago Herald and Examiner*, another of the city's six English-language dailies. The call was transferred to the desk of the city editor, who listened for a moment before hanging up and calling down to N. M. Meissner, head of the paper's film department.

"Have you got a cameraman ready?" the editor asked.

Meissner looked around the cluttered room. The only photographer in sight was Milton G. Norton, who was just then loading up his camera case with photographic plates and extra lenses. At forty-five, Norton was significantly older than most of his colleagues—newspaper work was very much a young man's game in 1919—but he was an able cameraman, especially good with a portrait. Meissner called out to him, asking whether he was ready for an assignment.

"All set," Norton replied. "What's the story?"

Meissner sent him to the city editor, who said that he'd just had a report about the blimp that had been flying over the city all day. The ship was supposed to land at the airfield in Grant Park within minutes. Norton was to go over there to get a few pictures of it for the next morning's edition—and to hurry, because a photographer from a rival newspaper was supposedly also on his way over.

Norton returned to the film department, grabbed his photography kit, and left immediately.[4]

* * *

As Milton Norton rushed across town from the Hearst Building, his path was thus converging with that of the other three men: Carl Otto, now sitting at his desk in the Illinois Trust and Savings Bank; Roger Adams, speeding north in his taxicab from White City; and Earl Davenport, already at Grant Park, trying to get his promised ride on the *Wingfoot*.

The blimp had landed some minutes earlier at the lakeside aerodrome, where Davenport was waiting for it. The publicist had already been thwarted twice that day. He was unable to get on the blimp's first run from White City to Grant Park—as the inaugural flight, it was considered experimental, and so Goodyear insisted that only its own pilots and mechanics ride. Davenport was also shut out of a two-thirty flight from Grant Park north to Diversey Avenue and back, since the seats on that run were taken by military personnel—among them a Colonel Joseph C. Morrow, who had been sent to Chicago to evaluate the blimp for the government—and two writers from the *Chicago Evening Post*.

And now, as five o'clock approached and the *Wingfoot* was being prepared for what would probably be its last flight of the day, there was another difficulty. So much hydrogen gas had been valved out of the blimp's bag on the first two flights that the ship could now safely carry only five people. The pilot had already reserved three of those places for himself and two mechanics, Harry Wacker and Carl Weaver. Undeterred, Earl was angling to get at least one of the remaining seats for himself.

Captain Jack Boettner, however, was reluctant. This had not been an easy assignment for him. The pilot had had his hands full all day, fending off crowds of spectators while trying to test-fly a new blimp in difficult circumstances. Having come to Chicago from Goodyear headquarters in Akron for the test, he knew little about the geography of the city he was flying over. And though he was an experienced dirigible pilot, he was unfamiliar with the *Wingfoot*'s engines. The twin Le Rhône rotary motors mounted above and behind the gondola were still experimental; as far as he knew, rotary engines had never before been used to power an airship, and he had no experience running them. True, the engines had behaved well on the first two flights, but Boettner was still learning their eccentricities.[5]

What's more, the attention attracted by the *Wingfoot* was becoming oppressive. Every time the blimp moored, thousands of people would gather around it. Local dignitaries and self-proclaimed aviation experts would materialize to present their credentials, ask questions, and try to cadge a ride. Since Goodyear regarded this project in Chicago as a publicity opportunity, Boettner had to be agreeable to these people, willing to act as tour guide even as he was supposed to be testing a blimp. The *Wingfoot* crew had received a letter to this effect from E. R. Preston, the company's advertising manager, indicating that prominent men should be encouraged to ride the blimp. (Preston had mentioned Henry Ford as an ideal candidate.)

So when Earl Davenport appeared at Grant Park asking for his long-promised ride, Boettner was inclined to oblige. He and the entire crew had come to like the genial publicity man in the days they'd been working at the White City aerodrome. So Boettner finally agreed to take him along. He kidded his passenger about his choice of footwear, and Davenport answered in kind, insisting that the tennis shoes would help him get a running start in case anything happened in the air. Laughing, Boettner replied that "a running start would be no good, that what he wanted to practice was a standing jump."

Meanwhile, the pilot and his crew continued their preparations for the day's final flight. They primed the engines and made adjustments to the controls. They checked the rigging that held the bag to the gondola. Mechanic Weaver burned a bit of stray oil off the twin engine propellers with a blowtorch.[6]

Just before they were ready to board, another figure emerged from the crowd—Milton Norton, with his camera kit on his shoulder. Seeing him, Davenport asked Boettner if the photographer could join them as the fifth person in the gondola. He pointed out that aerial pictures in the next day's *Herald and Examiner* would certainly be good publicity for Goodyear. Boettner agreed and allowed the photographer to ride. But given the amount of hydrogen gas left in the bag, he decided that no one else would be taken aboard on that flight.

The pilot issued each of his passengers a parachute harness belt. He demonstrated how a rope tied to the belt's D-buckle was fastened to one of the parachute packs attached to the outside of the fifty-foot gondola. If for some reason the passengers and crew were forced to jump ship, the ropes would pull their parachutes away from the packs and open them automatically. "All you have to do is jump," Boettner explained. "The parachute takes care of itself."

The two passengers made light of the idea of being tied to these glorified silk parasols. Parachutes were supposed to be for aeroplane pilots headed off into battle. How likely was it that a photographer and a publicist would need them on a joyride over the streets of Chicago?[7]

* * *

At exactly 4:50 p.m., Jack Boettner sounded a warning blast from his siren. The taut lines tethering the *Wingfoot Express* sprang loose, releasing the sleek gray blimp into a partly cloudy Chicago sky. The passengers in the gondola looked down, watching as the milling crowd of spectators in Grant Park seemed to recede, the throbbing pointillism of upturned faces and white straw boaters losing distinctness as it dropped away beneath them. Shrinking rapidly, the oblong shadow of the airship slid silently across the ground toward the glittering surface of Lake Michigan.

Captain Boettner, seated at the wheel in the prow of the gondola, turned the ship immediately to the east, toward the lake. The wind was steady. Twin American flags secured to the bow and stern of the bag rippled calmly as the engines purred and the two propellers spun in the warm early-evening air.

The men sat single file in the leather-covered wicker seats of the gondola. To those on the ground, they would have looked like oarsmen in a five-man canoe: first Davenport, seated directly behind Boettner; then Norton with his cameras and plates; and then mechanics Wacker and Weaver abaft, just under the whirring propellers.

When the blimp had gained some altitude, Boettner turned it north. The 150-foot-long airship, its bag enclosing ten thousand cubic feet of hydrogen, responded well. Each movement of the rudder was answered by a corresponding turn of the nose to port or starboard.

Finally, Boettner wheeled the airship west, toward the crenellated wall of buildings that lined Michigan Avenue like a rampart at the edge of the park. The pilot had decided that they would fly over the downtown Loop before heading south back to White City. That would give Norton an opportunity to take some spectacular photographs of the city's skyscrapers from above. It would also mean that the *Wingfoot* would be seen by thousands and thousands of Chicagoans as they left their offices at the 5 p.m. close of business. No one could ask for better publicity than that.[8]

Norton leaned over the edge of the gondola, snapping pictures. It was certain that no other newspaper would have anything like these photos tomorrow. From 1,200 feet up, the view of Chicago was magnificent. The entire city lay at their feet, humming like a fabulously complex machine, its miscellaneous components spreading out northward, westward, and southward from the shores of Lake Michigan and far into the distance. Directly below was the dense, teeming core of the downtown business district, a checkerboard of brooding modern skyscrapers and grim two- and three-story commercial buildings. Streets clotted with trucks, automobiles, and horse-drawn wagons threaded through these blocks of stone, intersected by silvery railway lines and, to the north and west, the snakelike curve of the Chicago River. And around this hub, its center enclosed by the rounded rectangle of the elevated Loop tracks, clustered the dozens of individual neighborhoods that together formed this huge and diverse metropolis. Here was Little Poland, Little Italy, the Black Belt, and Greektown, the silk-stocking districts and the New World shtetls, each one of which—whether made up of crumbling tenements, luxurious mansions, or neat little worker cottages—stood in many ways apart from the others, a self-contained enclave with its own ethos and mores. From this height, one could also see the engines that kept this collection of urban villages in operation—the interlocking feedlots and slaughterhouses of the stockyards district to the southwest, the enormous steel mills to the far south, the reaper works, the railcar factories, the gasworks, the warehouses and merchandise marts of the retailing trade, and the endless railyards full of trains that connected the city to the rest of the world. To call this conglomeration by a single name—Chicago—seemed wildly inappropriate. It was less like a city than a world unto itself, bringing together the artifacts and energies of a vast multitude.[9]

The *Wingfoot Express* continued westward and southward over this cluttered assemblage, attracting ever more attention as it sailed through the Loop. Automobiles pulled to the side of the road; commuters pointed at it from the platforms of the L; office workers stopped typing and hung up phones to watch it from the windows of their buildings.

But then, just as the airship crossed over busy State Street, Boettner felt something strange—a tremor in the fuselage, a shudder of the steel cables that held the gondola suspended beneath the blimp. He looked up and saw smoke and flames licking the bag just above its equator, and he knew immediately that the situation was dire. The pilot stood up and started waving his arms at the men behind him. "Over the top, everybody," he yelled as loudly as he could. "Jump or you'll burn alive!"

The other occupants of the blimp seemed confused at first, but then, looking up themselves, they comprehended the gravity of the situation. As they scrambled to heave themselves over the side, Boettner could see the flames moving rapidly above. The bag was crackling noisily as the fire spread out to consume the whole blimp. Just as the airship buckled in the middle and started to fold in on itself, Boettner jumped.[10]

* * *

People all around Chicago's central district watched in awed disbelief as the silver blimp in the sky crumpled and began to fall.

Roger Adams, the entrepreneur, was now at the airfield at Grant Park. His taxi from White City had been just a little too slow. "I got there just as [the *Wingfoot*] went up again," he would later say, "and I was too late to get on." Annoyed at the missed connection, he had been forced to content himself with taking pictures of the blimp as it floated away. But then he heard something troubling. "I heard both engines starting to backfire," he reported. "There was too much gasoline flowing through the carburetors . . . and I knew that [the blimp] was in trouble." He was horrified to see the distant airship burst into flames.

C. M. Kletzker and L. B. Blake, employees of the Horton Engraving Company, were looking on from the twelfth-floor windows of the Lees Building on South Wells Street. They had been watching the blimp when it first approached the Loop, but then returned to their desks to get back to work. A few minutes later, a colleague came into the office and asked to be shown the dirigible that everyone was talking about. "We went to the window to look again," Kletzker said. "We had barely located the airship when there was a flash of flame. . . . With the first flare, five [figures] jumped and their parachutes opened." Realizing that they were watching a tragedy in the making, they began to sketch the scene, hoping to create an eyewitness record of what was happening.

Much closer to the action, in the halls of the Board of Trade Building, Frederick Proctor was in the process of delivering one of Earl Davenport's invitations to fly. Proctor had moments before entered the office of Warren A. Lamson and asked the young broker whether he "craved a sensation." He explained that the publicity director of White City had offered Lamson and other board members an opportunity to take a ride in a blimp. Lamson demurred. "Exmoor and my Marmon are enough for me," he said, referring to his favorite golf course and his sporty automobile. At that moment, the two men heard a terrific crash just outside the office windows.

At Comiskey Park, not far south of downtown, thousands of baseball fans gasped and jumped to their feet when they saw flames erupt from the blimp hovering over the Loop. They had just watched their hometown White Sox win the first game of a doubleheader against the Yankees. Ace infielder Buck Weaver had singled in the decisive run in the bottom of the ninth inning, leading the Sox to a 7–6 win. Now, three innings into the second game, all action stopped as players and spectators alike anxiously watched the catastrophe unfolding in the distance. Reporters in the press stand immediately reached for their telegraph keys. "It was the most quickly reported accident that ever occurred," Sherman Duffy, the *Chicago Daily Journal*'s sportswriter, later reported. "The blazing balloon had not reached the ground before its fall had been telegraphed to newspaper offices both here and in New York."[11]

Witnesses could see the five tiny figures falling away from the flaming blimp. They saw four parachutes start to open—like long ribbons fluttering out of a magician's hat—as the ropes pulled the chute packs from the side of the gondola. One ribbon caught fire before it opened completely. This was Carl Weaver's chute. As the silk fabric dissolved in tongues of flame, the mechanic fell "like a rocket," crashing through the glass skylight of the two-story building below.

At least two of the other parachutes also seemed to be afire, though they were burning more slowly. Harry Wacker was able to control his descent somewhat, though he fell faster and faster as each square inch of silk above him was consumed. Plunging toward the street, he struck a ledge on the Insurance Exchange Building, nearly gained his footing on the masonry, but then fell again. Milton Norton, who had delayed jumping from the gondola as he worried over his camera and plates, was descending just as fast, spinning wildly round and round. He was thrown violently against a window of the Western Union Building. The window smashed, and Norton was snagged momentarily on the sill, but his momentum was too great and he, too, continued falling to the street.

Jack Boettner, being a trained pilot, had known to jump as far as possible from the flaming bag, and so his parachute had just been licked by the spreading flames as it opened. Even so, one edge caught fire. The pilot began to whirl in the air as he dropped. He couldn't see where he was going, but his feet soon struck the roof of a high building. Jolted by the impact, he rolled a few times and found himself peering over the edge of the roof, down into the street far below. Boettner didn't know it at the time, but he had landed safely on top of the Board of Trade Building, one of the tallest in the city.

Only one of the five figures did not fall away from the gondola. Earl Davenport had tried to jump with the others, but his rope had somehow become entangled in the blimp's rigging. He fell only about fifty feet and then just hung there, upside down, swinging back and forth. According to witnesses, he was kicking and struggling, but couldn't free himself from the tangle. All he could do was hang there helplessly as the flaming blimp collapsed in on itself, losing all buoyancy and then plummeting toward the roof of the Illinois Trust and Savings Bank below.[12]

* * *

Carl Otto sat at his telegraph desk, finishing up work for the day. Many of his colleagues had been surprised to see him when he showed up that morning. They had heard about his bout with influenza and knew he wasn't scheduled to return until Tuesday. But there he was, still busy at a few minutes before five, having put in a full day's work despite his lingering illness.

A number of the bank's other employees were also still hard at work on their tasks. The bank had closed to the public some time before, but there were still about 150 clerks, bookkeepers, and stenographers moving about the bank's central court, closing the ledgers for the day, finishing up their correspondence, and locking away bonds and other securities. Bank president John Mitchell had just left the building a few minutes earlier to go home.

The Illinois Trust, a small Greek Revival building tucked in among much higher skyscrapers in the southern Loop, was considered one of the most beautiful banks in the city, fronted by tall Corinthian columns that made it look more like a temple than a place of business. The ornate interior was just as grand. A magnificent central rotunda, rising two stories to a huge glass skylight, was surrounded on three sides by teller cages. Business with the public was conducted around the outside perimeter of these teller windows. The rotunda's central court, directly under the skylight and overlooked by a balcony, was reserved for the bank's internal business. Here were the telegraph stations and the stenographer pool, as well as the desks where clerks and bank officers did their work. As a security measure, this area could be entered only through one of two entrances in the perimeter of teller cages.

As the five o'clock hour approached, activity on the floor was waning. The women in the stenographic pool were finishing up for the day, pecking out a few last lines before pulling the covers over their typewriters and getting ready to leave. Helen Berger, the stout but ever-energetic chief stenographer, was attending to last-minute details with teller Marcus Callopy. Assistant cashier F. I. Cooper had left his desk and was accompanying a messenger to the vault area with some records.[13]

A few people noticed a change in the light around them as a shadow passed over the skylight above. This was followed by a sudden flash, which made some think that a photographer was taking a picture. Cooper the cashier, standing at the entrance to the bank's large time vault, heard a sound of breaking glass overhead and turned around to investigate. What happened next was horrifying: "The body of a man," he later said, "so badly burned and mangled that I could not tell at first that it was a man, came hurtling through the air and fell at my very feet." It was the body of mechanic Carl Weaver.

That was when the entire bank seemed to detonate.

"I thought a bomb had been exploded," one man said. Bombings had been in the news all year, and many bank employees worried that the Illinois Trust might be a target. But it instantly became clear that this was no ordinary explosive device.

A. W. Hiltabel was working in one of the teller cages at the south end of the room: "The first thing I heard was the breaking of the skylight," he said. "I looked up and saw fire raining down from the roof. There seemed to be a stream of liquid fire pouring down into the room."

Debris was suddenly falling everywhere. A huge engine and fuel tank slammed to the marble floor in front of him. "They exploded," Hiltabel said. "Flames shot high into the room and all over the place. I ducked under my desk."[14]

Carl Otto and his colleague Edward Nelson were in conference at the telegraph desk when they heard the terrific explosion above them. Suddenly they found themselves showered by "an avalanche of shattered window panes and twisted iron." Something sharp and heavy struck Nelson in the knee, throwing him to the ground. As hot sheets of flame billowed around him, he managed to crawl across the floor to an open teller cage. He scrambled up over the marble counter and out of the teller window to the lobby outside.

Carl Otto was not so lucky. The telegrapher took a direct hit from the falling engine and was instantly, horribly, crushed.

The initial shattering of the skylight had brought C. C. Hayford out of his office in the credit department. "I ran out and an explosion . . . hurled me over," he later explained. "I got up and someone ran into me, screaming, 'Oh my God, it's raining hell!'" Then Hayford saw great columns of fire rising almost majestically above the line of teller cages before him. He could make out silhouetted figures struggling in the flames. "The screams were indescribable," he said. "I turned sick. A man—I don't know his name—staggered out of the cage carrying the body of a girl. His own face was covered with blood."

By this time, the central court was, according to workers in the balcony, "a well of fire, a seething furnace." Clerks, stenographers, and bookkeepers, many of them with clothes ablaze, were clawing toward the two exits; others managed to escape through the narrow teller windows. "I saw women and men burning," said Joseph Dries, a clerk in the bond department. "I saw everybody trying to get out through the doors of the cages."

But many didn't move fast enough. Stenographer Maria Hosfield looked on in horror as her boss was burned alive: "I was sitting next to Helen Berger and saw her become enveloped in flames," she said. Several men ran to the chief stenographer and tried to extinguish her burning clothes. "She was saturated with gasoline," said bank guard William Elliott. "Everything was so confused . . . but I heard the screams, and I looked and saw flames eating her." He took off his coat and wrapped it around her. Pushing her to the ground, he rolled her on the floor to douse the flames, severely burning his hands. But he knew he had been too late.[15]

By now, police and firefighters were arriving on the scene. The intense heat of the fire, however, made it difficult for them to enter the caged rotunda. People were pouring out of the bank's windows like bees escaping a burning hive. Half-naked, dazed, and bloodied, many were now wandering numbly through the streets of the financial district. "When I got to the street," bank employee W. A. Woodward said, "I noticed that my face, head, and arms were covered with blood. . . . A man I had never seen before rushed up to me and said, 'Man, don't you know that you are badly hurt?' There was no ambulance near, so this man hustled me into a taxicab and took me to St. Luke's Hospital."

A crowd estimated at twenty thousand people had been drawn to the streets of the southern Loop to watch the disaster. Many were trying to help the victims. Several gathered around Milton Norton. The photographer lay in the street in front of the Board of Trade Building, still attached by rope to his smoldering parachute. By all appearances, the man seemed dead. But someone flagged down a passing automobile and ordered the driver to take the battered man to the hospital.[16]

Meanwhile, Jack Boettner had made his way to the street. After detaching himself from his burning chute on the roof of the Board of Trade Building, the pilot had found a fire escape and started down. It took a long time for him to reach street level. Amazed to find himself only slightly injured, he set off amid the confusion to search for his men. He was intercepted on the street by two police detectives, and when he told them who he was, they immediately arrested him and took him away for questioning.

Back at the Illinois Trust Building, firemen struggled to bring the blaze under control. Charred and bloody bodies were now being removed from the rotunda. Friends and relatives of bank employees ran frantically around the streets, looking for their loved ones. Bystanders were doing what they could, wrapping the injured in their own jackets and helping them to waiting automobiles. Even those people who had only witnessed the disaster were stunned, incredulous. No one could quite take in the reality of what had happened. How had this experimental blimp—this enormous, floating firebomb—been allowed to fly over one of the most densely populated square miles on Earth? Shouldn't someone have recognized the potential disaster and prevented it?

It was a question that would be asked numerous times over the next days, as the people of Chicago learned the details of what had happened that afternoon. The crash of the *Wingfoot Express*—the first major aviation disaster in the nation's history—had taken the lives of more than a dozen people, while injuring dozens more, and had brought utter panic to the heart of the second largest city in the country. To many, it was unthinkable that such a thing could occur, that people quietly conducting their business in a downtown bank could suddenly find themselves in the midst of a hydrogen-fueled inferno. Chicago had recently come through a world war and an influenza epidemic relatively unscathed. But in the new age of twentieth-century technology, there were exotic new dangers to fear, new sources of turmoil to be reckoned with.[17]

What no one could possibly realize at the time, however, was that the turmoil of the summer of 1919 had just begun. Over the next weeks, Chicago would plunge headlong into a crisis of almost unprecedented proportions, suffering an appalling series of trials that would push the entire city to the edge of civic disintegration. A population so recently preoccupied with fighting an enemy abroad would suddenly find no shortage of enemies within its own ranks, threatening residents' homes, their jobs, even their children. The result would be widespread violence in the streets, turning neighbor against neighbor, white against black, worker against coworker, while rendering the city's leaders helpless to maintain order. The Red Summer, as it would later be called, would leave Chicago a changed and chastened city, its greatest ambitions for the future suddenly threatened by the spectacle of a community hopelessly at war with itself.

All of this would happen over just twelve days. In retrospect, the crash of the *Wingfoot Express*—as horrifying as it may have seemed on that warm July evening—would come to be regarded as the least of the city's woes.

PART ONE

Collision Course

JANUARY 1 TO JULY 21, 1919

CHAPTER ONE

The New Year 1919

WET SNOW PELTED the city all evening, glazing the traffic-choked streets and wrapping every arc light in a gauzy halo of mist. In the chill hour before midnight, noisy groups of revelers rushed along the slippery sidewalks of the Loop. Music spilled from cabaret doorways; patrolmen blew their whistles; taxicabs caromed along the avenues, their thin tires throwing sprays of half-frozen slush toward the curbs.

Occasionally, the grimy trestles of the L would shudder as a crowded train rumbled past overhead.

December 31, 1918—proclaimed by the *Herald and Examiner* as "the most epochal New Year's Eve" in the city's memory. Despite the snow and a stinging gale off the lake, Chicagoans were coming out in huge numbers to celebrate. Every theater in the Loop was playing to sold-out houses, while hotels, saloons, and restaurants did record business, turning away latecomers at their doors. There were raucous dances at the Soldiers and Sailors Club, the Randolph Hotel, and even the normally staid Women's Club. At the Terrace Garden Restaurant, a skater dressed as Father Time performed a last turn on the ice while a little girl, representing the brand-new year to come, was lowered from the ceiling on a wire.

There were festivities for everyone in town, whether young or old, rich or poor, "old settler" or newly arrived immigrant. At the elegant Casino Club, Chicago's purest blue bloods watched Charlie Chaplin's recent comedy *Shoulder Arms* before settling down to songs and champagne before midnight. More daring souls jammed the cafés on Wabash and Van Buren, where frantic jazz—that scandalous new import from New Orleans—promised to continue until well past the mandatory 1 a.m. closing time. The city's destitute were also having their fun: At Michael "Hinky Dink" Kenna's tavern on Clark Street, where ten cents bought an evening's warmth and plenty of cheer, a homeless man named Curly Tim sat for hours over a pot of beer, singing a song about a "lemonade tree" in a "paradise where bums and little children live at peace."[1]

Chicago, in short, was greeting the new year in a spirit of high optimism. And why not feel optimistic? As the *Daily News* noted just that afternoon: "This year, the holiday breathes peace and contentment. The year 1919 is seen as the greatest in the history of Chicago, of America, and of the world." Long gone were the gloomy days of the German spring offensive of 1918. The Great War was over now. The Hun had been soundly defeated, and soldiers who had been leaving for combat in Europe a year ago would soon be returning home. Crime in the city was down, and the Spanish influenza, which in late 1918 had swelled the columns of death notices in the newspapers, seemed finally to be tapering off. Even the imminent arrival of Prohibition, almost certain to become law later in the year, had its hopeful aspects; though opposed by a large majority in the city, the abolition of alcohol held out the promise—in theory, at least—of significant reductions in vice, public drunkenness, domestic violence, and other urban ills.[2]

But perhaps the greatest hopes of Chicagoans on this snowy New Year's Eve were those stirred by the city's bold and wildly ambitious program for its own civic future. The so-called Plan of Chicago— a multimillion-dollar scheme to transform the city into a model metropolis more beautiful than the great urban centers of Europe— had been in the making for more than ten years. First conceived by the late architect Daniel Burnham (the creative force behind Chicago's

1893 World's Fair), the plan would expand, reshape, and modernize the entire city. It called for, among other things, redeveloping the Lake Michigan waterfront, widening dozens of roads, improving and expanding the park system, building major new bridges and highways, consolidating the city's railroad terminals, and even straightening a portion of the Chicago River. Considered one of the most ambitious urban improvement programs ever proposed, the plan promised to rationalize the city from top to bottom, creating "a practical, beautiful piece of fabric out of Chicago's crazy quilt." Advocates hoped that a more orderly and attractive urban environment would, in turn, create a new sense of community in Chicago, reducing social conflict and bringing out the best in all of its residents.

Naturally, there had been resistance to the plan at first. Many early skeptics had regarded the whole idea as too idealistic, too impractical, and altogether too expensive. But thanks to an all-out public relations campaign (which involved, among other things, distributing seventy thousand copies of a propaganda booklet to the city's schoolchildren), the effort had gradually gained acceptance. In the years since the plan's conception, numerous factions in the city had worked together to overcome a plethora of financial, legal, and technological obstacles. Property owners had been compensated for their land rights; railroads had been convinced to alter their rights-of-way; businesses had been compelled to move their factories and warehouses. None of this had been easy. For one project alone—the creation of a grand Michigan Avenue boulevard with a monumental bridge connecting the North and South Sides—the city had had to settle more than eight thousand lawsuits.

In 1919, the Chicago Plan would face some of its toughest hurdles to date. In July, the city council would have to pass a major ordinance allowing the plan's lakefront projects to go forward. And to finance the major bulk of the anticipated public works, voters would have to pass a series of critical bond issues in November. Given the shaky state of the city's postwar finances, accomplishing these tasks would require enormous political will. In fact, it was argued that the realization of Burnham's vision would call for an exercise of civic resolve unlike any the city had mustered in decades—at least since 1871, when Chicago rebuilt itself after its devastating fire.

Notwithstanding these challenges, however, enthusiasm for the effort was at an all-time high. "Chicago Plan Stirs Chicago Spirit to Realization" read the headline in the January 1 *Tribune*. "Project Truly Fine and Great Enters New Year in Full Swing." According to the paper, tangible progress was finally becoming evident to even the remaining doubters: "The visions that once seemed only heart-breaking images begin to settle into actualities. Great works are progressing day and night. Caissons are descending beneath the riverbed, skeleton structures arise on the banks, ragged glimpses are being knit up to make noble vistas, and at the end of them can be discerned faint outlines of visions that will endure."[3]

Of course, to believe all of this hopeful rhetoric about the Chicago of the future, one had to look past one major thing—namely, the Chicago that existed right now. Having grown unfettered from a small prairie village to a colossus of almost three million people in the space of ninety years, the city was still in many respects an awkward, oversize adolescent, and one whose upbringing had been in the hands of "hurried, greedy, unfastidious folk" more concerned with making a quick dollar than creating a model city. The result was an urban environment of barely controlled chaos: a two-hundred-square-mile jumble of wood, brick, and masonry structures, crisscrossed by four thousand miles of road (much of it unpaved) and chopped up by the trackage of twenty-six different railroads. Fifteen hundred trains, more than 20,000 streetcars, and 130,000 individual vehicles entered this muddle every business day, creating traffic snarls that wasted an estimated 100,000 man/days every year. Much of the city's housing stock, moreover, was substandard, ill-kept, unhygienic, and in short supply; working conditions in factories were often brutal and unsafe; and opportunities for escaping the squalor (at beaches, parks, and recreation centers) were inadequate or too expensive for many to consider. To make matters worse, the smoke from hundreds of coal furnaces, smokestacks, and railroad locomotives left a residue of soot and grime on every surface in the city.

The year ahead would also put exceptional pressures on Chicago's already stressed population. The war abroad may have been won, but many domestic conflicts seemed destined to erupt in the coming months. Labor problems—after a brief wartime truce between unions and employers—were on the rise again, soon to be exacerbated by high inflation, lagging wages, and the return of job-seeking soldiers just when the postwar economy was slowing. Racial strife was growing throughout the city, especially in border neighborhoods where African Americans were moving in ever greater numbers to escape overcrowding in the Black Belt. Friction was also rising among the city's numerous ethnic groups—Poles, Germans, Irishmen, Italians, and Jews—stoked by the nationalist passions of the recent war.[4]

But as Illinois governor Frank O. Lowden proclaimed in his official New Year's greeting: "The new year beholds a new world," and so Chicagoans were trying to put aside their worries and focus on the positive. The new world of 1919, after all, promised the fulfillment of many individual hopes and expectations as well. For someone like Emily Frankenstein, daughter of a prominent Jewish doctor in Kenwood, the coming year held many bright possibilities. Though she confessed to her diary that she didn't "dare even to dream" about the distant future, the ebullient twenty-year-old had an "enticing present" to contemplate—her recent graduation from the Kenwood-Loring High School, her exciting new course of study at the University of Chicago, and her budding romance with a young soldier named Jerry Lapiner, to whom she was secretly engaged to be married. Recently released from duty at a Tennessee army base, Jerry would be looking for a job in January, with an eye to making enough money to support a wife and home—a daunting prospect even in less uncertain times. But tonight the pair was determined to be carefree, braving the "blizzardy, rainy night" to take in a vaudeville show on Wilson Avenue before heading to a friend's North Side apartment for games and supper.[5]

Others were greeting the new year more quietly. Victor F. Lawson, owner of the *Chicago Daily News,* a paper that would go to great lengths in the coming months to reshape the city's future, remained in bed at his luxurious manor on Lake Shore Drive, nursing a broken foot. Lilian Sandburg, wife of a promising young poet soon to return from a wartime journalism assignment in Scandinavia, also celebrated at home, spending a "lonesome day" at their Maywood cottage caring for the five-week-old daughter her husband had yet to meet.

And *Tribune* columnist and sportswriter Ring Lardner, for whom 1919 would prove to be a life-changing year, had his own way of commemorating the holiday. Shunning the boisterous party scenes at the Pompeian Room, the College Inn, and the Edgewater Beach Hotel, the thirty-three-year-old writer instead set out for the "Hotel du Paragon" (that is, his home at 748 Buena Avenue on the North Side), where he found his three young sons engaged in a bacchanal as wild as any in town: "Two young men were lying on the floor, kicking each other, while a third stood on the piano bench, giggling insanely," Lardner reported in his next day's column. "None of the revelers wore evening dress. . . . One of them kept kicking off his slippers and laughing as if he thought it the height of comedy. The other two were continually leaving their chairs and running around the table, shouting at the top of their voices." Not surprisingly, the three young men soon exhausted themselves; by ten o'clock, they—and their long-suffering parents—were gratefully asleep in their beds.[6]

* * *

The snow continued to fall as midnight arrived, unleashing a citywide crescendo of noise, music, and merrymaking. "Hundreds of orchestras ushered in the new year with the strains of 'The Star-Spangled Banner,'" the *Tribune* reported, "and diners climbed on tables and cheered themselves hoarse." A block-long parade of soldiers and sailors materialized on State Street and proceeded north, "shouting and hammering and singing, gathering girls and women into the revel as it moved." Some of the carousing led to accidents. One young soldier home on furlough fell off a crowded streetcar into the path of an oncoming wagon. A distracted chauffeur crashed his employer's automobile into the display window of a Thirteenth Street shop. Taking advantage of this mayhem, car thieves managed to drive away with no fewer than ten vehicles in the first three hours of the year.

At one o'clock, police insisted that the doors of all saloons and cafés be closed to newcomers, though they allowed those inside to continue their celebrations for a while longer. Early breakfasts were served in the clubs; last songs were sung. By three, the city was beginning to settle down. Exhausted revelers nodded as they rode the late-night "owl cars" to the suburbs. A straggler named John Foll—standing on a street corner, calling for comrades to accompany him to Holland to kill the Kaiser—was quietly arrested and carted off to jail to sleep it off. Emily Frankenstein and Jerry Lapiner left their friend's soiree at two and—after a "cold-slippery-tired" ride on the L—got home at 4:30 a.m.[7]

It had been a grand night—the first New Year's Eve of the postwar era, heralding what many were convinced would be a time of reconstruction and new beginnings. And over the following few days, as Chicago recovered from its collective debauch, the city started to see corroborative signs of the positive changes to come.

Police chief John J. Garrity announced the hiring of one thousand new policemen to patrol the city and make it even safer. Governor Lowden announced a welcome 15 percent reduction in state taxes. Even Chicago's beloved White Sox got a new start. In a statement made public on New Year's Day, owner Charles Comiskey announced the replacement of manager Clarence Rowland with William "Kid" Gleason to lead the team in the upcoming season. While the Old Roman would not say why he was making the switch, reporters pointed to the team's sixth-place finish in the 1918 season, plus rumors that Rowland had lost control over several players disgruntled by salary issues. But the selection of Gleason—a former Sox coach with whom Comiskey was allegedly not even on speaking terms—came as a surprise to everyone. "The loyal patrons of the White Sox desired a change in manager," Commy explained with bland noncommitment, "and I have exercised the prerogative that I considered mine and made the change." The team's performance in the 1919 season, of course, would be the ultimate proof of whether Comiskey had made a wise decision.

Then, on January 6—as if to underline the passing of the old to make way for the new—the city learned that former president Theodore Roosevelt had died unexpectedly at his Sagamore Hill home. Shocked, Chicago went into mourning. Local dignitaries such as Jane Addams and Clarence Darrow published encomiums to the great man in the newspapers. Two days later—at 1:45 p.m., the exact time of Roosevelt's funeral—all business throughout the city stopped for five minutes. Streetcars and elevated trains shut down; schools and factories suspended operations; crowds gathered on street corners for a moment of silence. For three hundred seconds, the "mighty, roaring, sweltering, pushing, screaming, magnificent, hideous steel giant that was Chicago" came to a standstill.

And then it started up again as before, and moved on.[8]

Chicago was, in any case, more preoccupied with the future than with the past. The "youngest great city in the world" had important business to attend to—in particular, the upcoming mayoral election. In April voters would have to decide who would lead the city through its "greatest year" ahead. And that decision would ultimately amount to a referendum on the incumbent, the controversial figure who, for better or worse, had come to represent Chicago in the public mind both in the United States and abroad. Though many different candidates would compete in the race, all eyes would be on the current occupant of city hall: the blustering, flamboyant, unscrupulous, but always entertaining political phenomenon known to all as "Big Bill"—Chicago's mayor, William Hale Thompson.

CHAPTER TWO

The Mayor Announces

THE STREETS AROUND Arcadia Hall began to fill sometime after dusk on January 14. As evening fell, swarms of people began streaming from the North Side streetcars, joining pedestrians already on their way toward the large barrel-roofed structure at Broadway and Sunnyside in Uptown. By seven, large crowds—including many women, legal voters in Illinois municipal elections since 1913—had formed around the main entrance, spilling out into traffic on the street.

Once the doors opened, the cavernous auditorium quickly filled to capacity. Spectators crammed themselves into every available space, including the gallery at the back of the hall and the area behind the broad elevated stage. While some of these people were clearly Republican Party hacks and members of the campaign's "portable audience" (hired to fill out rooms around the city), many others had come of their own accord, simply to witness what they knew would be the best free entertainment in the city: Tonight, the mayor of Chicago would announce his candidacy for a second term.[1]

At eight o'clock, Samuel Hamilton, vice president of the Twenty-fifth Ward William Hale Thompson Club, called the assembly to order. He introduced the Chicago Marine Band, which warmed up the audience with a varied program of music, including a sing-along of the anthem "America," two violin solos by a young soldier named W. A. Dalpé, and "The Cycle of Life," a soprano solo sung by Mrs. Milton Severinghaus, wife of the program's musical director. Finally, the audience joined the singers on stage in a rousing performance of "The Man of the Hour," the latest Thompson campaign song, reading the newly minted lyrics from a signboard hoisted above the stage for all to see:

> *Over here we have a leader*
> *Who's been fighting for you and me.*
> *Ever since he's been elected*
> *He's been square as man could be.*
> *Though lying newspapers may lie,*
> *You hear the honest voters cry:*
> *We'll elect Big Bill for our next mayor!*

To warm applause, the members of the mayor's cabinet and other dignitaries filed onto the stage. The evening's emcee—Irene Pease Montoya, daughter of Republican warhorse James Pease—rose to give the introductory address, praising the man who had given Chicago "the best administration in its history." She then introduced City Health Commissioner John Dill Robertson, who whipped the crowd to further heights of enthusiasm until, with a shout, the guest of honor appeared in the hall to interrupt Robertson's accolades. Waving his trademark ten-gallon cowboy hat to acknowledge the riotous reception, he pushed his way through the cheering throngs, mounted the platform, and strode to the center of the stage. And there he stood for several minutes, jubilantly drinking in the applause and cheers he loved above all else: the man of the hour himself, Big Bill Thompson.[2]

No one could deny that the mayor of Chicago knew how to command a stage. A six-foot-plus bear of a man, his 225 pounds straining the seams of an indifferently tailored suit, he was not one to blend into a crowd. Decades of banquets and gravity had taken their toll on the former athlete's physique, but he was, at fifty-one, an impressive figure nonetheless, with a thick bull neck and a barrel-shaped chest that still seemed sturdy enough to stop a rushing fullback in his tracks. Rumor had it that a younger Big Bill had once knocked out three men in a bar fight in Wyoming. Those days were perhaps gone, but although he now sported a paunch (known as an "alderman" in the parlance of the day) as well as an extra chin or two, he still looked like the man you'd want to stand beside—or behind—when the bar stools and whiskey bottles started flying.

But the nickname "Big Bill" referred to more than just the mayor's physical proportions. There was something about the expansiveness of his personality, too, that made the title apt—his boyish enthusiasm, his flamboyant sense of showmanship, his sloppy and uncritical optimism, his Rabelaisian appetite for life. Thompson was naturally gregarious, so much so that even his enemies—of which there were many—admitted that they found him disconcertingly likable once they actually sat down with him. And the mayor's affection for Chicago, the city he grew up with, was nothing if not genuine and infectious. William Hale Thompson, as one of those enemies later wrote, "loved Chicago like a boy loves his dog—heavily and sentimentally."[3]

And, to a large extent, Chicago loved him back. Not, admittedly, the Chicago of prim-faced college professors, teetotaling clergymen, and settlement house do-gooders; but the rank and file of the city—the button makers and the livery drivers, the hotel porters and the packinghouse butchers, the small shopkeepers, the grocery clerks, and the tavern owners. These Chicagoans recognized Big Bill as one of their own. He spoke their language—"slangy, vulgar, and alive"—and seemed to understand their concerns better than an institute full of good-government reformers. Granted, maybe he wasn't entirely honest, but what politician was? Besides, he got things done. Under Big Bill's administration, unemployed sons and brothers-in-law were given jobs; viaducts and playgrounds were built; money was spread around. The best administration in the city's history? On this day, in this auditorium, and among this crowd, who would dare to deny it?

When the ballyhoo at his appearance finally abated, Big Bill stepped forward and thanked the audience for its generous and hearty welcome. "I have been requested by petition from more than 200,000 men and women voters of Chicago to become a candidate for reelection to the office of mayor," he announced. And then, with perfect dramatic timing, he added, in his familiar "big, boozy, bellowing" roar: "I take this opportunity to announce that *I will comply*!"

The hall erupted yet again with boisterous applause and cheering. Not that anyone in the audience had been in doubt about his intentions, but now it was official: Big Bill wasn't going to let them down. One of the most remarkable and controversial political figures in American history was about to pick up the cudgels and fight for a second term.[4]

* * *

He was not the likeliest of mayors, even in a city notorious for unlikely chief executives. Given the trajectory of his early life, it was remarkable that he had even entered politics in the first place. Born in 1867 to a wealthy Brahmin family on Beacon Street in Boston, he was brought to Chicago when he was still an infant.[5] His father, William Hale Thompson Sr., was a prominent businessman who had graduated from Yale, served with Admiral David G. Farragut at Mobile Bay during the Civil War, and then established himself as a successful Chicago real estate developer. Bill Jr. was groomed to follow in these footsteps. Related on his mother's side to one of Chicago's original founding families and on his father's side to an intimate of George Washington, he seemed destined to become a pillar of Chicago's educated and moneyed elite. Except, that is, for one small peculiarity: Young Bill really wanted to be a cowboy. Never one for study and discipline, he instead harbored dreams of busting broncos under a spacious Western sky. And so, at the age of fourteen, he had made a deal with his parents. After an embarrassing incident in which he was briefly jailed for riding his horse recklessly across the State Street Bridge (allegedly toward a make-believe Indian battle in Lincoln Park), he promised to make amends. He would buckle down and get a job in a grocery, he said—*if* his parents would allow him to use his earnings to pay for an extended adventure out West. They agreed to these terms, perhaps suspecting that the boy would lack the discipline to save money. It would not be the last time someone underestimated Billy Thompson's resolve. The following autumn, the boy was happily riding in the caboose of an empty cattle train, heading west.[6]

The Great Plains, as it turned out, suited Thompson perfectly. For the next six years, he spent the warmer months on the prairie (as a brakeman for the Union Pacific Railroad and a wagon driver at a Wyoming cattle ranch) and his winters back in Chicago (at the Metropolitan Business College, where he was known to appear occasionally in full cowboy garb). By 1888—convinced finally that their son really wasn't cut out for a career spent uneventfully multiplying the family fortune—the Thompsons purchased a ranch in Ewing, Nebraska, and asked Bill to run it. He was delighted to obey.

For three more years, he lived the life of the Western rancher, this time on a year-round basis. He led packs of his cowboy compadres on wild horseback rides down Ewing's Main Street. He hosted visits by city-slicker friends from Chicago (among them a young Flo Ziegfeld, well before his theater-producing days) and staged mock gunfights for them. High jinks aside, he also saw to the business of buying, feeding, and selling cattle at profit. Again exceeding low expectations, he turned the ranch into a highly lucrative business venture, clearing a profit of $30,000 (roughly $700,000 in current dollars) over the course of three years.

This western idyll, however, could not last forever. When William

Hale Sr. died suddenly in 1891 (leaving an ample estate of more than $2 million), the twenty-four-year-old cowboy was forced to return to Chicago to take over the family real estate business. But even then, politics was the furthest thing from Big Bill's mind. Instead, he threw himself into the nearest urban equivalent of cowpunching—amateur sports. At the prompting of his childhood friend Eugene Pike (another young millionaire with time on his hands), he joined the Chicago Athletic Club. Within a year, he was captain of the club's water polo team, competing successfully against teams from Princeton, Harvard, and Yale. In the national finals against the New York Athletic Club, Bill reacted to some aggressive play by unceremoniously walloping his opponent in the nose. His team ultimately lost the match, but Thompson himself won the adoration of Chicago's sports fans, who took to calling him "Fighting Bill."

From there, he moved on to other sporting triumphs—in baseball, football, diving, handball, even the aerial trapeze.[7] By the late 1890s, he had become a well-known figure around Chicago—not only on its playing fields, but also (to the chagrin of his mother) in the taverns and brothels of the Levee, the city's notorious South Side entertainment district. Then, one day in 1899, during a card game with friends at the club, Gene Pike tried to convince him to go into politics. Pike himself had just won election as one of the Second Ward's two aldermen. Now he wanted Big Bill to run for the ward's other council seat. But Thompson was unsure he wanted to jump in.

George Jenney, another club member, scoffed at Thompson's hesitation, claiming that Big Bill was afraid to run. Jenney took a fifty-dollar bill from his wallet and put it down on the card table. "This money says Bill Thompson is scared!"

It was a challenge no true sportsman could leave unmet. Acting before Pike could answer, Thompson put his hand out and covered the bill. "I'll take this one myself," he said. "George Jenney, you've got yourself a bet!"[8]

* * *

Once the Arcadia Hall crowd settled down after his opening announcement, the mayor wasted no time before launching into his campaign pitch. It was a speech that, in one form or another, he would deliver in countless venues before countless audiences over the next few months. As usual, he began on a positive note, his manner calm and confident, his diction almost formal. The fireworks would come later.

"An examination of the past four years," he declaimed, "will prove that I have given Chicago an honest, economical business administration, abounding with constructive achievements!"[9]

Holding up an index finger in one of his trademark gestures, he proceeded to enumerate these achievements—a reduction in crime citywide; the divorcing of the police from politics; preservation of the five-cent transit fare; and, of course, his ongoing building projects. He boasted shamelessly about the widening and improvement of city streets, the gargantuan Michigan Avenue development, and all of the other Chicago Plan endeavors that he had been working so hard to bring to fruition. All of this, he claimed, amounted to a mighty record of accomplishment, and yet it had been achieved without undue strain on Chicago taxpayers. The city's government, in fact, had been run "with less revenue . . . and with greater efficiency in every department than ever before!"

Arcadia Hall erupted once again with applause and shouts. Yes, this was the capable, can-do mayor Chicago had elected four years ago. Never mind the venal and incompetent Mayor Thompson depicted by the "lying newspapers." This was "the People's David," who fought for the common man's interests in the name of the common man. This was Big Bill the Builder!

"I know that a vast majority of the people desire good government," the mayor went on, shifting to a quieter tone, "[and that] the

most important element in securing good government is an intelli-
gent vote of the people. If people are to vote intelligently, they must
know the truth about their public servants and public affairs. [But]
how are the people to know the truth? What are their sources of
information?"

He let the question hang in that great space for a moment. The
audience, he knew, was in his hands now. And they, in turn, knew
exactly what was coming next. It was, in fact, the reason many of
them had attended the meeting in the first place. The mayor was
getting ready to start the real show of the evening. He was about to
go on the attack against his enemies. The fireworks were about to
begin.[10]

* * *

He had taken to politics immediately. Elections, after all, were not
so different from the sporting matches he loved—you played hard,
you worked your advantages, and at the end of the game there was
a winner and a loser. Big Bill liked being a winner, and so he had
thrown himself wholeheartedly into that first campaign. The Second
Ward in 1900 was a diverse area, embracing part of the red-light
district as well as the Prairie Avenue silk-stocking neighborhood, but
Thompson proved adept at appealing to both constituencies. Nomi-
nated at Freiberg's Hall, one of the Levee's most notorious dens of
vice, he nonetheless ran on a reform platform, promising to clean
up the streets and battle crime, which pleased the well-heeled progressive set. He also proved to be an indefatigable and openhanded
campaigner, buying drinks for prospective supporters at every one of
the ward's 270 saloons. "I'm spending $175 a day," he remarked to
friends during the campaign. "I've worn out two pairs of shoes and
I've gained 14 pounds. Fellows, politics is really the life!"

The strenuous glad-handing paid off. Thompson won the election
by a comfortable margin and joined his friend Gene Pike on the city

council. He proceeded to get married (to Maysie Wyse, a pretty secretary from his real estate office) and tried to interest himself in the day-to-day operations of city government. But Big Bill soon found that actually serving as alderman was somewhat less enjoyable than campaigning for the job. He proved to be an indifferent councilman, rarely attending sessions and racking up few legislative accomplishments. Tricked by his savvier colleagues in the First Ward (the legendarily corrupt Michael "Hinky Dink" Kenna and "Bathhouse John" Coughlin), he even naively voted for a redistricting ordinance that changed the boundaries of the Second Ward, essentially moving his own residence out of the ward and making it impossible for him to seek reelection. The erstwhile cowboy, it seemed, had shot himself in the foot with his own six-shooter.[11]

It was obvious that if Thompson wanted to go any further in politics, he would need a mentor. And he soon found one in the person of William Lorimer. Known as "the Blond Boss" of Illinois politics, Lorimer was head of the city's West Side Republican organization, and he saw in Thompson the raw material of a political comer. Lorimer discouraged Big Bill from trying to get revenge on Bathhouse John by running against him in the First Ward. "No one's going to beat Bathhouse," Lorimer told the young alderman. "You turn your ward delegates over to me and I'll put you up for county commissioner. That way you can run where there are some Republican votes. Tie to me, Bill."

Never one to balk at a blatant quid pro quo, Thompson gladly accepted the offer. Associating himself with the powerful Lorimer machine, he ran for county commissioner in 1902 and won. This was gratifying, especially since the position didn't require all that much work. But again Thompson ended up serving just a single undistinguished term. Losing his bid for reelection in 1904, he decided to quit public office and return to his sporting activities, reinventing himself this time as a successful yachtsman. Even so, he remained active in politics as a party committeeman, working tirelessly in the Lorimer cause as the Blond Boss managed to win himself a seat in the U.S. Senate. Meanwhile, Thompson cultivated other political connections, particularly with fellow wealthy pols George F. Harding and James Pugh (who had helped Big Bill during the 1902 campaign by sitting in the front row at Thompson's stump speeches and dropping a brick whenever the candidate forgot to smile).[12]

The most important connection Thompson made during these years, however, was with Fred Lundin, a one-term congressman who had quickly risen to become a major figure in the Lorimer organization. Widely known as "the Poor Swede" (evocative nicknames were something of an obsession in Chicago politics), Lundin was a true eccentric—a diminutive, bucktoothed "square head" who wore enormous eyeglasses and an old-fashioned black frock coat with flowing bow tie. Affecting the modest persona of an immigrant yokel with just an average citizen's interest in politics, he was actually a fiercely ambitious and ruthlessly manipulative operator, a former patent medicine salesman who had parlayed a one-wagon peddling enterprise into a substantial business empire. As such, he knew the value of hoopla and razzle-dazzle, especially when selling something, even a political candidate, to the public. "Get a tent," he was wont to tell his protégés in a lilting Swedish accent. "Give them a show, forget about the issues. Give them a good time and you get the votes."

In Thompson—a crowd-pleasing showman who loved the bare-fisted combat of campaigning—the Poor Swede recognized the perfect receptacle for this political wisdom. The fact that Big Bill wasn't overburdened with scruples or philosophical convictions only increased his appeal. "He may not be too much on brains," Lundin allegedly once said of him, "but he gets through to people." And so Lundin became Big Bill's new mentor and proceeded to lay the groundwork for his political future.[13]

Even so, it took over ten years and the demise of William Lorimer to put Thompson and Lundin in a position to make their move. In 1912, Lorimer, accused of bribing several Illinois state representatives to win election, was expelled from his Senate seat. For the Blond Boss, of course, this was a career-breaking disaster. For the Poor Swede it was a golden opportunity, a chance to pick up the pieces of a shattered political organization and rebuild it in his own image. And so, from the routed elements of the West Side Republican machine, he gathered together a core group that would come to be known as "the Five Friends," including Lundin himself, Thompson, George Harding, the brick-dropping James Pugh, and Thompson's old friend Gene Pike. Together they planned what one historian called "a thrust for power never before attempted by any little political group." Their goal, as far-fetched as it may have sounded at the time, was to elect from their number a mayor, a governor, and, finally, if they were lucky enough, a president of the United States.[14]

There was, of course, no shortage of people in Chicago determined to stand in their way.

* * *

He began, as usual, with the newspaper editors. As the Arcadia Hall crowd stirred with anticipation, Thompson started lashing out at the members of the Chicago press who had opposed him from the start of his career. All but the two Hearst papers—the *American* and the *Herald and Examiner*—had been consistently antagonistic to his administration, but his wrath was concentrated on the two major Chicago dailies: the *Chicago Daily News,* under its owner-publisher Victor F. Lawson, and the *Tribune,* run by Colonel Robert R. McCormick. To Thompson, these were the "lying, crooked, thieving, rotten newspaper editors"; they were the "great cancer gnawing at the very heart of our city of Chicago." Calling them "crooks" and "hypocrites," he claimed that they used their enormous influence "to destroy men in public life, men who had the courage to fight for the people!"

But Lawson and McCormick were not alone in their perfidy. There were other villains afoot in the city, such as the tack-head academics at the University of Chicago, the corrupt Democrats on the city council, and the treacherous reformers of the Municipal Voters' League, an alleged civic watchdog organization that had been especially hard on Big Bill's administration. All of them opposed the mayor because all of them were merely instruments of the "sinister interests." They were beholden, in other words, to the rich utility barons, who wanted to gouge the people with high gas and electricity rates, and to the rich traction barons, who wanted to bleed the people dry with high fares for streetcars and L trains. Those sinister interests, in fact, were the true enemy in the war against the people of Chicago. "Gold is their God!" the mayor proclaimed. And to get their gold, they had "betrayed and sold out the people!"

Fortunately, however, the people had a champion to defend them against those who schemed to get rich at the public expense. "The People's David" wasn't afraid to stand up against the interests. He had done so numerous times over the past four years, taking up arms against rotten traction ordinances, venal school officials, and the meddling of corporate lawyers in city affairs. Wasn't that the kind of mayor they wanted to lead Chicago forward to its "wonderful future"—someone willing to do battle for the common people? "I fought," the mayor cried, as applause once again echoed through the hall. "I fought for weeks and months to protect *you*!"[15]

＊ ＊ ＊

The first step in Lundin's grand plan was to get Big Bill Thompson into the mayor's office. The Poor Swede was convinced that this was possible—as long as his protégé did exactly as he was told. As the *Trib* would later put it, Thompson was to be the mouthpiece, while Lundin would supply the song. And so the two became an inseparable team. Big Bill made the speeches while the Poor Swede worked behind the scenes, calling in favors, making promises, patching together coalitions from the numerous factions that always fought for influence in this hugely heterogeneous city. The Republican Party was in disarray at this time—not just in Chicago, but in the whole country, torn apart by the rift between Roosevelt progressives and Taft party regulars. But Lundin was tireless, willing to compromise, and supremely well organized. Working with his soon-to-be notorious card files (containing records of favors owed and favors promised), he soon assembled the base of support necessary to put Thompson on the ballot for the Republican primary.[16]

On December 22, 1914, Thompson stood before a packed house at the Auditorium Theatre in the Loop. Onstage beside him stood a Christmas tree adorned with signature cards of 142,111 Chicago citizens, all of them ostensibly committed to sending Big Bill to city hall. Thompson feigned reluctance at first, but as he later said, in his best cowboy drawl: "I could no longer hold out agin 'em." Just as he would do some four years later at Arcadia Hall, the big man announced his candidacy for mayor.

At first, most people scoffed at the idea. Without the backing of an established political machine, they said, Thompson wouldn't even make it through the primary. Even when—thanks in part to an all-out effort to win the city's African American vote—he eked out a narrow victory to become the official Republican candidate, few doubts were shaken. Opponents were quick to point out that the hard-fought Democratic primary, won by Cook County clerk Robert Sweitzer, had attracted 50 percent more voters than its Republican counterpart. With so much of the town voting for the party of President Woodrow Wilson, everyone expected Sweitzer to run away with the election.[17]

Any less sanguine candidate than Thompson might have lost heart. The obstacles before him seemed insurmountable. Most of the city's newspapers, having initially discounted his candidacy, grew downright hostile once they realized that a creature of the disgraced

Lorimer might actually have a chance to become mayor. Thompson was "simply impossible," stewed Victor Lawson of the *Chicago Daily News*. Big Bill's opponent was equally dismissive. "Just who is this Bill Thompson?" Sweitzer complained. "I find he is a man who plays with sailboats."[18]

But while newspapers and political rivals jeered, an awful lot of regular Chicagoans seemed to like what they saw of Thompson on the hustings. For one thing, the man was an entertaining campaigner, always free with a joke or a gibe. And he knew the value of a campaign promise. Just about every voter heard from his lips an appealing pledge: To women, Bill promised a mother on the board of education; to blacks, he promised respect and equal opportunity; to workers, jobs on his big building projects; and to everyone else, an honest administration, a full dinner pail, and a cleaned-up city. He emphasized the bread-and-butter issues that would come to be a hallmark of his later campaigns—reduced gas rates, preservation of the five-cent car fare, greater home rule for Chicago. And always, the emphasis was on boosting the city he loved to a brighter future: "You're going to build a new Chicago with Bill Thompson!"[19]

On Election Day—following Lundin's dictum, "When in doubt, give a parade"—the Thompson forces hired extras from a circus menagerie to march through the city streets. The animals included three elephants, a bull moose, and a donkey (symbolizing the candidate's hoped-for appeal to Republicans, Progressives, and Democrats). The electorate seemed to take the hint. When the ballots were counted, Thompson stunned everyone by staging a landslide victory, winning by no fewer than 147,477 votes—the largest victory margin of any mayoral candidate in Chicago history.

"Hoorah for Bill!" cheered an incredulous Gene Pike that night at Thompson headquarters. Jim Pugh, meanwhile, danced around the room, yelling: "Bill, you're the greatest sonofabitch Chicago ever saw!"

But Thompson himself knew just whom to thank for his victory. "Fred, you're a wizard," he said to Lundin, heartily shaking his mentor's slender hand. "You did it all, and I'm not ever going to forget this!"

William Hale Thompson—surpassing low expectations yet again—had become the forty-first mayor of the city of Chicago. "In six months," quipped *Tribune* columnist Bert Leston Taylor, "we'll know if it's Big Bill or Big Bull."

It actually took more like three.[20]

* * *

After about an hour of fiery oratory, Big Bill finally started bringing his speech to a close. In that hour he had given his Arcadia Hall audience just the show they'd been looking for. He had lambasted his enemies in no uncertain terms; he had roared, whispered, crooned, and bellowed; and he had put the upcoming vote in terms easy to understand—as a fight "between the people, on the one hand, and the corporate interests, on the other," a story with good guys, bad guys, and a massive conspiracy to confuse the electorate about which was which.

And so he made his final plea: "If continued in the office of mayor of Chicago by the suffrage of the people," he concluded in grand style, "I shall go on yielding to *their* influence only. I shall sink personal and political considerations in seeking the good of the city. And I shall give myself unreservedly—henceforth as heretofore—to the support of *Law, Liberty,* and *Justice*!"

The band broke out with a rousing rendition of "The Star-Spangled Banner" as Big Bill, smiling his beaming, gap-toothed smile, waved his cowboy hat at the crowd and then strode off the stage. Anyone looking for signs that the audience was not 100 percent behind their mayor would have been hard-pressed to find any. According to one report, "the audience stood on its feet, and on the chairs, and cheered

and sang" for their candidate. Fred Lundin—looking on, one sup-
poses, from some inconspicuous corner of the hall—could not have
been anything but pleased. His great plan had faltered once or twice
since he first lifted Thompson from obscurity, but now his efforts
were definitely back on track. "A Mayor, a Governor, a President":
There was still a long way to go to achieve all of those goals, but winning for Thompson a second term in office—despite the rabid opposition of their numerous enemies—would be the vital next step.[21]

CHAPTER THREE

Enemies

WITHIN DAYS of the mayor's Arcadia Hall announcement, his foes in the Republican Party were already making plans to stop him. No one was expecting the task to be pleasant. Big Bill, they knew, would not surrender the nomination without a struggle, and anyone running against him would have to be prepared for a vicious campaign. Federal judge Kenesaw Mountain Landis, later to become the first commissioner of major league baseball, probably spoke for many of his fellow Republicans when—after being approached to become a candidate—he demurred with the comment: "I would just as soon have you ask me to clean a shithouse."[1]

Still, the city's various Republican factions did find their champions soon enough. First to move were those from the loosely organized progressive wing of the party. Convinced as always that Chicago's problems could be solved only by electing an incorruptible "expert" in municipal administration, the progressives threw their support behind one such prodigy—Captain Charles E. Merriam, a University of Chicago sociologist who had long served as an alderman from the Hyde Park district. According to Jane Addams (founder of Hull House and now something of a Chicago institution at age fifty-nine), Merriam was an "honest and fearless" politician who "would make Chicago the pioneer in the scientific administration of American cities." Merriam himself, promising Chicago "a clean, honest, progressive administration," adopted a somewhat more combative tone in declaring his candidacy. "The administration of Mayor Thompson is an epic of betrayal," he claimed, "a history of treachery without parallel in the annals of American history. . . . [Thompson's] continued rule would certainly undermine the foundations of democratic government."[2]

Fearing that the academic Merriam would have limited appeal to the average Chicago voter, GOP regulars lined up behind a more plausible challenger. Harry P. Olson, the so-called Harmony Candidate of the city's other two Republican organizations, was chief justice of Chicago's Municipal Court. Taking a more pragmatic approach than Merriam, Olson focused his attacks less on the immorality of the mayor's alleged corruption than on its practical effects. "Thanks to Mayor Thompson and his political blunderbuss," the judge said in opening his campaign, "the city's finances have broken down completely. Chicago is broke. Actually, honestly, broke." He proceeded to outline exactly how this had happened: "They made the school treasury a political feeding crib; they filled the payrolls with ward heelers and followers of the Lundin-Thompson political army." Olson also made sure to harp on the numerous scandals that had plagued Thompson's first term—the making of nine thousand "temporary appointments" to city jobs, the stacking of the board of education with unqualified toadies, the hiring at outrageous rates of an army of real estate assessors and legal experts in connection with city construction projects, and so on. Thompson and Lundin, he concluded, "have used the vast public expenditures, the great public enterprises, the enormous business activities of the city, to build up a personal machine for themselves."[3]

That such accusations were largely true is indisputable; less clear is how much these issues really mattered to the average Chicagoan just trying to make a living and raise a family. After all, machines such as the Thompson-Lundin organization may have been corrupt, but at least a portion of the monies they skimmed tended to percolate down rather than up the socioeconomic scale. For many in working-class Chicago the machine actually served as a kind of social service agency, a quasi-official organization with a "ceaseless devotion to getting a job for Tom, taking care of Dick's sick mother, and getting Harry out of the clutches of an over-savage or vindictive public prosecutor." All this in exchange for a simple vote. So why should a working-class voter care about "good government," especially when the term so often meant government that was good for the factory owners who exploited him, good for the utility owners who raised his car fares and gas rates, and good for the businessmen who charged ever higher prices for his meat, milk, and clothing?[4]

Besides, had Big Bill really been such a bad mayor so far? It often seemed to depend on whom you asked. Certainly, he had got off to a brilliant start. Riding high from his landslide victory, Thompson had begun his first term in 1915 with plenty of goodwill. On the day of his inauguration, Lundin organized a "Prosperity Parade," with seventy thousand banner-carrying citizens marching down LaSalle Street. Even the *Tribune* seemed impressed. "No mayor ever entered the City Hall with such a backing, such apparently universal good will and sincere spirit of cooperation," wrote *Trib* political columnist Charles Wheeler. "If he doesn't make good, he will be the most despised mayor of the whole lot."[5]

Determined not to let that happen, Big Bill offered an olive branch to many who had criticized him during the campaign. To McCormick he sent a conciliatory letter professing thanks for the "fair manner" with which his paper had treated his campaign, and the *Trib,* for its part, seemed willing to give the new mayor a chance. But the *Daily News* had not been quite so generous. Summoned to a meeting with Thompson shortly after the election, Victor Lawson listened as the expansive new mayor, surrounded by sycophantic lieutenants, crooned on about what a good mayor he would be, and how sure he was that the *News* would approve of his plans to build Chicago. Lawson was apparently unmoved. "Mr. Thompson," he said when

Big Bill had finished his pitch, "everything you do as mayor that is beneficial to Chicago will meet with the approval of the *Daily News*. I should be lacking in frankness, however, if I did not say to you now that I have no confidence in either you or your chief supporters." And with that, Lawson calmly rose from his chair and walked out of the room.[6]

But the mayor was feeling far too upbeat at that point to have his victory spoiled by an old prig like Victor Lawson. He had just won the most important ballgame of his life. The city he loved had shown its love back, and Thompson was determined—in that boyishly sentimental way of his—to make good. "We're going to drive every crook out of Chicago!" he vowed to his fans. "No shadow of corruption, dishonesty, [or] wrongdoing shall cloud . . . the city government during my term of office!"[7]

And for the first few months of his administration, it looked as if Big Bill might just be the man Chicago was hoping for. Early signs were promising. Seedy pool halls were closed; wholesome youth recreation centers were promised. Faced with a streetcar strike in June, Thompson locked representatives of both sides into his city hall office. "I'm not going to let them leave," the mayor told reporters, "until they make peace." Negotiations went on through the night, interrupted only when Big Bill took everyone into his lavatory to race his prize model sailboat in the bathtub. And when the doors opened at dawn, the strike was settled.

Then, later that summer, he had a chance to show another kind of leadership. On a bright Saturday morning in July, a steamship named the SS *Eastland* capsized at its mooring on the Chicago River, drowning 811 people who were about to leave on a pleasure cruise. Thompson was in California at the time, but he returned immediately by special train and coordinated the relief efforts. He established a charitable fund for victims and led a funeral procession through the Little Village neighborhood, home of many who had died. "I am here to emphasize the grief and indignation of this great city," the mayor told mourners. Chicago appreciated the gesture. Thousands began wearing wide-brimmed Stetsons on the streets—"Big Bill hats" they called them.[8]

Of course, there was the inevitable carping about campaign favors and the dispensation of patronage. A few days after the election, Thompson handed Lundin the city payroll, saying, "Here it is. *You* play with it." The Poor Swede obliged. His first step was to "advise" the mayor on filling his cabinet, peopling it with, as one critic put it, "a roster of his nearest and dearest friends, [adding] a name or two for tone." Some of the appointments raised hackles. When John Dill Robertson, Lundin's own personal physician, was made health commissioner, many in the medical community protested his lack of administrative experience. But for the most part, Chicagoans seemed willing to let their colorful new mayor surround himself as he and his advisers saw fit. Even after the newspapers started raising the alarm about those thousands of "temporary appointments"—made to circumvent civil service requirements for city jobs—few citizens seemed terribly exercised. What politician didn't repay his supporters with jobs and other sinecures? So what if Big Bill bent the rules a little to do so? That was how politics had always worked in the Windy City.[9]

Even so, it wasn't long before the Thompson administration started to make some less forgivable missteps. An early attempt to establish the mayor's reform credentials (by having him enforce the city's widely ignored Sunday-closing laws) quickly backfired, earning him the ire of Chicago's formidable legions of beer drinkers. And there were times when the Thompson-Lundin machine-building efforts proved to be a little too aggressive even by Chicago standards. Hoping to oust Theodore Sachs, the head of the city's Municipal Tuberculosis Sanitarium, in order to replace him with a more pliable machine crony, the mayor hounded the man so mercilessly that he ended up poisoning himself in despair. The doctor's dramatic suicide note—addressed "to the people of Chicago" and published prominently in the papers—was explicit: "Unscrupulous politicians should be thwarted. The institution should remain as it was built, unsoiled by graft and politics." Thompson maintained that the suicide had nothing to do with him, and he excoriated the press for trying to turn a troubled man's desperate act into a political football. But the episode was, if nothing else, a public relations nightmare.[10]

The machine's worst miscalculation, however, came two years into the term, when Lundin, with an eye on bigger political game, started angling to get Big Bill elected to the U.S. Senate. By early 1917, the Great War in Europe was looking hopeless, and when President Wilson began edging the United States toward engagement in the conflict, Lundin saw in the move a potential campaign issue. "The people don't want it," he told Thompson in a closed-door strategy session. "Any man who is against the war can be elected United States Senator on that issue alone."[11]

The mayor actually needed little persuasion on this point. Notoriously anti-British, he always fancied himself a proponent of America First, and so he embraced the isolationist stance with his usual gusto. When Marshal Joffre, hero of the Marne, came to the United States on a nationwide tour, Thompson did not rush to invite him to the city. "Chicago is the sixth largest German city in the world," he pointed out, quite accurately. "Some of our people might not be so wildly enthusiastic about it." Although the invitation was ultimately issued, Thompson continued to drag his feet on American involvement in the war, discouraging the sale of Liberty Bonds at city hall and even allowing a controversial pacifist organization to hold a meeting in downtown Chicago. "This war," he kept insisting, "is a needless sacrifice of the best blood of the nation on foreign battlefields."[12]

This position, of course, would hardly seem to be unreasonable, especially in a country that had just reelected its president on the slogan "He kept us out of war." There were also many reasonable public figures who shared the mayor's pacifism, including Chicago's own Jane Addams. But Thompson and Lundin had misread the change in Americans' sentiments once their country had actually entered the fray in Europe. Consumed by the reflexive jingoism that war inevitably inspires, otherwise rational citizens were now disposed to greet any expression of pacifism with instant and rabid denunciation. And so Thompson was soon pilloried in newspaper columns, speeches, and sermons—not just in Chicago, but all around the nation. "I think that Mayor Thompson is guilty of treason and ought to be shot," said one clergyman in Baltimore. Big Bill was variously maligned as "a disgrace to the city," "a low-down double-crosser," and (the name that would stick far longer than any other) "Kaiser Bill." And it only got worse as the war fever grew. The Rotary Club voted to expel him; Theodore Roosevelt condemned him for giving aid and comfort to the enemy; he was hanged in effigy on the lakefront by members of the local VFW. For a time, there was even talk of the Democrat-dominated city council voting to impeach him.[13]

Big Bill took none of this passively. He defended his America First agenda, put out a call for the conscription of excess war profits, and instituted libel suits against three of the Chicago daily papers. But these counterattacks weren't enough to salvage his hopes for a Senate seat. In the Republican primary of September 11, 1918, he lost the nomination by sixty thousand votes—to Medill McCormick, brother of the despised editor of the *Tribune*.

Clearly, Lundin had miscalculated badly. But there was a silver lining in the debacle. Though Thompson had lost the overall state vote in the Senate primary, he actually carried the city of Chicago by a significant margin. There were, it seemed, many Germans, Jews, Irish, and other ethnic voters in the city who had not found the mayor's antiwar stance particularly distasteful. His Senate loss, then, was seen as merely a temporary setback. As one Thompson-friendly newspaper pointed out after the primary: Didn't Abraham Lincoln lose to Stephen Douglas in the Senate race of 1858, and didn't Lincoln go on to do a thing or two of importance afterward?[14]

And now, at the beginning of 1919, Big Bill's popularity seemed to be on an upswing. With the war over (and the conflict at the peace table proving to be nearly as grisly), his alleged traitorousness was seeming less dire—except, perhaps, to the city's native-born Protestant elite, who were, in any case, losing influence in city politics as more and more of them moved to the suburbs. That left the city's working-class immigrants and blacks, many of whom were tired of war, tired of reform, tired of pious, intellectual do-gooders lecturing them about ethics and ideals and making the world safe for democracy. What they really needed were steady jobs, affordable streetcars, reasonable gas rates, and a local pol they could rely on for a favor. If Kaiser Bill was the man who could deliver those things, then Kaiser Bill was the man they would vote for. Or so, at least, Thompson and Lundin were hoping.[15]

* * *

Once it became clear who would be opposing Big Bill in the primary campaign, the Thompson camp wasted no time in returning fire. Merriam and Olson had both run for mayor in earlier elections without conspicuous success, so it was easy enough to dismiss them as merely inept and unqualified opportunists. "Who are the other two candidates for the Republican nomination for Mayor?" asked the editor of the *Republican,* the weekly mouthpiece of the Thompson-Lundin organization. "They are professional men, neither of whom has had any experience in practical business. . . . If there is anything more objectionable than a judge in politics, it is a college professor in politics."[16]

Within days, Thompson issued a challenge to Merriam and

Olson to take part in a debate. Both opponents accepted, but when the event finally took place—at the Masonic Temple on February 11—Olson was inexplicably absent. Not that this mattered to Thompson. With the crowded hall evenly divided between Merriam's partisans and his own, the mayor commandeered the podium and delivered a seventy-five-minute diatribe denouncing both of his opponents and the masters they served. Then he waved to the crowd and left the hall before Merriam had said a word.

Flummoxed, Captain Merriam, a trim, handsome figure who made a point of wearing his uniform in all of his campaign photos, stepped to the podium and began his part of the "debate." Before he could utter more than a few words, however, the hall erupted with hissing, catcalls, and booing. Unable to speak uninterrupted, Merriam jettisoned his prepared remarks and resorted to shouting out the 1919 equivalent of sound bites: "Mayor Thompson has disgraced Chicago!" he screamed. "[He is] a shirker in times of peace and a slacker in times of war!" To much hooting and groaning, Merriam brought up the old disloyalty charges: "I want to say to the Mayor of Chicago that this is not the sixth German city in the world, but the first *American* city in the world!" He even dragged the mayor's deceased father into the fight. "If Lt. Commander Thompson could speak from his grave tonight," Merriam proclaimed, "[even] *he* would rebuke this un-American mayor!"

But it did the captain no good. No one seemed to be listening, and the event soon degenerated into a shouting match between the opposing camps. Unable to make himself heard, surrounded by zealous Thompson-ites yelling "rather uncomplimentary things" at him, Merriam could finally only give up and slink from the stage.[17]

Then, on February 18, Thompson distributed a campaign flyer that made it absolutely clear just whom he regarded as his real opponents in the struggle for Chicago's future. "FIGHT FOR YOUR RIGHTS!" the mayor urged voters in the one-page screed:

Defeat the traction and gas barons and other greedy interests, the newspapers which support them, and the political bosses who serve them! These interests and the *Chicago Daily News,* the *Chicago Tribune,* and the Municipal Voters' League—which always has a corporation lawyer at its head—are trying to get you to vote against yourself and for some candidate who, if elected, will do what they want done.

It was by now a familiar litany of villains: Robert R. McCormick and the *Tribune.* Victor F. Lawson and the *Daily News.* The Municipal Voters' League. These were the enemies Thompson had been fighting for years. Against them he already had all of the ammunition he needed.

So the game plan for the mayor's reelection was clear. He wouldn't run against Merriam and Olson; they were just figureheads. He would run instead against the symbols of entrenched wealth and power in the city. He would run against McCormick and Lawson.[18]

CHAPTER FOUR

The Fourth Estate

THEY WERE, it must be admitted, easy targets:

Colonel Robert R. McCormick—imperious, aloof, dogmatic, and visibly, extravagantly, undeniably rich—was just the kind of figure that working-class Chicago loved to hate. A nephew of Cyrus McCormick (manufacturer of the mechanical reaper), he had been educated at English boarding schools, Groton, and Yale, and spoke with the faux-British accent to prove it. As patrician as Thompson was populist, he was notorious for showing up at *Tribune* editorial meetings in jodhpurs, often with a trio of noisy German shepherds in tow. Occasionally, he would repair to the roof of the newspaper's downtown headquarters to practice polo on a mechanical horse. "The Colonel," as the six-foot-four, thirty-eight-year-old McCormick was always called, had served honorably in the Great War and had come back to Chicago determined to turn his "World's Greatest Newspaper" into a leading force for good government and the conservative Midwestern values he held dear. But his aristocratic mien, his country estate in the western suburbs, and his overweening sense of superiority and entitlement ("Working for McCormick is a little like working for God," an employee once confessed) made him easy prey for any politician hoping to incite class resentments.[1]

Where the *Tribune*'s publisher was eccentric and often slightly ridiculous, Victor Lawson, the sixty-eight-year-old publisher of the *Daily News,* was dignified and bland, a deeply religious man whose formal manner and gray Vandyke beard made him appear a relic of the nineteenth century. One of the founders of the Associated Press, he had taken a small, struggling Chicago daily and turned it into the third-largest-circulation newspaper in the world. Severe, even prudish at times (he once fired a *Daily News* pressman for dancing at work), he professed to exacting standards of newspaper ethics, even making a point of personally testing advertisers' claims before he would accept their ads for publication. But although he touted his paper as an independent and objective voice in city affairs (in contrast to the sharply partisan *Tribune*), he was united with his rival publisher on the issue of Thompson, whom he considered "a man of mental and moral poverty." Needless to say, Thompson had no problem depicting him as a rich Gilded Age holdover in cahoots with the "sinister interests."[2]

Against these two pillars of privilege, then, the Thompson campaign could position itself just as it wished. Chicagoans had traditionally harbored a deep distrust of their hometown newspapers, whose idea of civic righteousness often seemed to coincide conveniently with the preservation of the rights of wealth and property. By pounding the daily press, Thompson could make himself a populist hero while at the same time explaining away all of those news stories about his administration's alleged venality. "Some newspapers, as evil as they are powerful, have mercenary reasons for their attitude toward your city government," the mayor maintained in one of his campaign booklets. "Their hands are befouled with ill-gotten school funds, thefts of taxes, and corrupt profits derived from gigantic corporate and public utility interests." Thompson slyly focused on two high-profile newspaper "scandals," the first involving the *Tribune*'s below-market lease on some land owned by the city schools, the second concerning a $17.32 annual tax bill paid by Victor Lawson for his million-dollar North Side home. Neither issue was truly a scandal. The long-standing *Tribune* lease, while certainly an advantageous deal for the newspaper, was entirely legal, while Lawson's minuscule 1911 tax bill was merely a prorated payment intended to compensate for overpayment the previous year. But such subtleties were easily glossed over in the heat of the campaign. To Thompson (and, he hoped, to the majority of Chicago voters) these were clear indications that the two most powerful newspapers in the city had their hands in the public till. McCormick, Thompson declared, was "robbing the school children of Chicago," while Lawson was nothing but a "tax dodger."[3]

The *Tribune* and the *Daily News* did their best to correct these blatant mischaracterizations, but with indifferent success. No matter what they printed in their own defense, Thompson merely repeated the charges ad nauseam. Even Big Bill's main target admitted that the tactic was effective. In a letter to fellow newsman Arthur Brisbane, Lawson (who fancied himself something of an advertising expert) pointed out that the mayor's practice of "iteration—and iteration—and iteration" was actually an ingenious application of the new science of selling. "Thompson is a good advertiser," Lawson wrote, "but of bad wares."[4]

So the newspapers did what they could to bury the master advertiser's message. The *Tribune* and the *Daily News* both gave extensive coverage to the two challengers' attacks while providing far less ink to the mayor's responses. And as the February 25 primary approached, the tactic seemed to be having some effect. "Mayor's Men Panicky Over Swing to Olson," the *Daily News* reported in mid-February. To some, this probably seemed more like hopeful cheerleading than objective journalism. But even in his private correspondence, Victor Lawson was allowing himself some cautious optimism. "I think 'stocks are up' as respects the mayoralty outlook," he wrote to E. D. Hulbert on February 15. "Indications are very strong that Thompson is losing ground."[5]

But there were also other concerns preoccupying the Chicago electorate. On January 16, Nebraska had become the thirty-sixth state to approve the dreaded Eighteenth Amendment, meaning that Prohibition would soon become the law of the land. Two days later, the much-anticipated Peace Conference got under way in Paris, with all eyes on President Wilson and his controversial Fourteen Points. Closer to home, the first sizable contingents of Chicago soldiers had begun returning from Europe. Emily Frankenstein was one of the thousands of Chicagoans who gathered in the Loop to welcome home the 333rd Field Artillery of the Blackhawk Division, the first group to arrive. Securing a good vantage point at the window of a family friend's office on the fourth floor of the Willoughby Building, she watched the procession as it made its way up Michigan Avenue toward city hall. Two weeks earlier, Emily had been approached on the street by a "shell-shocked soldier" who had followed her home, asking if he might call on her. The incident had unsettled the young girl—some of the returning soldiers seemed quite changed by their ordeal in the trenches—but today she was happy to cheer them on, disappointed only that the parade was more subdued than she had expected. Mr. Caspery, the family friend, told her not to worry, that the really big celebrations were yet to come. "Wait until the Rainbow and Prairie Divisions come in," he said, referring to the two Chicago-based forces that would arrive later in the spring. Whether Chicago would be able to house and employ this influx of demobilizing troops, however, was a question that was already being asked with some trepidation.

Also a question was how—and how many of—the returning soldiers would be voting in the upcoming elections. The conventional wisdom (in the newspapers, at least) was that the vast majority of soldiers would naturally support anyone *except* Kaiser Bill, the man who had allegedly undermined their efforts during the war. But the United States was being agonizingly slow in repatriating its armed forces after the close of hostilities. With the deadline for voter registration looming, it was possible that few soldiers and sailors would be back in time to make their voices heard in the April 1 general election. In a close race, a disenfranchised military could very well mean the difference between defeat and victory for the Thompson forces.[6]

In any case, the vast majority of soldiers certainly wouldn't be registered in time for the primary, and so in the final days of the campaign for the nomination, both papers intensified their attacks on Big Bill. The *Daily News* printed a withering "Case Against Thompson" on its editorial page, enumerating the many "counts in Chicago's indictment" against its mayor. The *Tribune* followed with a forceful endorsement of Olson as the only Republican with any hope of unseating the pernicious incumbent. The editorial was blunt: "[Thompson] has failed in everything that could be hoped for him. . . . It will be a good thing for the city of Chicago if he is not returned to office."[7]

Big Bill was unperturbed. "Actions speak louder than words," he declared at the dedication of the Monroe Street Bridge, a Chicago Plan improvement whose opening was carefully timed to coincide with the culmination of the primary campaign. For Thompson, this kind of event was pure political gold. Early in his first year in office, when Charles Wacker, chairman of the Chicago Plan Commission, had come to the mayor's office to lobby for Burnham's grand scheme, he'd found a receptive audience. As George F. Harding would later say, "Bill grabbed the Chicago Plan and raced away with it like a gridiron star tearing down the field . . . for a touchdown." After all, the plan promised something for everyone—jobs, pride-inducing public works, rising real estate values, and photo ops galore. It also offered a virtually inexhaustible source of patronage and graft, all in the name of creating "a city finer than any the world had ever seen."

And now, with just a few days left before the primary, Thompson was playing his role as Big Bill the Builder for all it was worth. Flashing a union card identifying himself as a member of Local 182 of the Bridge Operators' Union, he personally pulled the lever that lowered the brand-new drawbridge into place. "This latest addition to our traffic facilities," he announced, as fireworks boomed above a fluttering American flag, "emphasizes the 'I Will' spirit of Chicago, which rises superior to all obstacles!"[8]

On the eve of the primary, all three Republican candidates employed contingents of soldiers to lead street-corner demonstrations and pass out campaign flyers. At Thompson's final rally at Cohan's Grand Opera House, one soldier—a Lieutenant L. M. Thorpe, allegedly wounded at the Battle of the Argonne—announced himself from the audience as a Merriam supporter. He was roundly booed, but the mayor was gracious. "Bill Thompson is glad to have any soldier of the nation talk in this meeting," he said, helping the lieutenant climb to the stage.

"Why are you in politics?" someone in the hall shouted.

"I'm in politics," Lieutenant Thorpe said, turning to face the crowd, "because I don't want to be a citizen of a German city. . . . I'm in politics to have an *American* put into office!"

Taken by surprise, Thompson grabbed the soldier by his Sam Browne belt and tried to shove him back into the crowd. Declaring the meeting adjourned, the mayor promptly stalked off the stage and found the nearest exit. According to a reporter for the *Daily News*: "Pandemonium reigned in the audience for several minutes before order was restored."[9]

Such embarrassments aside, the Thompson-Lundin forces were supremely confident going into the primary the next day. Most of the newspaper straw polls were in his favor, and Lundin's get-out-the-vote machine was primed and ready. And sure enough, when the polls closed on February 25—amid allegations from Olson about a "city-wide plot among the crooks and vice element to steal the election"—Thompson cruised to an easy victory, defeating Olson 124,194 votes to 84,254. As for Captain Merriam, although he had qualifications that, according to one observer, should have attracted every Chicago voter "who had eyes to see and ears to hear," only 17,690 turned out to be so qualified. The reformist professor hadn't even been able to carry his own Hyde Park district.[10]

Thompson and Lundin were jubilant. "Our cause is crowned with victory," the mayor proclaimed in a brief statement to the voters. "I highly resolve to dedicate myself to carry out your mandate." Granted, a second term was not yet secured, but as Thompson crowed on primary night: "We beat them today and we'll beat them on April 1!"[11]

Certainly the prospects looked good. The winner of the Democratic primary, Robert Sweitzer, was the same man Thompson had defeated in 1915, and there were rumors that several other candidates would make third-party or independent runs. As usual, in other words, the Chicago electorate was likely to be split many ways—and that was exactly the kind of environment in which the Thompson-Lundin machine worked best.

The city hall crew and their supporters were able to celebrate their primary victory for a day or two. But then, in the early-morning hours of February 28, something happened that could potentially change the entire complexion of the upcoming election. At about 2 a.m., a bomb went off in the downstairs hallway of a South Side rooming house. The explosion knocked thirty people out of their beds and killed a young girl sleeping with her grandmother. Significantly, all of the residents affected were black, and the rooming house was one that had been newly purchased by a black man from its white former owner.

The city's response to this tragedy was going to be closely watched. Chicago's black population—a key element in virtually all of Big Bill's election victories to date—would be looking to Thompson to take the lead in addressing this outrage and punishing the perpetrators. No matter who proved to be responsible for the bombing, it was clear that the Black Belt's unwavering support of the mayor was about to be tested.[12]

CHAPTER FIVE

A Bomb in the Night

THE FORCE OF THE explosion at 3365 Indiana Avenue shook the neighborhood for blocks around, shattering windows up and down the street. Within minutes, crowds of neighbors—most of them white—were gathered outside the brick row house to assess the damage. Debris littered the pavement in front of the building, and from the broken windows on the first and second floors, torn curtains billowed in and out of the cold night air.

Police arrived shortly thereafter to investigate the blast. In a front room on the second floor, they found Ernestine Ellis, a six-year-old child who had been sleeping in her grandmother's apartment. The girl had been blown vertically out of her bed. The impact of her body against the ceiling above had fractured her skull. She died while being transported to nearby Provident Hospital.

At first, investigators assumed that the explosion had been caused by a leaky gas pipe. But no trace of fumes lingered in the wreckage, and the building's owner, Charles Thomas, claimed that all of the fixtures in the house were electric. The only gas on the premises, he said, was in canisters used for cooking purposes. Those canisters were still intact. Thus, only one conclusion was possible: The house had been intentionally bombed—"the violent result," according to detectives, "of prejudice against the Negro inhabitants."[1]

This was not the first racially motivated bombing to occur in Chicago in the past several months. In fact, the Indiana Avenue explosion was only the latest in an apparently systematic bombing campaign dating back to July 1917, when the home of Mrs. S. P. Motley, an African American woman who had moved her family into a formerly all-white block of Maryland Avenue, was damaged by explosives. Eleven other bombings occurred in 1918, followed by several more in the new year 1919—most of them targeting black-inhabited dwellings or properties held by black real estate agents, and mostly on blocks where families from the Black Belt were moving into formerly all-white neighborhoods. Numerous protests had been lodged by the black community, especially since Chicago police had yet to make a single arrest in any of these cases. But the February 28 incident was the first to cause an actual fatality, so it was certain to intensify pressure on city officials to do something about the bombings and about the rising racial tensions they manifested. The death of Ernestine Ellis could not be ignored.[2]

* * *

Throughout its history, Chicago, though hardly a bastion of interracial harmony, had earned a reputation as a relatively tolerant city. The area's first permanent resident, in fact, had been a black man—a Caribbean-born entrepreneur named Jean Baptiste Point du Sable, who established a trading post near the mouth of the Chicago River in 1779. In the years following the establishment of an actual town in 1833, Illinois state law prevented many blacks from settling in the area. Even so, Chicago was a center of abolitionist sentiment during the Civil War, and after the war, a steady stream of blacks began moving in, most often taking work as domestic servants in households newly prosperous from the city's rapid economic development. The number of black Chicagoans increased significantly in the rebuilding period after the Great Fire of 1871, but the city's overall population was growing so fast that African Americans remained just a small proportion of inhabitants. Black neighborhoods were scattered widely throughout the city, with a large concentration developing on the South Side, just below the Loop.

All of this began changing in the decades after the end of Reconstruction and the striking down of the federal Civil Rights Act of 1875. The resulting rise of lynchings and Jim Crow discrimination made life ever more difficult for blacks in the former slave states. Many began to regard a move north as the only path to economic betterment, especially once a boll weevil infestation began destroying agricultural prospects in the Cotton Belt. The steadily growing exodus increased markedly, moreover, once the United States entered the Great War in 1917. The loss of thousands of workers to the armed forces, combined with a marked wartime contraction in immigration, created an acute labor shortage in Chicago's meatpacking, steel, railroad, and other industries. Private labor agents began to go south to recruit workers for Chicago factories, while some widely circulated black newspapers—most notably, the *Chicago Defender*—exhorted southern blacks to leave "the land of suffering" and come to the new Canaan in the North. Not just Chicago, but Detroit, Cleveland, and many other cities saw sudden and massive influxes from the South. "Anywhere north will do [for] us," wrote one would-be southern migrant. "I suppose the worst place there is better than the best place here."[3]

The result was what came to be known as "the Great Migration." In the three years after 1916, half a million southern blacks flocked to the large industrial cities of the North. In some cases, ministers transplanted entire congregations at once, chartering special train cars for the trip. Chicago alone saw more than fifty thousand new arrivals in the years from 1916 to 1919, doubling the city's black population in less than three years. Southern business interests tried to stop the hemorrhage of cheap labor by publicizing tales of frigid winters and difficult lives up north, but to no avail. "Every time a lynching takes place in a community down south," observed one city official, "colored people will arrive in Chicago within two weeks."[4]

For some this sudden increase in the black population was unambiguously a boon. The *Defender* saw its circulation balloon from ten thousand to over ninety-three thousand by the end of the war. Banks, retail outlets, and other "race" businesses in the Black Belt flourished, while attendance at Schorling Park, home of the all-black American Giants baseball team, soon exceeded that at Comiskey or Cubs Park on many afternoons. But although Chicago may have become, as one observer suggested, "the greatest experiment-station in the mingling of races and nationalities . . . rich with the noblest possibilities for the future," many people soon began to regard the influx as a source of concern. "Half a Million Darkies from Dixie Swarm to the North to Better Themselves" ran an all-too-typical headline in the *Tribune*. McCormick's newspaper had seen trouble brewing as early as the spring of 1917. "Black Man, Stay South!" the *Trib* pleaded in May of that year, arguing that the migration was "a huge mistake" that would soon be regretted by whites *and* blacks. By summer, the paper was even offering financial aid to blacks who would agree to leave Chicago and head back south.[5]

To be sure, problems did begin to appear soon after the migration's wartime crest. Numerous factors, some of them purely racist in origin, sparked white resentment of the newcomers. Egged on by the ever-helpful *Tribune*—which consistently overreported black crime and tended to depict the migrants as lazy, banjo-plucking idlers—many white Chicagoans soon found confirmation of their ugliest prejudices wherever they looked in the Black Belt. Places like "the Stroll," the main commercial stretch of State Street from Twenty-sixth to Thirty-ninth Street, were indeed hotbeds of gambling and vice—but mainly because police, responding to pressure from whites, kept forcing vice establishments to move from white residential and commercial districts to African American neighborhoods. Black-occupied houses were indeed overcrowded and dilapidated—but mainly because black tenants were compelled to take in boarders to help pay inflated rents, and could not persuade their landlords to make necessary repairs. And South Side street-cars were indeed full of black laborers in dirty, threadbare work clothes—but mainly because African Americans were the only major group of industrial workers forced to live beyond walking distance from their workplaces. Since most of the migrants came from rural areas, moreover, they were often not attuned to city living conventions, and thus appeared on the streets in housecoats, dust caps, and other casual attire—a perfectly acceptable practice where they came from but a sign of dissipation and turpitude to many "respectable" urban whites.[6]

In the workplace, too, blacks were soon causing friction. Since strikebreaking had long been the only route for African Americans into many industries, the words "Negro" and "scab" were often seen as synonymous by many labor groups. At the Union Stockyards, where the number of black workers increased by a factor of twelve in the years from 1915 to 1918, efforts were made to recruit the new workers into existing unions. But many of the migrants, relegated to subordinate, all-black locals and denied access to high-paying jobs, were rightfully suspicious of organized labor and refused to join. (As one black stockyard worker said of the unions, "You pay money and get nothing.") These workplace conflicts just intensified as many white soldiers returned from the war only to find their old positions filled by black interlopers from the South.[7]

But it was in the area of housing that racial strains were most keenly felt. New residential construction had all but stopped in Chicago during the war, and so the new arrivals faced an acute housing shortage. The South Side Black Belt, already home to almost 90 percent of the city's blacks, simply could house no more within its existing boundaries. With Lake Michigan to the east and largely industrial and commercial zones to the north and west, the neighborhood could feasibly grow only to the south and southwest, into previously all-white sections of Kenwood, Hyde Park, and other nearby areas—setting off an "invasion" that longtime residents regarded with increasing resentment.[8]

At first, efforts to halt the integration were peaceful. Neighborhood organizations such as the Hyde Park–Kenwood Property Owners' Association launched initiatives—often under the cover of promoting cleaner, safer streets—to keep their districts "clear of undesirables." Real estate agents were discouraged from renting or selling to African Americans, and propaganda campaigns urged residents to protect property values by preserving the "lily white" character of the area. When these efforts failed, however, the tactics turned uglier. Mobs armed with brickbats and other weapons gathered around black-occupied dwellings. Intimidating handbills were circulated: "Look out; you're next for hell," read one. Another, addressed to black tenants of a building on Vincennes Avenue, was more explicit: "We are going to BLOW these FLATS TO HELL and if you don't want to go with them you had better move at once."

And then the bombs started going off for real. Although the *Defender,* at least, was convinced that these acts of "attempted assault and murder" were committed by members of the Hyde Park–Kenwood Association, no conclusive evidence was ever found to link the organization to the incidents. In any case, the bombing effort was doomed to fail. By the end of the war, Chicago's black population was still on the rise and still on the move into white neighborhoods, and there was little that anyone in the city could do to stop it.[9]

* * *

One of the major beneficiaries of this mushrooming of Chicago's black population was William Hale Thompson. Where the *Tribune* and other bastions of the white establishment could see only problems, Big Bill and Fred Lundin saw opportunity. Blacks were still overwhelmingly Republican at this time; they would not begin abandoning the party of Lincoln until the 1930s, when FDR's New Deal lured them to the Democratic side. African Americans in Chicago, eager to embrace the franchise they were denied down south, also voted in higher percentages than their white counterparts. And for the first time, blacks made up a significant portion of a northern city's population. Recognizing these facts, Thompson and Lundin were among the first Chicago politicians to see the voters of the Black Belt for what they had now become—what Carl Sandburg would later call "the strongest effective unit of political power, good or bad, in America."

Thompson, whose father fought the slave-owning rebels at Mobile Bay, had actually been attentive to black concerns since the beginning of his political career. One of his few accomplishments as an alderman had been sponsoring an ordinance to build a playground in a black section of his ward—allegedly the first municipal playground in the nation. "White people from nearby came over and said they wanted it in their neighborhood," he would later boast in speeches. "I said to this, 'I see you have a fine house and yard with fences around it and nice dogs but no children; I'll build a playground for children and not [for] poodle dogs.'" Later, at a celebration of the fiftieth anniversary of the Emancipation Proclamation, he threw away his prepared speech and spoke plainly to his audience of fifteen thousand African Americans: "My task is not easy," he said. "Prejudices do exist against Negroes. . . . But to deny equal opportunity to the Negro in this land would be out of harmony with American history, untrue to sacred history, untrue to the sacred principles of liberty and equal rights, and would make a mockery of our boasted civilization."[10]

At a time when alleged progressives were falling pitifully short in their support of equal rights, such words showed significant political courage. And Thompson did not back down from them when he ran for mayor. "I'll give you people the best opportunities you've ever had if you elect me," he told a black audience during the 1915 campaign. "I'll give your people jobs . . . and any of you want to shoot craps, go ahead and do it." That he was appealing more to new migrants than to the respectable black middle class is obvious from that last comment, but both ends of the spectrum ended up showing him strong support. The Second Ward's black voters gave Big Bill the margins he needed in 1915 to win in both the primary and the general election.[11]

Whether Thompson's election was truly a boon for Chicago's blacks is debatable, but he *did* deliver on many of his promises. Aside from helping to sweep into office the first African American alderman in the city's history (Oscar De Priest), he also appointed blacks to prominent posts in his administration. Edward Wright and Louis B. Anderson were named assistant corporation counsels (Anderson later became Big Bill's floor manager in the city council), while the Reverend Archibald Carey was made an investigator in the city's legal department. By the end of his first term, Thompson had also doubled the number of blacks on the police force. Nor did he neglect the more symbolic expressions of support. He appeared frequently at holiday celebrations and civic functions in the Black Belt, and one of his first official acts as mayor (a decision later reversed by a judge) was to ban the showing of D. W. Griffith's notoriously racist *The Birth of a Nation*. Thompson denounced the film as an abomination and an insult to millions of American citizens.[12]

Many whites disapproved of these efforts. Writers in the daily press began referring to city hall as "Uncle Tom's Cabin" and questioned the wisdom of some of Thompson's appointments. Big Bill did back down on at least one choice (of a black physician to the Municipal Tuberculosis Sanitarium), but on the rest he stood firm. "The persons appointed were qualified for their positions," he argued. "In the name of humanity it is my duty to do what I can to elevate rather than degrade any class of American citizens." This from a man derided by his allegedly more enlightened enemies as "a blubbering jungle hippopotamus."[13]

The black community responded with understandable enthusiasm to Thompson's various expressions of support. The *Chicago Defender* in particular was lavish in its praise of the mayor, comparing him frequently to Abraham Lincoln and calling him "the best friend politically our people have had in the past half-century." According to the *Defender,* the members of the race owed him their votes. "He has treated us fairly and squarely," an editorial claimed in late 1918, during Thompson's unsuccessful Senate campaign. "We have waited too many long, weary years for such a friend, and we should be loyal to him."[14]

But there were some in Chicago's Black Belt who were not quite so entranced with Big Bill Thompson. For those working to mitigate the squalor of black neighborhoods, the mayor's bruited support often seemed all talk and grand gestures, with very little real conviction behind it. Wasn't it Thompson's police department that was pushing vice and gambling establishments into the Black Belt, degrading the neighborhood and providing black youths with an easy road to crime and vice but no route to respectable success? And wasn't it that same police force that was now just standing by as black homes were being bombed? Clearly someone needed to point out that fine words and a few token jobs were not enough to earn the mayor comparisons to the Great Emancipator. And there was at least one black leader in Chicago determined to do just that.

*   *   *

On the night of March 19, a little girl playing on a South Side pavement watched as two men in a roadster drove past and tossed a package from the passenger side. It landed on the steps of 4724 State Street, the offices of black banker and real estate agent Jesse Binga. Curious, the girl turned to a woman standing next to her. "Let's see what it is," she said. But the woman held her back, warning, "No, it might be a bomb."

A few seconds later, the package exploded, rocking the neighbor-hood and showering the sidewalks on both sides of the street with broken glass.

Only one person—a frightened man who jumped out of a third-floor window at the sound of the blast—was hurt. Another bomb a few minutes later on Calumet Avenue, apparently thrown from the same roadster, hurt no one at all. But for Chicago's black population, the implications of this new attack were ominous: The pace of bomb-ings was accelerating, and it seemed clear that the Chicago Police Department was unwilling to do anything to stop them.[15]

Admittedly, the police weren't doing much to fight crime else-where in Chicago, either. As the spring of 1919 progressed, crime suddenly seemed to be out of control everywhere in the city. Hold-ups, shootings, stolen automobiles—all were now on the rise, making a mockery of the hopeful New Year's sentiments about "Chicago's greatest year." In the first twenty days of March alone, the city had seen eighteen murders, two major bank robberies, three payroll hold-ups, and scores of assaults, muggings, and other offenses. John Gar-rity, Mayor Thompson's chief of police, was on the defensive. Crime was rampant nationwide, he explained. There were simply too many soldiers returning from war and failing to find jobs. In Chicago, he added, the problem was compounded by the presence of five thou-sand unemployed African Americans newly arrived from the South. With so many idle, rootless black men in the city, it was no wonder that crime was so high.[16]

To Ida B. Wells-Barnett, the well-known South Side journalist and anti-lynching activist, this was simply too much to take. Not only were blacks being disproportionately victimized by the rising tide of crime in Chicago; now, apparently, they were also going to be blamed for it. And this by the administration of a man who claimed to be the best friend of the Black Belt!

Born into slavery in Holly Springs, Mississippi, in 1862, Wells-Barnett had been a controversial figure for most of her adult life. Called everything from "the mother protector" of her race (by the *Illinois State Journal*) to "a slanderous and nasty mulatress" (by the *New York Times*), she had been on a one-woman "crusade for justice" since her early twenties, when she filed suit against the C&O Railroad for ejecting her from a first-class coach on a train out of Memphis. (When the conductor tried to pull her from her seat, the diminutive young teacher "hooked her feet under the seat in front of her, began scratching the conductor with her nails, and then bit his hands deeply enough to draw blood.") Several years later, in response to the lynching of three black men in Memphis, she wrote a newspaper editorial so scathing that a mob of the city's "leading citizens" ransacked the paper's offices and warned the editorial's author (who was in Philadelphia at the time) that if she ever returned to Memphis she would be hanged in front of the courthouse. This, of course, only cemented her resolve to keep writing. "They had destroyed my paper . . . , made me an exile, and threatened my life for hinting at the truth," she later wrote, "[so] I felt that I owed it to myself and my race to tell the *whole* truth."[17]

Since moving north to Chicago in its world's fair year of 1893 (when she caused a stir with her controversial pamphlet "The Reason Why the Colored American Is Not in the World Columbian Exposition"), she had married and raised six children. But family life had done little to curtail her activities. When called upon to make speaking tours, she would simply pack up whatever child was still young enough to require her attentions and bring him or her along. She also organized several women's political and suffrage clubs, served as Chicago's first black female probation officer, worked with Jane Addams to prevent school segregation, and once even represented "the colored people of Illinois" in a court case against a sheriff who had failed to prevent a lynching in Cairo. ("Mother," her thirteen-year-old son had said to her when at first she seemed reluctant to take on the task, "if you don't go, no one else will.") Anticipating that Chicago's burgeoning black population would soon need a reliable source of social services, she and her husband had founded the Negro Fellowship League in 1910. Conceived as a kind of black version of Hull House, the league was to serve as a "lighthouse" for black migrants, finding them jobs and housing and providing them with alternatives to the saloon and the brothel as places to spend their idle hours.

Now a white-haired and matronly woman of fifty-seven, Wells-Barnett had become a familiar figure on the streets of the South Side, marching resolutely from one political meeting to another ("She walked as if she owned the world," her daughter once said), always willing to take up a cause. And although she did admit that Chicago was now the "one spot in this entire broad United States [where] the black man received anything like adequate political recognition," that didn't mean the city's current racial situation was in any way satisfactory to her. True justice, she knew, required a constant goading of the powers-that-be, and as her son might have put it, if she didn't do it, no one else would.[18]

The lax official response to the recent bombings just confirmed the need for strident protest. Big Bill Thompson, a mayor for whom she had once campaigned, had done nothing to prevent the ongoing attacks on the people who regarded him as their champion. And now Chief Garrity's blaming of them for the high crime rate merely added insult to injury. Furious, Wells-Barnett called a meeting of the Negro Fellowship League on March 24. In a contentious session, they adopted a series of resolutions denouncing the mayor and his associates. Branding Garrity's charges "a willful and malicious libel against the Negro," the league depicted the statement as an attempt to make blacks the scapegoat for police incompetence: "It is bad enough that we are being discharged from work and made idle through no fault of our own without being held responsible for all the crime in Chicago in an attempt to excuse Big Bill's inefficient police force."

These were hardly mincing words, but the league saved the worst for last: "We urge all self-respecting, law-abiding Negroes in Chicago to resent this insult against the race by going to the polls next Tuesday and voting for Maclay Hoyne for next mayor of the city."[19]

To many in black Chicago, this was tantamount to blasphemy. Hoyne, the Cook County state's attorney, was running for mayor as an independent, but he was a longtime member of the Democratic Party—the party of the southern whites they had come to Chicago to escape. And, besides, how could blacks turn against the mayor they had so long regarded as their friend?

Clearly, any attempt to turn the Black Belt against Thompson was going to face staunch opposition. But given the closeness of the polls, even a slight shift away from the mayor was potentially dire to his and Lundin's plans. The "Second Lincoln" was counting on his usual flood of African American votes to give him his victory on Election Day. The last thing he needed was Wells-Barnett, the eternal troublemaker, stirring up resentment among his most reliable base of support.

CHAPTER SIX

Election

THE ELECTION WAS—as hoped—turning into a free-for-all. By mid-March, there were four major candidates actively campaigning to wrest control of the city away from its incumbent mayor. Each had vulnerabilities. Democratic nominee Robert M. Sweitzer, who had lost to Thompson in 1915, was an affable, somewhat Falstaffian county clerk burdened with inconvenient ties to the local gas interests. Sweitzer had the dominant Democratic faction behind him, but his support in the party was likely to be sapped by the independent candidacy of State's Attorney Hoyne, an "iron-jawed Irishman" whose family had been prominent in Chicago since it was a village. Never much concerned about vice and corruption until a Republican captured city hall in 1915, Hoyne had since become a persistent thorn in the side of the Thompson-Lundin forces, launching several high-profile campaigns against prostitution, police malfeasance, and illegal gambling. Meanwhile, Labor Party stalwart John Fitzpatrick and Socialist candidate John Collins, hoping to capitalize on the growing disaffection among the city's union and radical elements, were also running hard—neither likely to win, but each capable of drawing away crucial votes from the main contenders.

And now even Ring Lardner had thrown his homburg into the ring. In a series of columns entitled "Me for Mayor," the ever-sardonic journalist was amusing *Tribune* readers with his run as "the People's candidate." In his daily column he was making a joke of the whole

election, casting his campaign promises in verse ("The fire department will be my special delight / So that I may fire someone every
night") and vowing to make "a strong play for the Walloon vote."
He also made sure to point out that, if elected, he would be the thin-
nest mayor in Chicago history.[1]

On this last point Lardner definitely had the advantage of his main
opponents—rather voluminous figures all—but for sheer absurdism
he had plenty of competition among the city's pols. Chicago had the
pleasure, for instance, of watching Judge Harry Olson, who during
the primary campaign had warned that reelecting Thompson would
"ruin the Republican Party for years to come," suddenly change his
mind and come to the ruinous mayor's support in the general election.
Other Republicans—with the exception of intellectual progressive
types like Charles Merriam—were also miraculously finding virtues
in the man they had so recently lambasted. This, of course, was not
unusual behavior in the Windy City. Deal making among political
enemies was a venerable Chicago tradition. It was no accident, after
all, that Charles Dudley Warner, the editor who coined the old saw
about politics and strange bedfellows, spent several formative years
practicing law in Chicago.[2]

The mayor's nemeses in the press, on the other hand, were proving to be more than just fair-weather enemies. Victor Lawson of the
Daily News again took a practical approach: "None of the mayoral
candidates is of the type which should be chosen for the high office of
Mayor," he admitted to Arthur Brisbane in mid-March. "But under
the circumstances, the controlling consideration is to deliver Chicago from the menace of four more years of the Thompson-Lundin
combination." Since, by Lawson's arithmetic, "Sweitzer can beat
him; Hoyne can't," the *Daily News* adopted the cause of the official
Democrat. McCormick at the *Tribune,* trying to be equally practical,
came to the opposite conclusion: "The Thompson-Sweitzer issue was
fought out four years ago," a *Tribune* editorial noted on March 3,

"and Thompson cleaned Sweitzer with the precise and meticulous violence of a high wind taking the shingles off a decayed farmhouse. . . . We do not say that Hoyne is a fair-haired boy who would meet the unqualified approval of the City Club. But he is immeasurably a better candidate than Thompson or Sweitzer."[3]

But while the anti-Thompson forces may have disagreed on who qualified as the least of three evils, they did seem united on at least one point—that Big Bill was most vulnerable on the issue of his alleged disloyalty during the war. Crime, scandals, the growing city deficit—all were given their due in the screeds against Thompson delivered throughout the month of March. But candidates and newspapers alike seemed to doubt the potency of these issues, which had failed to do much damage to the mayor in the primaries. Instead, hoping to arouse the sentiments of a city joyfully welcoming home its sons in arms, critics focused their attacks on Kaiser Bill—Thompson the antiwar apologist, the snubber of Marshal Joffre, the mayor of "the sixth German city" of the world. Thompson, according to celebrity lawyer Clarence Darrow, who was campaigning for his colleague (and frequent courtroom opponent) Maclay Hoyne, "used his influence to weaken our power, to discourage our people, and to strengthen our enemy." Hoyne himself was even more caustic, accusing Thompson of failing the nation in its hour of greatest need: "He disgraced Chicago in the eyes of the world, and in fact became a national menace." The state's attorney recounted stories of German fliers who allegedly dropped extracts of Big Bill's antiwar speeches into American trenches during the war "in an attempt to make our soldiers believe that their own country was not united back of them." This last point was much emphasized by the newspapers, which reprinted numerous letters from soldiers decrying their hometown mayor. "A guy was ashamed to acknowledge that he was from Chicago when he was mixing with other troops," ran one of these alleged testimonials reproduced in the Daily News. "They [always] wanted to know if it was a fact that Chicago had a German spy for a mayor."

One letter—from a First Sergeant Alfred B. Backer to his family—was even more dyspeptic: "Honestly, I believe if that big fat Bolshevik crook is elected to office again, I don't want to come back to Chicago to live."[4]

Thompson could only parry these attacks with blunt and categorical denial. He was *not* a traitor, he insisted, and in fact had been the soldiers' greatest defender against exploitation by war profiteers who put their greed above human lives. He reminded the electorate of his numerous libel suits against the newspapers for raising the specious disloyalty charges in earlier elections. Thompson, of course, was trying hard to turn his wartime behavior into a nonissue, but in truth the hint of pro-German sentiments did not work entirely against him in certain quarters. After the primaries, Fred Lundin had determined that Thompson could win the general election by capturing big margins among three important demographics: blacks, the Irish, and Germans. None of these groups had been particularly pro-war—blacks because of widespread racial discrimination in the armed forces, the Irish because of anti-British sentiments, and Germans for obvious reasons of ethnic loyalty. ("Damn him," one German voter would later say, "we know he's no good, but he made life livable for us in 1918, and [so] he gets our votes.") Always known for sounding off on national and international topics, Thompson had no problem campaigning on emotional issues that would seem to have little to do with a local city election, so he made a point of espousing Irish home rule, calling for "the dissolution of the British yoke of oppression," and railing against England's aggressive posture in the Paris peace talks.

The mayor was also careful to cultivate his old friendships in the Black Belt. Ida Wells-Barnett's efforts to turn the black vote to Hoyne were troublesome, and Thompson and Lundin were taking nothing for granted. When the "Old Eighth" (the 370th Infantry, an all-black regiment) returned to Chicago from active duty in France, Big Bill was on the scene to greet them. Bursting into the hall of the Coliseum, where the troops were being feted by large (and largely black) crowds, Thompson rushed to the podium and, amid cheers and applause, hailed the returning heroes in lofty terms. "You have come back decorated for distinguished service on the battlefield," he intoned, "and for your glorious service, your devotion to our country, and your heroism in battle, I bespeak for you that justice and equality of citizenship which shall open the doors of opportunity to you." These were fine words indeed, and they were received with gratitude by the returning soldiers in the crowd. The fact that such "justice and equality" had been denied them so often in Woodrow Wilson's segregated army—where they routinely faced abuse from white officers—just highlighted the mayor's enduring appeal to the city's African American community. Big Bill's actions may have left much to be desired, but at least he was saying the right words, at a time when few other politicians were doing likewise.[5]

Whether Thompson and Lundin were seriously worried about their support among blacks is impossible to say. The Poor Swede had already managed to broker his deal with the heads of the other two GOP organizations, and his formidable army of ward committeemen, precinct captains, and election workers—in the Black Belt and throughout the city—was firmly in place. But there was another uncertain factor that could possibly prove decisive in the contest—namely, the soldier vote. According to Illinois law, anyone voting in the April 1 election had to be registered by March 11. Because of delays in bringing the troops back from Europe, many Chicago soldiers would not arrive until after that deadline. In fact, members of the Rainbow Division (the 149th Field Artillery, composing one of the largest contingents of potential Chicago voters) were expected to arrive after the registration deadline but before the election. Given Thompson's unpopularity among the returning white soldiers, allowing these men to vote would pose a distinct threat to the mayor's reelection chances.[6]

Back in January, Robert Sweitzer, among others, had proposed emergency legislation to allow unregistered soldiers to vote if they could present their discharge papers at polling places on Election Day. A measure to this effect, sponsored by a state senator named Edward Hughes, had been introduced in the legislature at Springfield and was now swiftly advancing through the readings process. The bill was expected to pass in time, but before becoming law, it would have to be signed by the Illinois chief executive—Governor Frank O. Lowden. A Republican who owed his election in 1916 to the support of the Thompson-Lundin organization, Lowden could choose to stop the emergency bill by refusing to sign it. But his decision would be influenced by a few major considerations: namely, that Lowden would be running for the upcoming 1920 Republican presidential nomination; that Thompson was likely to be reelected chairman of the Illinois delegation to that convention; and that the two men, once friends and political allies, were now sworn enemies.

On March 20, the Hughes bill, which had already passed in the state senate, passed in the house by a unanimous vote of 130 to 0. The bill would now go to Governor Lowden for his signature. Thompson and Lundin would be watching to see what the governor of Illinois did next.[7]

* * *

Of all the powerful figures standing in the way of Thompson and Lundin's aspirations to political ascendancy, Frank O. Lowden was perhaps the one they despised most. Outright enemies like Victor Lawson or Colonel McCormick could be battled head-on; political rivals like Harry Olson or the members of the Democratic organization could be bargained with; idealists like the progressive reformers could simply be marginalized. But allies who turned around and betrayed their friends were another story. In machine politics, after all, ingratitude and disloyalty were the greatest sins a man could commit. Lowden was guilty of both.[8]

Like that most famous presidential aspirant from Illinois, Frank Lowden had risen from humble beginnings. Son of a blacksmith-farmer from rural Iowa, he had educated himself whenever his farming duties allowed, eventually working his way through the University of Iowa and then Union (now Northwestern) College of Law. A flourishing Chicago legal practice had given him enough stature to meet and marry an heiress—Florence Pullman, daughter of multimillionaire George Pullman of railroading fame. Always a solid, middle-of-the-road Republican of high principle, Lowden (blessed, according to Hamlin Garland, with the looks of "an English earl") had nonetheless been enough of a pragmatist to agree to an uneasy alliance with the Thompson-Lundin machine in his run for the governor's mansion in 1916. At the time, Lundin had been eager to proceed to step two of his grand plan to make "a Mayor, a Governor, a President," and he saw in the distinguished-looking Lowden a politician appealing enough to win and ambitious enough to play ball to do it. And so, at a much-whispered-about colloquy in a country house near Eagle Lake, Wisconsin, the three men reportedly struck a deal: Lowden, it was agreed, would support Thompson for leader of the Republican National Committee if Thompson and Lundin would support Lowden for governor. It was just the kind of horse trade for which Illinois politics was notorious, and—in this case as in many others—it bore fruit. In May 1916, with Lowden's help, Thompson became chairman of the Illinois delegation to the Republican National Committee. In November of the same year, Lowden, with the support of the mayor and his mentor, was elected governor of Illinois.[9]

For Lowden, apparently, the deal ended there. But Thompson and Lundin had other plans. In their version of the game, elective success was naturally followed by expressions of gratitude, mainly in the form of patronage and other spoils of victory. And in Illinois these were always in abundant supply. For technical reasons having to do with the state's antiquated constitution, major cities in Illinois had to be run by a number of independent "governments," each responsible for a different part of the city's operations. Chicago alone had twenty-seven of these entities—including several park districts, the Chicago Board of Education, the library board, the courts, and so forth—each acting independently to raise and spend money to accomplish its various mandates. What this created (aside from administrative chaos) was a plethora of boards, commissions, and bureaus, each of which had to be filled by appointment or election. With so many choice, well-paid positions to dispense, Illinois officials could—and did—use them as a kind of political currency, trading a commissionership here for a bit of election support there, promising a veto of a bill today for control of a parks board tomorrow. This was politics as usual in the Land of Lincoln in 1916, and—albeit to a lesser extent, thanks to constitutional and administrative changes over the years—it's the way the game is still played today.[10]

But Frank Lowden had other priorities upon becoming governor in January 1917. Once in office, he launched a full-scale effort to streamline the state government and modernize its tax structure, effectively doing away with many of the lucrative no-show jobs with which politicians repaid their supporters. Worse still, the plum appointments that remained within the governor's gift were hardly disposed of in line with the desires of the mayor and Lundin. In fact, as Lowden's biographer has observed, "an endorsement from Thompson seemed almost equivalent to a blackball" for any aspiring machine ally seeking state patronage.[11]

Needless to say, the city hall crowd was furious. On the occasion of one of the governor's visits to Chicago that spring, Lundin and several of his associates stormed Lowden's suite at the Blackstone Hotel, pushed past his secretary at the outer door, and confronted the governor within. To hear one writer tell it: "It was a hectic interview. Lowden lit many cigarettes, throwing them half-smoked in the fireplace. He pleaded that appointments were personal, not political." But the Poor Swede would not hear of it. "Lundin pressed the Governor. He demanded promised patronage and support for the City Hall organization. But when the final showdown came, the Governor refused point blank."[12]

Since then, relations between city hall and the Illinois governor had just gone from bad to worse. The two Republican executives had clashed repeatedly since 1916, especially over the mayor's pacifist stance during the war, which Lowden regarded as tantamount to treason. And so in March 1919—as the fifty-eight-year-old Lowden lay in bed in Springfield with a mild case of the flu—he had a delicate decision to make about the upcoming Hughes bill. With his eye on the 1920 presidential nomination (which he very much wanted, despite pro forma expressions of reluctance), he could conceivably allow the bill to die unsigned and make it impossible for many soldiers to vote. Doing so would certainly win him some needed points with the alienated Thompson-Lundin organization and perhaps ease his path to the nomination. But it would also go against every pro-military conviction he had as the so-called war governor of Illinois. And in any case, if Thompson lost the mayor's office, he would be a significantly less formidable enemy to Lowden, even if he managed to retain his position as a power broker at the 1920 convention. So when the bill came before him, the governor did not hesitate long. On March 27— just five days before the election—he signed it into law.

Thompson and Lundin, loath to be seen as anti-soldier but certain to be hurt by the bill, could say nothing publicly against the decision. But the governor's move underlined a conviction that had been forming in their minds for three years—namely, that if they were to have any hope of realizing their greater political goals, Lowden was an obstacle that would have to be eliminated.[13]

* * *

It was the last week of the campaign, and prospects were starting to look worrisome for the Thompson camp. March had been a turbulent month in Chicago. The crime wave had just grown worse and worse, a development attributed by the *Daily News* not to a rising black population, but rather to the "criminal politics" in city hall. Labor unrest was growing, with one meeting in the hall of Chicago's journeyman plumbers union degenerating into a fatal gun battle. Wage demands by the streetcar unions were at the same time pushing the car lines to the verge of crisis: "It is impossible to exaggerate the seriousness of the situation," announced Leonard Busby, president of the Chicago Surface Lines, "both to the investors and [to] the public." Meanwhile, the entire city was fretting about Bolsheviks in their midst. On March 10, an alleged Chicago-based plot by the Industrial Workers of the World was revealed, its object "the overthrow of the government of the United States by means of a bloody revolution and the establishment of a Bolshevik republic." Chicago police had even formed a special "Bolshevik squad" to investigate the bomb threats that were becoming ever more numerous.[14]

The toll these events were taking on the mayor's reelection prospects was clear. Even the election bettors in the city saloons, where Thompson had long been the favorite, were now holding back their wagers, "awaiting next week's developments." Then, just a few days before the election, McCormick and the *Tribune* opened up a bold new line of attack against the Thompson-Lundin forces. Filing a plea in the mayor's libel suit that charged him with sedition during the war, the *Trib* cited acts and conduct that "did obstruct and embarrass, hinder and interfere with the United States" in its war effort. The timing of this plea was clearly an election tactic, the last blast in a concerted effort to remind Chicago voters of Big Bill's war record, but it had its effect. Some were now saying that Sweitzer would run away with the election. Even the news that Ring Lardner had dropped out of the race (he decided that he'd rather make a run for the office of king) could not bring the mayor any cheer.[15]

If ever Thompson and Lundin needed to shore up their base, it was now. So they turned to the people who had given them the winning edge in 1915—the voters of the Black Belt. No arrests had yet been made in the racial-bombing incidents, and black voters clearly needed some reassurance that the mayor hadn't turned his back on them. At a March 24 rally at the Pekin Theatre, Thompson was in top form: "I always feel at home here in the Second Ward," the mayor crooned to the all-black audience. "I feel as though I were among friends."

"You're our brother!" cried a voice from the second row.

Amid general laughter the mayor turned serious. "That's no jest," he said. Then, in a not-so-veiled reference to Wells-Barnett's efforts against him, he added: "Enemies have tried to divide us—they are trying to divide us now—but we have always stood together and we always will."

The rally eventually turned into a virtual lovefest. Ignoring accusations of his inaction in the recent bombings, Thompson made sure to remind his audience of their frequent descriptions of himself as the second Abraham Lincoln. His advice to black voters was to deny the naysayers and remain united: "Vote as a unit and you will protect yourselves from your enemies; lose your solidarity and you will fall prey to them."

"And now," he concluded to riotous applause (and with perhaps more candor than he intended), "go out and get as many ballots in the box as you can."[16]

The campaign, meanwhile, reached a crescendo in the days leading up to April 1, with Thompson, Sweitzer, and Hoyne each predicting a victory margin of more than one hundred thousand votes. "Never, on the eve of a Chicago mayoralty election, was there more uncertainty than tonight," the *New York Times* remarked on March 30. The *Tribune* described the scene in vivid detail: "Downtown Chicago stood on its head," the paper reported. "[Partisans] ran around in circles, got mixed up in a dozen clashes, tore down lithographs and smashed banners, paraded, yelled, swamped the betting places, and went mad." There was widespread hooliganism in the Loop—including, according to the *Herald and Examiner,* the "hurling of stink bombs"—as anti-Thompson crowds grew increasingly desperate. One group painted a Kaiser-style mustache on a poster of the mayor's face and followed his limousine to all of his campaign stops. "Whenever [Mayor Thompson] drew up at the curb," the *Trib* reported, "the crowd was there with the picture and insisted on sticking it into his face."[17]

Early on Election Day, voter turnout seemed on track to break all previous records, with an estimated four hundred thousand ballots cast by noon. Amid a "general belief that party lines were [being] thrown to the wind," no one could predict the outcome with anything approaching confidence. The Cook County ballot qualified as one of the longest and most complicated in the world, so one could never guess precisely what a confused electorate might do. This vote, though, was considered even less predictable than usual. Irma Frankenstein, Emily's mother, went to vote with her husband, Victor, and described the process in her diary: "We knew a little about the candidates but there were so many of them [that] the ballot was a disturbing puzzle." She tried to recall the recommendations made by the Women's City Club, but could remember only a few. For the rest of the offices, she decided to vote "100% American," rejecting candidates with Polish, German, Bohemian, and Swedish surnames (an odd choice, surely, for a woman named Frankenstein). "I fell for one poetic name," she admitted, "Earl somebody or other. His name was in two places. I voted for him once. So much for poetry." After an hour, she emerged from the polling station only to find that Victor had taken even longer to decipher the ballot. But she was apparently satisfied with her vote. "I found a system," she concluded, "and I daresay I voted as intelligently as most voters."[18]

Mrs. Frankenstein may or may not have been right on that last point, but when the votes were tallied—again amid widespread charges of ballot fraud and voter intimidation by armed thugs—the message was clear: The city (or at least a plurality of its voters) wanted four more years of Big Bill Thompson. Granted, the mayor's total of 259,828 votes was nearly 140,000 less than he'd gotten in 1915, but in a field divided among Sweitzer (238,206 votes), Hoyne (110,851), and the minor-party candidates, it was enough to squeak by.[19]

"Truth and justice have again prevailed," the euphoric and much-relieved mayor announced at his victory celebration that night. "The voters have rendered their verdict. In spite of the malevolent attacks made upon me by the interests that seek to prey upon the public, my administration has been approved by the people!"[20]

The national press, fully invested in the image of Thompson as a traitorous buffoon, was incredulous: "Chicago's Shame!" screeched the *New Haven Journal-Courier.* The *New York Times* could only scratch its editorial head: "It is difficult for outsiders to understand the complicated interplay of machines and personalities and more or less artificial issues . . . that enter into a Cook County municipal election," the paper admitted. Somehow, voters in that "bedraggled and dirty" city had seen fit to reelect an "eccentric Caliph," and one who had proven himself "a bitter joke as a patriot." It was apparently more than the members of a truly civilized East Coast electorate could fathom.

The local newspapers seemed to have a better grasp of what had happened. The much-hoped-for surge of anti-Thompson votes—among soldiers and others hostile to the mayor—had been dissipated by the presence of too many alternative candidates in the race. Calling Thompson's victory a "fluke," the *Daily News* tried to make much of this huge but splintered opposition vote: "He becomes a minority mayor, holding office not by virtue of any confidence still felt in him by the community . . . but simply because the anti-Thompson voters did not work together."

The *Chicago Daily Journal,* however, was far less diplomatic. "Negroes Elect 'Big Bill' " was the banner headline on their special election edition, over a story explaining how Thompson's overwhelming support in the Black Belt accounted for virtually his entire 17,600-vote margin of victory. "The Negroes were in a frenzy of delight when they learned that their votes had put Big Bill in the mayor's chair for another four years," the paper reported. "South State Street, South Wabash Avenue, and the other thoroughfares in the district witnessed a demonstration of hilarity seldom seen on an election night." In an already divided city, then, the election results provided just one more point of contention, just one more reason for many embittered whites to resent the city's ever more powerful black population.[21]

The mayor himself offered a different analysis. "I have been maligned. I have been misunderstood," Big Bill announced. "[But] I hope during the ensuing four years to be understood." Turning to his perennial trump card, the Chicago Plan, he tried to refocus the city's attention on its hopeful future. "I want to make Chicago a great city," he effused. "I want to build her a lakefront, to finish widening streets and building bridges. I love this city! My love for her was inherited! I love Chicago with all my heart!"

For Fred Lundin, the triumph of his protégé meant a second chance to extend the reach of his organization beyond the city to embrace his greater state and national objectives. Before that could happen, though, there was a lot of work to be done. In the days after the election, he was already busily tallying up the contributions of their friends during the campaign, in order to know who was to be rewarded and who was to be shunned. The calculus of political obligation could be arcane, but no one knew it better than the Poor Swede.

One thing that did not escape his notice: Among the customary letters of congratulations, conciliation, and contrition—the bread-and-butter missives that came from both Republicans and Democrats, from both friends and enemies—one was conspicuously missing. From the governor of Illinois there was nothing.[22]

CHAPTER SEVEN

On the Warpath

BARELY CHASTISED by the close call of his narrow reelection victory, Big Bill Thompson moved quickly to punish his enemies and reassert his authority over a city where discord and divisiveness now seemed to be worsening every day. "Re-Election Starts Mayor on Warpath," the *Daily News* reported on the day after the election. In words "bristling with militancy," the mayor made it understood that he was ready to do battle with the full gamut of "greedy plunderers of the people." He would launch an official investigation into the "rotten influence" of the Municipal Voters' League, begin an effort to purge the board of education of his opponents, and take aim at the utility and transit interests that wanted to bleed the people with higher gas prices and transit fares. All this, he claimed, was to "restore to the people their constitutional powers to govern themselves."[1]

The hidden agenda behind these multiple crusades was not lost on the members of the press. "Thompson Men Plan to Extend Rule in State: Have Visions of Lowden Forced into Line," the *Tribune* warned on April 3, citing rumors that the governor's political future was now in Big Bill's hands. "Mayor Thompson let it be known that he will shoot full of holes . . . Governor Lowden's alleged hope of entering the Republican lists for the presidential nomination," the *Herald and Examiner* reported. "If the Governor wishes the Mayor's assistance, he will have to plead on his political knees." Lowden, in other words, was going to have to start giving the Thompson-Lundin organization what it wanted—or else suffer the consequences.[2]

In his official statements, of course, Big Bill adopted a different tone and was mostly magnanimous in victory. When asked in a sit-down interview with *Tribune* reporter Charles Wheeler if he wanted to say anything to the newspapers, Thompson chuckled. "I guess we gave you a pretty fair fight, didn't we?" he said. "But seriously, I am not apologizing for my fight against you. I am ready for more if you want it." After a moment, though, the mayor relented and offered to let bygones be bygones: "I am here for four years more. Let's try to forget our personal likes and dislikes for a while and see if there isn't something good and big and enduring we can all do for Chicago."

Apparently hoping to get past this genial rhetoric, Wheeler went on to press the mayor on possible changes to his cabinet and on the coming wars with the MVL and the new city council. But just when Big Bill seemed ready to be more candid, the office door burst open and Fred Lundin rushed in. "Hello there, old-timer," Lundin said to the veteran reporter, with a smile that "hung on either earlobe."

When Wheeler asked the Poor Swede for his own perspective on the election results, Lundin (who owned a hardware business) merely threw up his hands. "Don't know a thing about politics," he cried. "I'm just selling doors."

"Isn't he a wonder?" Thompson beamed.

And that was the end of the interview.[3]

Whatever their real plans, the Thompson administration continued to insist publicly that its first priority was to unite the discordant city behind "a constructive program to boom Chicago"—translation: to rally support for as much of the Chicago Plan as money could be found for. "Be a Chicago booster!" the exultant mayor now cried at every opportunity in his speeches. "Throw away your hammer! Get a horn and blow loud for Chicago!" Such enthusiasm would certainly be needed to accomplish the goal. Given the current state of the city's finances, funding Big Bill's big plan would not be easy. Because of strict limits on the city's taxing and bonding powers, special legislation would be needed to aid Chicago in the months ahead—not just to raise the money for long-term projects like the Michigan Avenue extension but even for current expenses. In a time of rising prices and growing government debt, such legislation was sure to meet with stiff resistance from some quarters. "A new spirit must control public officials chargeable with expenditures of public money," Governor Lowden warned in his public statements that spring. "The war is over. We must now plan to pay the cost." He threatened to veto any tax increase bill "unless it is one absolutely necessary."[4]

Fiscal conservatism, however, was not high on Big Bill's agenda in 1919, and with his new leverage over the governor, any rumblings about a veto could likely be made to disappear. In late April, Thompson and his entourage traveled south to Springfield to lobby for passage of the required aid bills in the state legislature. At a distinctly awkward luncheon with the Lowdens on April 29 (at which the chastened governor, it was reported, offered his "delayed congratulations" to Thompson on his recent reelection), the mayor turned up the pressure on Lowden to support the bills. That afternoon, Big Bill made a more public pitch before a joint committee of the Illinois house and senate. Alluding to "conditions over which the municipal government of Chicago has no control" (among them, the anticipated loss of revenue due to the coming of Prohibition), the mayor, now that he was safely reelected, made no secret of the city's dire financial condition. Under present law, he averred, Chicago could expect to raise revenues of some $20 million for the year; the sum required to run the city, however, would be $33.5 million. The conclusion was simple: "The city of Chicago must have relief if it is to continue functioning as a city."

It proved to be an effective plea. Although the measure faced predictable opposition from southern and rural elements in the legislature (the struggle between "the city" and "downstate" was—and still is—a recurring theme in Illinois politics), the mayor ultimately got his way. The bills passed, and Lowden, apparently persuaded that it would be in his interest to find the tax hikes "absolutely necessary," signed them into law, however reluctantly. For Thompson and Lundin, the pleasure of seeing the proud and aristocratic governor bow meekly to their will must have been exquisite. But passage of the bills was also an important political victory. Although individual bond issues would still have to be voted on by the taxpayers, Chicago had essentially had its credit limit substantially raised. The mayor and his Mephistopheles, as some were now calling them, had cleared yet another hurdle on their way to doing that "something good and big and enduring" for the city of Chicago—no matter what the cost.[5]

* * *

In the meantime, the citizens of the Windy City were finding refuge from their worries, as always, in sports and other amusements. Baseball season had opened in mid-April, and both Chicago teams had won their first games handily—the Cubs beating the Pirates 5 to 1 and the White Sox trouncing the St. Louis Browns 13 to 4, with the "Gleason gang" collecting a total of twenty-one hits off four different pitchers. ("I wish you could of [sic] seen this ball that Eddie [Collins] hit in the third inning," Ring Lardner reported in the *Trib* the next day. The ball had been hit so hard, according to Ring, that Browns second baseman Joe Gedeon "doesn't know yet if he caught it or not.") In May, the city's two big amusement parks—Riverside on the North Side and White City on the South—opened with all appropriate fanfare. It was White City's fifteenth summer season, and park officials had high hopes for the anniversary year. True, White City's aerodrome was still being used for the construction of blimps and other aircraft, but the park had plenty of other attractions on tap, including a freak show, a riding academy, and "The Garden Follies," a musical extravaganza featuring the spectacle of "100 dainty dancing ankles." One big unknown was Prohibition's likely effect on attendance. Because there was still no ratified peace treaty officially ending the war, the Wartime Prohibition Act, a grain-conservation measure banning alcohol consumption in most states, was set to go into effect on July 1, six months before national Prohibition. But park officials hoped that the demise of alcohol might actually increase business at the park, forcing saloon habitués to seek a more wholesome venue in which to spend their dollars and their leisure hours.[6]

Fears of Bolshevism, unfortunately, also carried over from spring into summer. The success of the Russian Revolution had put the fear of God (or, rather, godlessness) into many U.S. officials, and now a full-blown domestic spying campaign was under way to root out Americans considered of dubious loyalty—a category that could include everyone from pacifists to union leaders to persons insufficiently enthusiastic about buying Liberty Bonds. During war, in fact, even Mayor Thompson himself had complained of being spied on. "My enemies have recently bored holes in the walls of my apartments, installed pictographs, tapped telephone wires, stationed operators in adjoining rooms, and employed spies to hound me," he complained. Hearing this, many Chicagoans suspected that the mayor might be succumbing to outright paranoia, but federal records indicate that Big Bill was indeed under surveillance at the time.

And now, in 1919, the possibility of violent revolution in the United States was considered very real indeed. The Red Menace appeared to be everywhere, with Chicago's "Bolshevik squad" turning up rumors of sabotage conspiracies all over the city. Then, in late April, a genuine nationwide bomb plot was uncovered. On the 28th, an explosive device "big enough to blow out the entire side of the County-City building" was found in the mail of Seattle mayor Ole Hanson. The next day, a package addressed to Georgia senator Thomas R. Hardwick exploded in the hands of a servant in Atlanta. A clerk at the New York Post Office proceeded to turn up sixteen undelivered packages in a back room; all contained explosives. By the end of the week, a total of thirty-six package bombs had been found, addressed to prominent figures such as J. P. Morgan, John D. Rockefeller, Attorney General A. Mitchell Palmer, and Chicago's own Kenesaw Mountain Landis. It was enough to make even the wildest conspiracy theories appear plausible.[7]

Chicago's ongoing labor unrest, meanwhile, also played into these rising fears of worker revolution, as the faltering national economy put pressure on employers and employees alike. With inflation eating into every worker's paycheck (the cost of living had risen 75 percent since December 1914), unions were demanding hefty salary increases; but industry, scaling back production from wartime highs, refused to make any concessions at all. So, as spring ended, the number of unions threatening to strike was mounting precipitously. Not just the steel, meatpacking, and transit unions were restive; there were strike threats from Western Union telegraphers, municipal sweepers and garbagemen, members of the building trades, and even city engineers.

Closely observing this increasingly grave labor situation was a man whose name would eventually have very different associations in the national psyche. Carl Sandburg, a Chicago resident since 1906, had already earned a reputation as a poet by 1919 (his *Chicago Poems* had been published to some acclaim four years earlier), but he still needed a day job to support his wife and three children in their little house in suburban Maywood. Finding himself unemployed shortly after Mayor Thompson's reelection, Sandburg decided to make a pitch to *Chicago Daily News* editor Henry Justin Smith to be taken on staff as a labor reporter. "I believe there are some big, live feature stories" to be covered in the labor field, he wrote to Smith on May 31, mentioning the looming troubles in the transit unions and employment problems of the newly repatriated doughboys. "How are the returned soldiers going to work," he asked, "and what does life mean now to the steelworkers who went overseas?"[8]

Convinced by this argument, Smith hired the poet immediately and set him to work covering the national convention of the American Federation of Labor. The assignment proved to be a good fit. A former member of the Socialist Party ("I am with all rebels everywhere" is how the poet once described his political leanings), Sandburg had been active in left-wing politics for decades. Recently, upon returning from a journalism assignment in Sweden, he had even been interrogated by federal authorities for agreeing to deliver ten thousand dollars in bank drafts and some revolutionary literature to a Finnish agent in New York. Always sympathetic to the cause of labor, he was clearly moved by what he saw at the AFL convention—namely, the coming of "fundamental, seminal changes" in labor-management relations. Unions, he reported, were indeed becoming more radicalized, and if the current situation in Chicago was any indication, a major confrontation between workers and their employers across many industries was all but inevitable.[9]

Conflict also surfaced in the city's patchwork of ethnic neighborhoods. Postwar Europe's shifting currents of civil strife—"a sorry world," as Colonel McCormick called it, "everywhere unrest, revolution, Bolshevism"—were having repercussions among Chicago's foreign-born populations. On May 21, a mob of twenty-five thousand eastern European Jews stormed downtown Chicago to protest the pogroms in Poland, jamming streets and sidewalks and stopping traffic in the Loop. On June 8, fearing a pogrom on their own soil, eight thousand West Side Jews gathered at the corner of Twelfth and Kedzie to fend off a rumored "invasion" by a mob from an adjacent Polish neighborhood. The invasion never materialized, but incidents of Polish harassment of Jews continued to occur. Eventually, they grew so numerous that a delegation of Jewish peddlers demanded a meeting with police chief John Garrity to discuss special police protection. In a sense, the city's collage of ethnic enclaves had become a small-scale version of the European continent, so that conflicts occurring there were naturally being played out in miniature on the streets of Chicago's neighborhoods.[10]

Ethnic dissonance of a kind was also being felt at the Frankenstein household down in Kenwood. In March, Emily's parents had forbidden her from seeing any more of Jerry Lapiner, her still-secret fiancé. Part of the problem was Jerry's background. The Frankensteins, members of Chicago's long-established German-Jewish community, were wealthy, highly educated secular Jews—Victor a doctor, Irma a college-trained intellectual who (despite her rather cavalier attitude toward voting) wrote poetry and read widely. Jerry, who came from a working-class family of eastern European Jews, was not well spoken and had never gone to college. The cultural gulf separating them was starting to become an issue, especially for Emily's parents. Like many of those belonging to Chicago's assimilated old immigrant groups (which had come mainly from northern and western Europe), the Frankensteins tended to look down on less assimilated, less educated new immigrants (who were mostly from southern and eastern Europe). Worse, Jerry was still flirting with conversion to Christian Science. All in all, he was not considered by the Frankensteins to be marriageable material for their daughter.

The Christian Science issue troubled Emily as well. Sharing many of her parents' values, she largely eschewed traditional religious observance but found spirituality "in literature, my schoolwork, reading and thinking for myself." Christian Science seemed to her an alien and unhealthy system of belief. Still, characteristically eager to see things "in a new or different light because of the experiences I have," she had made a secret visit in February to a Christian Science lecture to try to understand its appeal. But she had come away unimpressed. The lecture had seemed more like a sales pitch than anything else, and on looking around the audience she'd seen "so very, very few healthy, robust people."

"Was madder than ever after leaving [the lecture]," Emily wrote in her diary that night, "and more helpless." Even so, she was determined to change Jerry, to get him interested in "things sensible—history, literature, even some kind of science. Just so he'll see the difference."[11]

Emily, of course, was still very young and subject to girlish romanticism, but she felt she really did love Jerry. The previous summer, at the height of their untroubled first months of courtship, they had sat together in the swing on the side porch of the Frankenstein home on Ellis Avenue, baring their souls to each other. "Isn't it funny," she'd written in her diary afterward, "a lovely June evening, on a vine-covered porch, makes it so easy to say what one has to say." Emily felt it was important that they have no secrets from each other. So she told him about her past suitors, of which there had been no shortage—Lenny, the boy who had been cruel to her; Albert, the overeager one whose annual proposals she always turned down flat; and Harrison, the son of one of her father's medical colleagues, who had tragically died in an army camp during the war. She wanted to make sure Jerry knew about all of them, especially since she and Jerry were already thinking about marriage. It wouldn't happen immediately; Jerry, like many of the other former soldiers in Chicago, still could not find work, and he was resolved not to wed until he could support a wife properly. But Emily insisted that this didn't matter. "I told Jerry I never wanted to marry a rich man," she wrote. "In fact, I've always preferred a poor man, so I could help him. I felt that that was a true test of love."

It had been an idyllic evening. After a time, Jerry asked if he could put his head on her lap. Nervously, Emily agreed. "I could hardly believe it was I on the swing—with Jerry's head in my lap," she wrote. "I looked down and saw his body clad in khaki—[and] I sort of sighed." She began running her hand through his hair and patting his cheek. "No one ever taught me what to do," she said, worrying about her inexperience with the physical side of courtship. But Jerry was reassuring. "'That doesn't need any teaching,'" he told her.

Later, he persuaded her to say aloud that she loved him, and they kissed. "God is good, all good," he said happily.

A few days later, on a shopping excursion to Marshall Field's, he gave her a ring that had belonged to his mother. "Wear it as long as you love me," he said.

That had been ten months ago, and Emily was still wearing the ring—but on a chain around her neck, so that her disapproving parents wouldn't see it. She would kiss the ring every night before going to bed. And despite her parents' admonishments—and although she was publicly dating other boys, all of them from far more appropriate Jewish backgrounds—she still considered herself engaged to Jerry. Fretting about the situation was even causing her to lose weight. "I wish I'd stop worrying about this," she wrote in her diary. "I try to, but it disturbs me."[12]

* * *

On the early morning of April 7, a black-powder bomb exploded on the porch of a flat building at 4212 Ellis Avenue—just three blocks away from the Frankenstein home in Kenwood. Another device went off on April 20 at a black-owned realty office on Indiana Avenue. Two more, both targeting the same address on Grand Boulevard (the home of black Shakespearean actor Richard Harrison), followed on May 18 and May 28. On May 29, a flat on Wabash Avenue was hit.[13]

In 1919 Chicago, of course, one could never be sure of the motivation behind any individual bomb or bomb threat. For many disaffected groups in the city, dynamite and black powder had become the preferred means of communicating a message, and police were often hard put to determine whether a given incident was part of the political, ethnic, racial, or labor conversation in the city. But these five bombings, along with two more in June, were clearly connected to black incursions into white residential neighborhoods, and signaled an accelerating deterioration in the city's racial situation. As early as April, the *Broad Ax,* a black weekly, had proposed its own radical solution to the problem: "Well, Negroes," the paper argued in an editorial on April 5, "you must get guns, guns I said! Then more guns and keep them loaded with buckshot. The awful day will surely come, and we might just as well die fighting in America as to die fighting in France."[14]

Cooler heads chose less incendiary, but no less confrontational, approaches. After the second bombing on Grand Boulevard, Ida Wells-Barnett (who with her family had just moved into a handsome Queen Anne–style residence on that street) resolved to take her case to Mayor Thompson personally. Her attempt to turn black voters against him in the recent election had failed, but that didn't mean she was ready to give up her campaign to spur the Thompson administration to action. So, after gathering together a committee of concerned citizens—including the mother of Ernestine Ellis, the girl who had died in the February 28 bombing—she marched them to city hall and demanded an audience with the mayor. Big Bill, perhaps hoping to punish Wells-Barnett for her support of Hoyne, refused to see the committee. Through his secretary, Charles Fitzmorris, he instructed them to take the matter to Chief Garrity. But they got no satisfaction there, either. Garrity, who at least agreed to speak with the committee, told Wells-Barnett that the department was doing its best, but that "he could not put all of the police in Chicago on the South Side to protect the homes of colored people." The committee members could only walk away in frustration.[15]

Big Bill was, in any case, too busy playing politics to worry about a little unrest in the city he had just been reelected to run. Governor Lowden had been getting altogether too much favorable press lately. The success of Lowden's sweeping reorganization of the state government was attracting nationwide attention, and now the governor was being mentioned for president by more and more Republican organizations. For Thompson, this was distinctly irksome. Some of his own followers had hopes to boom Big Bill for the same office, and though the mayor himself professed to be more interested in booming Chicago these days, he did admit that "no man is big enough to refuse a nomination for President if it is offered him."[16]

Given the lingering questions about Thompson's loyalty during the war, any notions of his becoming president (at least in 1920) were probably far-fetched even to him. But that didn't mean he wanted Lowden to get the nod. Indeed, the Thompson-Lundin organization's designs on greater power increasingly hinged on getting rid of the troublesome governor. With more than a year still remaining in Lowden's term, and with the governor's popularity growing every day, they could not afford to wait. Whenever the inevitable confrontation between the two chief executives came, Thompson and Lundin needed to be ready for it.

The extent of the political estrangement between mayor and governor became painfully obvious in late May, as the city prepared its welcome for the Thirty-third "Prairie Division," by far the largest group of returning Illinois soldiers to date. The planned celebration was to be vast, a ten-hour demonstration of "smiles, tears, hugs, [and] kisses," culminating in "the greatest parade the old town ever saw." Governor Lowden, the official host of the festivities, would preside over the parade from a reviewing stand set up on the east side of Michigan Avenue, right in front of the Art Institute. Joining him on the platform would be General Leonard Wood (another likely candidate for the Republican presidential nomination) and a host of other military and political dignitaries. Kaiser Bill, who had been conspicuously absent from all previous homecoming parades (except, significantly, that of the all-black Old Eighth), was pointedly not invited to join them.[17]

On the day of the parade, however, a defiant Mayor Thompson had his own reviewing stand set up on the other side of Michigan Avenue, a few blocks north of the governor's. To hear the *Tribune* tell the story, spectators were surprised to see the mayor present. "Gee, he's here!" a young boy allegedly remarked, within earshot of the Thompson party. "I been lookin' for him a long, long time since the soldiers started comin' home."[18]

The boy—or at least his quote—was probably an invention of the *Trib*'s reporter, but the scorn felt for Mayor Thompson by many at the event was undoubtedly real. As the parade progressed—amid the cheers of thousands who had gathered on its route—many soldiers walked right past the mayor without even a salute, pretending not to be aware of the second group of dignitaries. "I failed to see the Mayor's stand," Colonel Abel Davis of the 132nd Infantry told a reporter afterward, with barely disguised irony. "Somehow missed it altogether, but [I] found the Governor, General Bell, and General Wood in a splendid position. It's impossible to see everything in a parade of this sort."

It was, perhaps, the first time anyone ever claimed that Chicago's monumental mayor was inconspicuous in a crowd.[19]

One month later, the mayor and the governor crossed paths again at a convention of the Loyal Order of Moose in Aurora, Illinois, where both men had been invited to speak. By accident, they and their entourages ran into each other on the platform before the convention opened. It was an uncomfortable meeting—one that both men had probably hoped to avoid—but they made the best of it. "Why, hello," the mayor said with easy geniality. "Won't you have something to eat with me?"

"Just had my luncheon," the governor curtly replied.

They shook hands, and then the governor was hurried away by a convention delegate.

It would be the last time for years that the two men would even pretend to be friendly to each other.[20]

CHAPTER EIGHT

Going Dry

AT 11:59 P.M. on Monday, June 30, every saloon, tavern, and beer hall in Chicago was filled to bursting. Men—and more than a few women—were packed three to ten deep at every bar, with long lines of would-be patrons snaking out into the beer-soaked streets. Rowdiness prevailed across the city. People sang songs and danced on tables; tipsy wags held mock funerals for John Barleycorn on street corners; two drunken men "bowing to the Board of Trade Building" were struck by an automobile on LaSalle Street and knocked unconscious. It was Chicago's farewell party for Demon Rum. At midnight, wartime Prohibition would go into effect, and the entire city would be dry.

Police tried their best to keep order on the streets. Chief Garrity had earlier sworn "dire vengeance" on any proprietor who served a drink after midnight, but enforcement proved to be problematic. When the Fountain Inn closed its doors at the appointed hour, furious patrons tried to kick them down, and when detectives attempted to arrest the ringleaders, a small riot ensued, forcing the officers to call in reinforcements. At a saloon on Van Buren Street, a group of young men stole a barrel of whiskey just before closing. With a crowd of five hundred trailing behind them, they rolled it east along Van Buren to State Street. There they tried to tap it, blocking traffic on the city's main shopping avenue. A patrolman moved in to disperse the gathering, but he was driven back by the unruly mob until he was cornered in a cigar store, where he had to draw his revolver to defend himself. The store clerk telephoned the Central Police Station for backup, but when reserves arrived, the troublemakers—and the barrel of whiskey—had disappeared.[1]

It went on like this all night, and by the time "the biggest carnival night in the history of Chicago" was over, the jails were full, several people were dead, and the rest of the city was suffering from hangovers of both the literal and figurative variety. One paper estimated that more than $2 million had been spent on liquor on that one night alone. For the city's overwhelming majority of wets, it had been a night to remember, but now the era of the legal drink had passed. Over the next few days, as saloons reopened in their new guise as soft drink emporiums (to decidedly smaller crowds of customers), the city's drys were ecstatic. Billy Sunday, for one, expressed the highest hopes for the new alcohol-free society. "The slums will soon only be a memory," the reverend predicted. "We will turn our prisons into factories and our jails into storehouses and corn-cribs."[2]

Well, not exactly. Although Prohibition would indeed make it more difficult for a poor Chicago laborer to enjoy a glass of beer after his hard day's work, most of those with a little money and/or foresight would have little trouble finding a drink. Robert McCormick, for instance, had allegedly stocked the cellar of his country estate with so much scotch that he would still have plenty left when the Eighteenth Amendment was repealed thirteen years later. And for the non-millionaires in the population, there were other options as well. Sales of raisin cakes soared (each one came with explicit instructions on how not to "mistakenly" allow it to ferment). Fifteen thousand doctors and fifty-seven thousand retail druggists applied for licenses to sell "medicinal" alcohol to customers who demonstrated the need. Ring Lardner tried to be helpful by printing a recipe for homemade champagne in his *Tribune* column. ("Take a glass of sweet cider, drink it, and knock your head against the wall until it aches.") And for the truly desperate, there would always be embalming fluid, antifreeze solution, and rubbing alcohol.

Such expedients, however, would prove necessary only for a brief time. Before long, the ingenuity of the city's criminal class would come to the rescue, putting in place a bootlegging infrastructure more than adequate to supply as many speakeasies and backroom taverns as the city could support. Alcohol, in short, would soon be readily available to any citizen willing to flout the laws of the land. In Chicago that would prove to be just about everyone.[3]

* * *

As the summer progressed, this spirit of lawlessness, whether alcohol fueled or not, seemed to be as contagious as the Spanish influenza. On June 17, a gang of white teenagers—allegedly members of a South Side "athletic club" called Ragen's Colts—attacked a black man who had entered a de facto white saloon. Around the same time, a melee broke out on a State Street trolley when a white sailor slapped a black woman who had asked him not to step on her children's toes. In the parks, interracial violence was becoming a daily event. A black parent at the boathouse in Washington Park struck a white principal for failing to protect her children from stone-throwing white boys; the resulting conflict led to twenty arrests. Eight days later, fights erupted again in the same park. "A race war, threatening for weeks, assumed sinister proportions on Chicago's South Side last night, when 200 extra police were rushed to the Washington Park District," the *Herald and Examiner* reported on June 23. According to the paper, a "small army" of white men had run wild in the park with the avowed intention of "cleaning out the blacks." By the end of the evening, one black man was dead and another lay dying. Then, on June 30, a black former soldier named Charles W. Jackson fired his service revolver at a group of whites who had beaten his brother, this time on the West

Side; he managed to wound five of them before being chased down an embankment and killed.[4]

As July 4 approached, many law enforcement officials feared large-scale mayhem. Notices were posted along the Garfield Boulevard boundary of the Black Belt urging neighbors to "get all the niggers" on the holiday. Friendly whites told black residents to "prepare for the worst." Just as ugly as these racial threats, moreover, were rumors sweeping the Polish neighborhoods that a Jewish grocer had killed a Polish boy for his blood; three thousand Poles took to the streets around Eighty-fourth and Buffalo on the Southeast Side over the weekend, leading to eighteen arrests. Meanwhile, persistent fears of an Independence Day anarchist bombing plot kept the entire city on edge.[5]

The holiday ended up passing without serious incident—to the palpable relief of the newspapers and most residents—but the tensions did not subside. Many worried that the inevitable eruption had merely been postponed. Carl Sandburg, now working on a series of *Daily News* articles about the Black Belt, could see evidence of the coming conflagration all around him. He was spending days roaming the South Side, "interviewing shopkeepers, housewives, factory workers, preachers, gamblers, pimps," and it was obvious to him that resentment was seething. "We made the supreme sacrifice," one black soldier told him, "[and] now we want to see our country live up to the Constitution and the Declaration of Independence."[6]

Ida Wells-Barnett was more blunt. Two years earlier, she had seen the portents of disaster in the weeks before the East St. Louis race riot of 1917. "There had been a half-dozen outbreaks against the colored people by whites," she wrote in an open letter to the *Tribune* published on July 7. "Two different committees waited upon Governor Lowden and asked him to investigate the outrages against Negroes before the riot took place. Nobody paid any attention." The result had been one of the worst outbreaks of racial violence in American history.

And now the signs of another, perhaps even worse outbreak were proliferating. Just that week, several days of rioting had broken out in Washington, D.C. How long would it be before the same thing happened in Chicago, where bombings and violent attacks had become commonplace? "It looks very much like Chicago is trying to rival the South in its race hatred against the Negro," Wells-Barnett wrote in her letter. "Will the legal, moral, and civic forces of this town stand idly by and take no notice of these preliminary outbreaks? Will no action be taken to prevent these lawbreakers until further disaster has occurred? . . . I implore Chicago to set the wheels of justice in motion before it is too late."[7]

City officials, though, seemed more concerned about the worsening labor situation. "Labor unrest to an extent never before known in the city's history has gripped Chicago," the *New York Times* warned on July 19. By that time more than 250,000 Chicago workers were either on strike, threatening to strike, or locked out. Most government war contracts had expired, meaning that many employers could now ignore federal requirements for union recognition, collective bargaining, and nondiscrimination. As a result, there were confrontations—often violent—at International Harvester, the stockyards, the American Car and Foundry Company, the city building trades, several garment factories, and the steel-rolling mills. One analyst estimated that more than one out of every four industrial wage earners in the city was involved in a labor dispute of some kind that summer.[8]

Of most concern was a threatened strike by transit workers that could potentially disrupt the functioning of the entire city. Wage negotiations between the streetcar lines and the unions had been deadlocked since July 11. Workers were demanding a massive pay hike from forty-eight to eighty-five cents an hour, with time and a half for overtime; the companies were arguing that any such raise, without a concomitant doubling of transit fares, would bankrupt the lines; city officials, however, insisted that a fare hike of any size

would violate long-standing traction ordinances. "The traction volcano," wrote the *Chicago Evening Post,* "which has been rumbling
these many months, has blown its cap off, and the straphanger is
anxiously estimating the prospective depth of the lava." On Friday,
July 18, the threatened eruption seemed imminent. With no settlement even remotely in sight, the unions voted by a 50-to-1 margin to
walk out the next day.[9]

Governor Lowden, hoping to stop the chaos before it started,
ordered the Illinois Public Utilities Commission to step in and avert a
strike. "Frank is much concerned over strikes and threatened ones,"
a nervous Mrs. Lowden wrote in her diary for that date. The governor had reason for concern. His presidential run had just been
officially launched in Washington the week before. A major profile
about the new candidate (a puff piece under the headline "LOWDEN
OF ILLINOIS: Blacksmith's Son, a School Teacher at 15, Takes Field
for Presidential Nomination") was to run in the *New York Times* on
July 20. The governor's handling of the transit crisis would be one of
the first things that potential voters in the East, where he was as yet
little known, would hear about him.[10]

Mayor Thompson, seeing the potential for a coup, rushed to
appoint his own board of arbitration to settle the transit mess. Having campaigned on a promise to preserve the five-cent car fare, he at
first had been content to let the governor take the heat for any breakdown in negotiations, citing legal obstacles to intervention by the
city. Now those concerns were brushed aside. Thompson proposed
that the unions bypass the state commission and meet with his own
nine-member mediation committee to pound out a compromise. But
the president of the elevated railway employees union rebuffed the
mayor's proposal. "Never," he stated categorically when asked if he
would agree to the intervention. "That committee arbitrate? I should
say not." The unions did, however, agree to hold off on the strike for
at least another few days.[11]

The situation was looking grim, but even with this citywide crisis looming, the mayor was still pushing hard on his "Boost Chicago" effort. The lakefront ordinance and other important Chicago Plan measures were to be voted on in the city council on Monday, July 21. It would be, as the *Evening Post* put it, the council's "most important meeting since the world's fair days," and Thompson and Lundin were determined not to let the current strife distract the city from its "dream coming true." Waving aside the *Tribune*'s complaints about the exorbitant cost of the projects, the mayor pointed to the Michigan Avenue Bridge in particular as the kind of improvement that would pay back its investment many times over. "This bridge'll bring property values around here up by the millions," he argued. "They'll be building big skyscrapers here when that bridge is finished, and some of [the people] that'll build them will be the very ones that are howling at me now." The city may have been falling apart all around him, but Big Bill the Builder still had his eye on the future.[12]

And as for other dreams coming true, how bad could things really be in Chicago when the Sox were doing so well? On the afternoon of July 19, the South Siders had come back from a four-run deficit to defeat the Washington Senators 6 to 5 in eleven innings—against ace pitcher Walter Johnson, no less—convincing many fans that "the Sox are after the pennant." Emily Frankenstein was supposed to go to that very game with her perpetual suitor Albert Chapsky, but she canceled the date at the last minute to secretly meet Jerry at home while her parents were away. Jerry had implied that he might be losing interest in Christian Science, a development that lifted her spirits considerably. "Maybe, after all, there is some hope of dreams coming true," she wrote in her diary. "Maybe—but, oh, maybe—"[13]

* * *

The following Monday, July 21, 1919, dawned sunny and warm. Mayor Thompson, arriving at city hall, had a busy day ahead of him.

One day last week, he had been approached in a corridor by a man named Earl Davenport—the publicity representative for the White City Amusement Park—who had asked if the mayor wanted to ride on a blimp that would be making flights over the city on Monday. Big Bill claimed he would love to accept the invitation, but there were simply too many crises demanding his attention. After all, the transit situation was calling. At noon, therefore—as the *Wingfoot Express* was making its preliminary flight over the city—the mayor was not aboard. Instead, he was meeting with members of his arbitration board to try to break the transit deadlock before the governor's commission could do likewise.

The outlook was more hopeful at the city council meeting later that afternoon. With the mayor presiding over the vote, the council triumphantly passed the Chicago Plan ordinances, making July 21 what Chicago Plan Commission president Charles Wacker called "the greatest day, barring none, in Chicago's history."

"It marks a new era," Wacker announced when the final tally was announced. "It is the beginning of the making of Chicago." The council's courageous decision, he said, "will make Chicago the most beautiful city in the world."

That new era, however, was about to get off to a decidedly shaky start. Before the meeting had ended, news arrived that sent a shock through the buzzing council chamber. A bizarre accident, it was said, had occurred in the Loop just a few blocks south of city hall. The *Wingfoot Express*—the blimp that the mayor himself might have been on that very day—had just fallen from the sky in flames and crashed into the Illinois Trust and Savings Bank.[14]

PART TWO

Crisis

CHAPTER NINE

Tuesday, July 22

B Y TUESDAY MORNING, people from all over the Chicago area were traveling to the Loop to view the site of Monday's bizarre disaster. A contingent of sixty patrolmen tried to keep order as thousands of curious onlookers milled around the ravaged bank, blocking traffic and mobbing the doors in order to get a glimpse of the wreckage inside. Thanks to some overnight volunteer work by scores of the city's locked-out construction workers, the bank had managed to open to the public at the usual hour, and now its rattled employees—some with bandaged heads or arms in slings—were attempting to conduct business as usual. Fortunately, most of the damage from the crash had been confined to the building's interior courtyard. The grand public areas had escaped relatively unscathed, and aside from some $95,000 worth of charred but still negotiable Liberty Bonds, the bank's material losses had been remarkably small. "Reports that we lost any money or checks or bonds are not true," bank president John J. Mitchell announced at 10 a.m. "Our greatest loss lies in the list of dead and injured."[1]

As the reality of those casualties began to sink in, many Chicagoans found that their initial distress over the loss of life was giving way to feelings of indignation and anger. The blimp crash, as one newspaper columnist put it, violated "all preconceived notions of safety," allowing death to "burst into that modern monastery—a strong, conservative, and previously imperturbable bank." Somehow the freak event seemed to strike at basic assumptions of urban order and security, leaving many city dwellers feeling vulnerable in ways they hadn't just twenty-four hours earlier. "That girls working at their desks in the security of a bank building should be killed by flying steel and burning gas is an outrage against our civilization," the editors of the *Evening Post* wrote in an editorial. "It is due, as so many other disasters are due, to the American habit of taking no preventive action till the disaster has occurred."[2]

The natural impulse was to hold someone accountable. The *Chicago Daily News,* describing the crash as "the most sensational tragedy since the end of the war," fixed the blame firmly on the pilot and his employers, who irresponsibly put an entire city at risk for the sake of a "joyride" with no clear purpose. "The flight of the dirigible was a holiday stunt," the paper maintained, "and helped advertise an amusement park." The *Tribune* sounded a similar note: "There seems little question that the flight was experimental. Why, then, was an experiment carried out over the heads of thousands of persons, over the Loop of Chicago, when there are millions of acres of unoccupied land in the United States, to say nothing of a lake nearly 100 miles wide within a few blocks of the hangar?"[3]

City and county officials wasted no time in apprehending the apparent culprits. Within hours of the crash, State's Attorney Maclay Hoyne, still in his old job after his unsuccessful run for mayor, had ordered the arrest of everyone associated with the *Wingfoot Express.* Fourteen men, all employees of the Goodyear Tire and Rubber Company, had been held and interrogated. Most had been promptly released, but two—pilot Jack Boettner and project director W. C. Young—remained in police custody. Under intense questioning by the state's attorney and Chief Garrity, Boettner made what were called "serious admissions" about the construction and operation of the blimp. The pilot acknowledged that the *Wingfoot's* rotary engines were "experimental" and that this was the first time they were being used to power an airship. When asked whether the blimp had carried any fire extinguishers, he answered that the craft was indeed equipped with such a device, "but it was in the wrong place; by that I mean it was not handy." As explanation for what had started the fire in the first place, Boettner could offer only "the theory of spontaneous combustion."

Even more disturbing was the testimony of W. C. Young. A former mining engineer, the twenty-seven-year-old project director confessed that he was totally unfamiliar with engine technology and in fact "did not know the difference between a spark plug and a carburetor." Despite his inexperience, however, he had apparently taken an active part in the blimp's construction. Insisting that the airship be assembled "in the quickest possible time," he had even attached small makeshift hoods over the engines' cylinders to address a problem with splashing hot oil. Hearing this, prosecutors felt they had enough evidence to request an indictment for criminal negligence, and so ordered that the two men be held overnight for a grand jury hearing.[4]

Chicago's city council had also acted with uncommon dispatch. Remaining in session after news of the *Wingfoot* crash reached the council chamber, the city's aldermen spent Monday evening debating an emergency resolution intended to prohibit all aviation in the urban area. "It is unnecessary to state reasons for the adoption of this resolution," said Alderman Anton Cermak, who introduced the measure. "This accident shows we must stop flying over the city sooner or later, and we had better do it sooner." Further debate convinced Cermak to modify the wording of his resolution to call for regulation, rather than outright prohibition, of urban aviation. But by 11 p.m., the measure had been passed and sent on to the corporation counsel for further action. Having thus—as the *Post* complained—once again taken steps to prevent a disaster only after it had occurred, the council adjourned the session and the aldermen were able to go home before midnight.[5]

* * *

At morgues and hospitals across the city, loved ones of the victims held vigils through the night. At the Central Undertaking Rooms on Federal Street, Catherine Weaver, wife of blimp mechanic Carl Weaver, sat alone outside the room where her husband and several other victims lay awaiting identification. Arriving at the morgue in a state of hysteria, she at first had been denied admission to the room. She had taken a seat in a straight-back chair just outside the door and remained there for hours, pale and trembling, whispering, "He can't be dead, he can't be dead." When Carl's body was finally wheeled out to her for identification, she broke down completely, weeping uncontrollably until doctors led her away.[6]

At St. Luke's Hospital, several other victims were barely clinging to life. The family of Marcus Callopy, a clerk in the bank's foreign exchange department, waited anxiously while surgeons labored to save the young man's life, though the prognosis was grim. In an outer office of the hospital, Alice Norton spent the night on a bench with two friends while her husband, Milton, was attended by doctors. Early signs had been hopeful; the photographer's legs had been broken in the parachute jump, but he appeared to have no internal injuries. His condition, however, had deteriorated during the night. Early on Tuesday morning, Mrs. Norton was taken to his bedside, but though he was able to recognize her, he could not speak. Doctors held out little hope for his recovery.[7]

Others were already planning funerals. Elsie Otto—wife of Carl Otto, the bank telegrapher who had returned to work a day early—was making arrangements with her husband's Masonic lodge to hold a memorial service at the Graceland chapel. She had first heard about the tragedy when a *Tribune* reporter approached her on Monday evening, as she was sitting on the porch of their North Side cottage with their adopted son, Stanley. "Are you the wife of

Carl Otto?" the reporter asked. Instantly suspecting the worst, Elsie asked, "What's happened to him?" She screamed when the reporter told her that Carl had been seriously hurt. "He's dead! I know he's dead!" she cried. "I told him not to go back to work today!" Leaving Stanley with some neighbors, she called a taxi and raced to St. Luke's Hospital. Carl was still alive when she arrived, but she had only a few minutes with him before he died. Doctors gave her morphine and held her at the hospital until she had calmed down enough to go home.[8]

Earl Davenport's wife had reacted even more dramatically. Shortly before the accident, the publicity man had apparently telephoned her. She was ill in bed at the time and had asked him not to go up in the blimp, since she'd "had a premonition that something was going to happen." Earl had promised her that he wouldn't ride that day. But several hours later, a family friend called the house and spoke to the couple's daughter-in-law, who was looking after Mrs. Davenport. "Earl was in the ship," the friend told her.

"But where is he now?"

"Well," the friend temporized, "he's not in the hospital. . . ."

When she heard the news, Mrs. Davenport collapsed and did not regain consciousness until Tuesday morning.[9]

Survivors with less tragic stories were meanwhile repeating them all over town, regaling friends, relatives, coworkers—and newspaper reporters—with their various close calls. "All I can say is, I thought the end of the world had come," bank worker Katherine Bruch told rapt neighbors on the porch of her Kenmore Avenue home. "Everything around me seemed [to be] on fire. I was lying on the floor, [and] I thought I might just as well stay there and burn. Then I saw a girl running, and I jumped up and ran, too. I got out, but I have no clear recollection how I did."

"I was working in the bond department," Maybelle Morey told a reporter at the Iroquois Hospital, where she was being treated for cuts and burns. "I was in the front part of the office and I heard something flash. I thought they were taking pictures. Then boom! came the big explosion, and the whole place seemed in flames. . . . I had to jump out the window. When I came to, they were pouring whiskey down me. I don't know where they got it, with the town so dry. . . ."

Even those who were nowhere near the bank that day could not stop talking about the crash. Literally tens of thousands of people had witnessed at least one of the blimp's three flights that day, and it was only natural that they were eager to share their war stories with all who would listen. Some of their tales, of course, were embroidered or exaggerated for effect. The number of people who claimed that they themselves would have been on the blimp, but for this or that lucky break, would probably have filled a whole fleet of airships.[10]

Shortly before noon on Tuesday—in room 1123 of the County Building, the other half of the enormous neoclassical pile in the Loop that also housed the city hall—county coroner Peter M. Hoffman convened the official inquest to determine responsibility for the deaths of the victims. Two six-man juries—one consisting of engineering specialists and one of assorted businessmen—had been impaneled the previous evening ("while the airship was still burning," according to the *Daily Journal*). They would now hear testimony from a wide variety of witnesses and aviation experts. It proved to be a frustrating session. The first two people called—Boettner and Young, now represented by Goodyear attorney Henry A. Berger—refused to testify on advice of counsel and were excused. Several subsequent witnesses gave conflicting testimony about what might have caused the blimp to catch fire on its final flight. After just two and a half hours, Coroner Hoffman decided to adjourn the session and reconvene on Wednesday, when Goodyear representatives, now en route from Akron, could be present.

As he closed, the coroner stood up and said he had an announcement to make. During the inquest session, a note had been passed to him with news from St. Luke's Hospital. "You gentlemen now have to view the body of another victim," he told the jury. "Mr. Norton is dead."

The toll from the crash had now reached twelve.[11]

* * *

Mayor Thompson, distracted by the transit situation and other city business, seemed to be paying little attention to the tragedy that had struck the Loop the day before. Given Big Bill's reputation for empathy (not to mention his instinct for the effective sound bite), this was surprising. The *Eastland* disaster—the excursion-boat capsizing that had occurred early in his first term—had seemed to bring out the best in the mayor; the *Wingfoot* disaster, by contrast, seemed not to arouse his sense of public duty, despite the fact that he'd almost been one of its victims. Granted, the death toll in the earlier accident was far greater, and it had occurred during his political honeymoon period, when the local press was more willing to publicize any manifestations of his leadership ability. But if surviving newspaper reports are any indication, the mayor seemed far too consumed by "the traction mess" to show much sympathy for the victims of an aviation tragedy, no matter how spectacular.

Certainly he had an excuse for being preoccupied. The heads of the surface and elevated lines, having rebuffed the mayor's own arbitration committee, had decided to meet in closed-door sessions with the governor's commission to discuss fare hikes. City hall was furious. "Mayor's Forces Resent Lowden's 'Interference'" ran the headline in the *Daily Journal*. At issue, according to Thompson, was the city's fundamental right to determine its own fate. He insisted that the transit situation was an affair strictly between the people of Chicago and the owners and employees of the car lines; the State of Illinois had no business being involved. "The Mayor's position," the *Daily Journal* maintained, "is that the 1907 ordinances give the city exclusive control over streetcar fares, and that this control has been assumed illegally by the utilities commission." Seeing an opportunity for some grandstanding, the mayor and his men attempted to depict the "star-chamber sessions" as a power grab by downstate elements in cahoots with the car companies and other big business interests. "Chairman Dempcy of the utilities board is from East St. Louis," one of the mayor's spokesmen announced. "It ought to gall every Chicagoan to think of the Governor sending a man here from such a dinky city to settle a big Chicago question."[12]

Especially provoking were rumors that the governor's commission might choose to raise fares by as much as 60 percent without a public hearing. Thompson (the self-styled "defender of the five-cent fare") was not about to let that happen. He indicated that he was more than prepared to put up a fight on the issue. And for once he had some newspaper support: "If our state constitution were properly constructed," the *Herald and Examiner* argued in an editorial, "the people themselves would have a chance to decide whether this city might control its own peculiar affairs or not. . . . We would have a Chicago utilities body delving into the present mix-up in the open light of day and with authority to deal out justice to employer and employee."

Thompson, having named just such a Chicago utilities body (in the form of his nine-member mediation committee), only to have it rejected, found himself in complete agreement with this analysis. By evening, he was already threatening to take the governor and his state commission to court.[13]

* * *

With all of the upset in the city that day—the fallout from the *Wingfoot* disaster, the conflict over the transit situation, the ongoing epidemic of strikes and lockouts—it was perhaps not surprising that police at the Chicago Avenue station on the city's North Side were somewhat slow to respond to a missing-person report they received in the late afternoon. Mr. and Mrs. John Wilkinson, Scottish immigrants who ran a local grocery store, had come to the station at about 6 p.m., frantic about their six-year-old daughter, Janet. Early that morning, they said, Janet had left the family's apartment on East Superior Street to accompany two friends to a nearby park on the lakeshore. The three girls had registered their names with a park official and played there for several hours. At noon the park closed for the midday break and they had to leave.

According to one of the friends—a seven-year-old named Marjorie Burke—the three girls had ambled home for lunch through the busy North Side streets. Near the corner of Rush and Superior, they stopped to look at magazine covers in a shop window. But then they had to part ways. The two girls said good-bye to Janet and watched as their friend, dressed in her favorite blue sailor dress, walked down the block toward the Wilkinsons' apartment. They saw a man with glasses—someone they recognized as a neighbor—beckoning to her on the sidewalk a few steps from her door. Janet stopped and spoke with the man for a moment, but then the girls turned away to head back to their own homes.

A few hours later, Janet's older sister Berenice returned from an outing and was surprised to find the apartment empty. The lunch she had prepared for Janet a little before noon was still sitting untouched on the table. The girl had apparently never come home, and she had not been seen or heard from since.[14]

CHAPTER TEN

Wednesday, July 23

T HE SEARCH BEGAN in earnest on Wednesday morning. An assortment of neighbors, friends, grocery store customers, and more than fifty volunteer boys and girls joined scores of police in scouring the Gold Coast neighborhood on the city's North Side, looking for any trace of Janet Wilkinson. Some knew the girl by sight; others relied on the police description: "6 yrs; 3'9"; 42 lbs; blond straight hair; deep blue eyes; wore a dark blue sailor frock and black oxfords; no stockings." The more optimistic of the volunteers searched for the girl by examining the faces of children on the street, scanning the crowds in parks and playgrounds, and asking questions of nearby merchants and residents. The police, however, were using other methods. They poked sticks into dark, foul-smelling sewers. They turned over fly-specked piles of trash in alleys. They used crowbars to tear up old wooden floors and dug through dusty basement coal bins, looking for—and hoping not to find—the young girl's body.

By late afternoon, searchers would have a photo on the front page of the *Evening Post* to work from. It depicted a rather homely child with a grave, oddly accusatory expression on her face, her eyes disconcertingly intense. In the photo, Janet's hands were tightly clasped over a frilly white dress with a wide flaring skirt.[1]

Police had only one real lead in the case, but it was a solid one. The man Marjorie Burke had seen talking to Janet just after the girls had parted on the corner fit the description of Thomas Fitzgerald, who ran a small boardinghouse with his wife in the other half of their duplex apartment building. Several months earlier, Janet had come home complaining about Fitzgerald, alleging that he had invited her into his apartment and "annoyed her." The Wilkinsons had confronted the man at the time, but ultimately chose not to prosecute, fearing the ugliness of a public investigation. Now they were convinced that Fitzgerald had something to do with Janet's disappearance, and the police agreed. At 2 a.m. on Tuesday, they located the man at the Virginia Hotel on Rush Street, where he worked as a night watchman, and brought him into the Chicago Avenue station for questioning.[2]

Fitzgerald—a slight, mild-mannered man in his late thirties who wore round gold-rimmed spectacles—denied categorically that he knew anything about the girl's whereabouts. He admitted that he had stopped her on the street to exchange a few words, but claimed that they had parted again almost immediately, and that he'd then merely continued home to go to sleep, his wife being away in Michigan visiting friends. At six in the evening, he said, he had gotten up as usual and headed to work, where he'd remained until his arrest. He insisted that he had heard nothing about the disappearance of "Dolly"—the neighbors' pet name for the child—until police asked him about it at 2 a.m.[3]

The interrogation went on all night. Under intense pressure from Detective Sergeant Edward Powers and Lieutenant William Howe, Fitzgerald revealed that in 1902 he had served sixty days in the county jail on a charge of larceny. He had been arrested twice more—once in 1905 and again in 1913—on the same charge. More pertinent, however, was the discovery by police that Fitzgerald had been arrested about a year ago on complaints from two neighborhood mothers for his "conspicuous interest" in their young daughters. The case had eventually been dropped for want of prosecution, but it pointed to a pattern of behavior that, in the current circumstances, could only be regarded as ominous.[4]

When asked about the "bothering" incident with Janet, Fitzgerald claimed it had all been a misunderstanding. "It was around Christmastime she came into my home," he explained. "She and another girl were coming up the stairs. I had some candy in the house and some funny papers. I invited them in." He gave the girls some of the candy and let them leaf through the comics. When another resident of the building—a roomer in the Fitzgerald boardinghouse—happened to come in, Fitzgerald asked her what she thought of "my two little girls." (The roomer, questioned later, claimed to have no recollection of the incident.) According to Fitzgerald, the roomer and the other little girl left after a few minutes, "but Dolly stayed a little longer." Even so, nothing untoward had happened when they were alone. "She came into the house another time," he went on, to prove his point. "My wife gave her some bread and jelly. She was a nice little girl. I always liked her."[5]

At one point in his interrogation, Fitzgerald made an offhand comment about perhaps finding Janet's body in the lake, and so the marshy waters off Chicago Avenue were dragged. Police cut away the reeds growing along the shoreline—still undeveloped in 1919—and searched the entire area. But nothing was found, and no trace of Janet was discovered either in the duplex apartment building or at the Virginia Hotel. By evening, police were running out of obvious places to look for the girl. Though theories about Janet's disappearance abounded, the evidence for any of them was scant. And so the search went on.[6]

* * *

The blimp inquest was also generating its share of unprovable theories. While awaiting the expected late-afternoon arrival of Goodyear officials from Akron, Coroner Hoffman called a number of expert witnesses on Wednesday, including Colonel Joseph C. Morrow, who had been a passenger on the *Wingfoot*'s second flight on Monday.

Though not an aviation specialist, Morrow had served in the army's air service during the war, and he had given the blimp a quick inspection before the flight. "At that time everything was in good condition," he testified.

"Was there any motor trouble while you were in the air?" Coroner Hoffman inquired.

"No, sir."

"Did you notice any leakage in the gasoline pipes?"

"No, sir."

When asked whether he considered the *Wingfoot*'s flight "experimental," Morrow was emphatic: "No, it was not. The motor was not of a new type, though it is true that the government had loaned it to Goodyear to be tested in flight."

Colonel Morrow went on to express total confidence in pilot Boettner's competence. "The pilot was experienced," he asserted. "I have never observed him making any mistakes in flying a ship."

At the conclusion of Morrow's testimony, Goodyear attorney Berger rose and announced that, in a reversal of his advice of yesterday, Boettner and all other members of the *Wingfoot* crew would cooperate completely with the investigation and answer any questions asked of them. He also added that Goodyear was willing to pay all expenses caused by the crash. "Any families who have suffered because of this accident will only have to present bills to our company to have them paid," he said. "We are doing this gladly and entirely of our own free will."[7]

Other expert witnesses were then called to the stand, but—to the consternation of Coroner Hoffman and the two juries—none seemed able to give a definitive opinion on the cause of the fire. Static electricity, abrasion between the blimp's interior balloonettes, sparks from the rotary engines, even radio waves from a nearby tower were all proposed by one expert or another. At one point, Coroner Hoffman declared that unless it could be proved that the blimp was improperly constructed, or that the pilot or mechanics were incompetent, or that flying an untested balloon over a city constituted criminal careless- ness, official blame for the deaths might never be established. With- out a definitive ruling from the coroner, moreover, State's Attorney Hoyne would find it problematic to bring a case against anyone. Since no real precedent existed in Illinois law, any prosecution for man- slaughter would have to be brought under the Old English common law—"which," as the *Chicago Daily Journal* observed, "did not con- template airships falling through the tops of buildings."[8]

Sometime late in the afternoon, the officials from Goodyear finally arrived. After conferring briefly with attorney Berger, they echoed his promise of full cooperation and insisted that the company itself was also conducting its own internal investigation. In an official state- ment, they assured the jury that "every precaution known to the art of air navigation" was taken at all times in the building and opera- tion of the blimp, and that the Goodyear employees involved were "a skilled aeronautical crew." But since it was too late in the day for any of the new arrivals to testify individually, the inquest was adjourned for the day. Among the topics to be explored when hearings recon- vened on Friday morning were uncorroborated rumors in the press that mechanic Harry Wacker, still recovering from his injuries at Presbyterian Hospital, had made several damaging admissions about the blimp's condition and about pilot Boettner's behavior during the fatal flight. It was hoped that Wacker would be well enough to testify for himself on Friday.[9]

While the inquest was still in session, the first of the disaster's victims was laid to rest. Funeral services for Marea Florence, a ste- nographer at the bank, were held at 2 p.m. in the little chapel of the Western Undertaking Company on Michigan Avenue. More than two hundred relatives and friends gathered to hear Henry J. Armstrong of the Fifth Church of Christ, Scientist, read from the Scriptures and eulogize the young woman. "If you ever saw her smile," Armstrong said to the assembled mourners, "you would never forget it." Later, her body was taken to Rosehill Cemetery for burial.

At about the same time, Marcus Callopy, the teller from the bank's foreign department, succumbed to his injuries at St. Luke's Hospital. He thus became the disaster's thirteenth, and final, victim. Of the remaining twenty-seven injured, all were now expected to recover.[10]

* * *

By the end of the day on Wednesday, prospects for a settlement of the transit issue seemed to be stalled. Emerging from their closed-door sessions with the car companies and the public utilities commission in late afternoon, union leaders were pessimistic. Rumors were flying that surface line president Leonard Busby had proposed a compromise contract that would raise salaries to sixty-two cents an hour, with a standard nine-hour day, but the unions claimed to know nothing about it. "That [rumor] is either a dream story or is one of Busby's tricks to discover what would happen to the proposition if he made it," union leader W. S. McClenathan told reporters. But he insisted that any such offer "would be turned down cold. It would be a waste of time to take it to the men." According to McClenathan, the workers were fighting for their very livelihood. "There are certain basic principles that are not open to arbitration and compromise, and the right to live and get a living wage are two things that are not arbitrable."

Even so, all participants seemed determined to keep talking, and the press was convinced that progress would be forthcoming. "Statements by both sides in each meeting today," the *Daily News* reported, "made it clear that everyone concerned is trying to avert, if possible, a strike which would paralyze the city's transportation system." Union leaders were promising that there would in any case be no strike until the governor's commission had completed its investigation.[11]

The mayor of Chicago, still complaining about being excluded from the talks, was apparently optimistic enough about the situation to go ahead with some long-standing plans for a summer holiday. Having accepted an invitation to be guest of honor at the annual Frontier Days Roundup in Cheyenne, Wyoming, Big Bill was already packing for the trip, stuffing "a lariat and a pair of chaps in his valise" in preparation for a return to his beloved old stomping grounds out West. And he wouldn't be traveling alone. At the suggestion of Cheyenne's roundup committee (who urged the mayor "to bring everybody who voted for [the mayor], if he wished"), Bill was planning to take along the entire Chicago Boosters Club, consisting of more than one hundred of his closest friends and supporters, including Fred Lundin, city comptroller George Harding, and even police chief John Garrity. A special train was due to leave the city shortly before midnight. According to the *Daily Journal,* the train's baggage car would be "well stocked with ice for lemonades and other soft drinks. What each guest may carry in his grip is a personal matter."

Of course, some people questioned the prudence of the mayor's leaving town with the heads of most of the city's departments. At such a critical time, with bombs going off and strikes threatening everywhere, shouldn't city hall be fully staffed? Big Bill had decided, therefore, that corporation counsel Samuel Ettelson would be left behind to mind the shop while the boss and his minions were gone. However, given that Ettelson was widely considered to be the creature of utilities baron Samuel Insull—a person deeply interested in the outcome of the ongoing transit negotiations—this precaution was likely to reassure no one. Perhaps as a concession to these fears, Thompson decided at the last moment that Comptroller Harding would remain in town as well.

But the mood was boisterous as the mayor and his entourage boarded the special train at Union Station. Big Bill assured reporters that he would be in close contact with his advisers the whole way, and that, because of the weekend, they'd be missing only two and a half working days. If all went as scheduled, the mayor and his men would be returning to Chicago early on Monday morning, refreshed and ready to start a new workweek. And after all, how much could possibly go wrong in just four short days?[12]

CHAPTER ELEVEN

Thursday, July 24

A S IF TO RATIFY Big Bill's decision to leave town on nonessential business, the city turned relatively quiet on Thursday. Transit talks remained at a standstill. Traction company owners, union leaders, and the Lowden commission held several meetings throughout the morning, but no one was budging on the question of the eight-hour day, and the unions were refusing even to broach the topic of wage concessions until that issue was settled. The *Wingfoot* inquest, meanwhile, was on hiatus while funerals for seven of the victims were held at various locations across the city.

Shortly before noon at the Illinois Trust and Savings Bank, all business came to a halt for five minutes to honor the dead. As the *Tribune* later reported, "Not a typewriter clicked, not a pencil moved, and the telephones went unanswered. The employees rose to their feet and bowed their heads—a silent tribute to their coworkers who were killed."[1]

A few hours later, officials at Goodyear, rising to the occasion, issued a public apology for the accident and announced the naming of a special three-man committee to arbitrate all claims for compensation from the families of the victims. They requested only that Goodyear and its employees be given a fair hearing. "In justice to our men," the company said in its statement, "we respectfully ask a suspension of public judgment as to their responsibility until the facts are reliably established."[2]

Legislators were meanwhile acting to ensure that accidents like the *Wingfoot* crash would not be repeated. In Washington, D.C., Illinois's own Senator Lawrence Sherman introduced a federal bill designating specific lines of aerial traffic that would steer clear of crowded downtown districts. Closer to home, the Chicago City Council, having passed its emergency resolution on Monday, was now working on legislation to give the symbolic measure a more enforceable form. Even Mayor Thompson, still en route to Cheyenne, made sure to chime in on the topic. Speaking to reporters at a brief stopover in Omaha, the mayor was apparently eager to appear "still on the job." "I am going to do everything I can to help establish laws for the regulation of airships of every kind when they fly over Chicago," he told the press corps. "I am opposed to permitting any airship which uses inflammable and explosive gases to pass over a city."[3]

Even the Janet Wilkinson case was stalled for most of the day. Despite being subjected to round-the-clock interrogation—including relentless "man-to-man questioning" by Lieutenant Howe—Thomas Fitzgerald stubbornly maintained his innocence throughout the early-morning hours of Thursday. Toward dawn, Howe brought John Wilkinson, Janet's father, into the basement interrogation room. When Wilkinson reminded the prisoner of Janet's claim that he had harassed her last winter, Fitzgerald shook his head vigorously and insisted that the child had been misquoted. Wilkinson, he told Lieutenant Howe, "has it in for me and is telling lies."

This was too much for the grieving father to stand. "You hound!" he allegedly shouted in his heavy Scottish burr. Without warning, he sprang on Fitzgerald and started strangling him, "driving his fingers tightly into his throat." Howe and another detective rushed to pull Wilkinson off the much smaller man, who sank to the floor in a swoon.[4]

Later in the day, other witnesses were brought in for questioning. Edward C. Watson, another roomer in the Fitzgerald boarding-house, and S. C. Darby, an old family friend who had dropped by the apartment "acting in a peculiar manner," were both detained and subjected to a grilling. One issue of concern was the whereabouts of Mrs. Fitzgerald. Her husband claimed he didn't know how she could be contacted—that she had gone to Michigan at the invitation of some friends who owned a cottage there, but he didn't know exactly where. Oddly, Edward Watson knew that the cottage was in Bangor. Suspecting a kidnapping conspiracy (as well as an illicit relationship of some kind between Mrs. Fitzgerald and her boarder), Howe had Watson send her a telegram asking her to return to Chicago; Howe himself then spoke to her via long-distance telephone and gave her the details. Insisting that her husband was innocent of any wrongdoing, Mrs. Fitzgerald promised to catch the first train back to Chicago, at which time she would prove to police that her husband had nothing to do with Janet's disappearance. Howe wasn't convinced. After the conversation, he had a picture of Janet rushed to police in Bangor in order to initiate a search for the girl there.[5]

By afternoon, Howe thought that he might actually be making progress with Fitzgerald. A box of stale chocolate candy had been found in the boardinghouse, and although the suspect initially denied that it was his, he later recanted, admitting that he had bought it two weeks ago from a Chicago Avenue druggist. Having thus caught the suspect in one lie, Howe hoped that more admissions would follow. He cleared the interrogation room and pressed Fitzgerald further, questioning him in classic good-cop fashion by trying to play on his sympathies. "Think of that child's mother," he said to the prisoner, "worried, hysterical, dying for news of her baby. If you have any idea where she may be, where her body may be found, tell us and relieve the mother's suspense."

At this point, Fitzgerald apparently wavered. He opened his mouth and his eyes "took on a peculiar beaten expression." To Howe, he appeared ready to give in and finally tell what he knew. But at that instant a door opened and a station porter stuck his head into the room. The moment was lost. Fitzgerald "shut up like a clam" and refused to utter another word.[6]

At an afternoon press conference, Detective Sergeant Powers could barely conceal his frustration. "It is possible Fitzgerald lured [Janet] into his home on the promise of giving her some of that stale candy," he told reporters, "but then what happened? And where is the girl? If she was killed, where is the body? It was daylight. The slayer couldn't have taken her on the roof unless he went up the fire escape in front. He would have been seen."

The obvious alternative was that Fitzgerald had taken the body to the basement of the duplex building. But Powers dismissed that possibility: "We searched [the basement]," he said. Then, becoming perhaps more graphic than was absolutely necessary, he added, "There was a fine fire in the boiler, but there always is. Janet's body was too big to shove through the boiler door, unless it was dismembered, and there were no blood spots anywhere."

In short, the police were baffled. "It is possible that Fitzgerald could have got away from his work Tuesday night, before he was arrested, to dispose of the body—if you accept the theory that he murdered the little girl. His employers admit that. But so far as they know, he remained at work all that night."[7]

As the interrogation of Fitzgerald continued without a break, scores of anonymous calls were coming into the Chicago Avenue station from people who claimed to have seen Janet. One person alleged she had witnessed Janet being abducted in an automobile by a well-dressed woman. An iceman's son reported that he had sold the girl some ice. Someone else was certain she had seen Janet playing on a Logan Square playground. Police dutifully checked out these and numerous other leads, but without success. One tipster called the station insisting that the girl could be found in room 400 of the Morrison Hotel. Police rushed to the scene only to find that the hotel had no room 400. They searched the entire building nonetheless.[8]

The case took a sensational turn late in the day when Muriel Fitzgerald walked into the Chicago Avenue station at 6 p.m. A slender, well-dressed woman with delicate, attractive features, she appeared to be significantly younger than her husband. In her meeting with Lieutenant Howe, she again expressed confidence in Fitzgerald's innocence. "The reports about his peculiarities are born in the brains of gossiping people," she maintained. "I shall stand by him until he is vindicated."

Lieutenant Howe, having become convinced of Fitzgerald's guilt over the course of forty hours of continuous interrogation, was skeptical. When Mrs. Fitzgerald asked to speak to her husband privately, Howe agreed, but he first made sure to send Detective Sergeant Powers to conceal himself behind the prisoner's cell. When Mrs. Fitzgerald was led to the basement and left alone with her husband, Powers was ready with pen and pad in hand. What the detective heard next was remarkable:

"You did it, you did it," Muriel Fitzgerald hissed to her husband the moment she thought they were alone. "When I received that telegram telling me to come home, I knew what was the matter. You stick to your story and all will come out all right."

Fitzgerald, apparently seeing his wife as his only ally, pleaded for her help, though he admitted nothing explicitly. "Go to the package room of the Virginia Hotel and get a small package I left there," he told her. "Whatever you do, Muriel, stand by me!"

When Mrs. Fitzgerald left the basement, she was immediately seized by two police detectives. She objected vehemently, but then Howe showed her the notes that Detective Sergeant Powers had taken. When she could offer no plausible explanation for her words, she was formally arrested and taken to Women's Detention House No. 1 to be held overnight.[9]

Eager to follow this new clue, police rushed to the Virginia Hotel to search for the package. At first, they could find nothing, though they apparently examined every parcel in the room. Eventually, they brought Fitzgerald himself over to the hotel, and he reluctantly showed them where to look. The package was found and opened.

Inside was a brand-new .32-caliber revolver, nestled in a soft chamois case. Every chamber was loaded. A quick inspection indicated that the gun had never been fired.

This discovery convinced Lieutenant Howe that the case might be a kidnapping after all, and that Janet could still be alive. Moving quickly, he dispatched a pair of police detectives to Michigan to retrace Muriel Fitzgerald's movements in the days after Janet's disappearance. But he insisted that there be no letup in the local investigation. Police continued to follow up on all tips, which were coming in with increasing frequency, especially after John Wilkinson announced a $500 reward for any information leading to Janet's recovery.[10]

By now police were also dealing with a flood of another kind of report as well. Inspired by the publicity of the Wilkinson case, parents across the city were coming forward in astonishing numbers to complain that their own children had been assaulted by strange men. An Anna Clark of West Pierson Street claimed that her daughter Florence had been attacked by an older man on July 17. A Helen Lipschutz reported a similar incident with her five-year-old daughter, Anna. Apparently this problem—until now largely suppressed by parents unwilling to expose their children to unwanted publicity—was far more widespread in Chicago than anyone had imagined. By late Thursday, there were rising cries for Deputy Chief John Alcock, acting as chief in Garrity's absence, to immediately arrest and institutionalize all suspected "morons" (1919 parlance for "mentally deficient deviants"), at least until some plan for the protection of the city's children could be devised. Whatever the ultimate explanation of Janet Wilkinson's disappearance, the "moron problem" in Chicago was seemingly out of control. As in the *Wingfoot* disaster on Monday, Chicagoans had been suddenly and brutally awakened to an insidious new urban danger—and in this case, the source of that danger was apparently their very own friends and neighbors.[11]

CHAPTER TWELVE

Friday, July 25

EARLY ON FRIDAY MORNING, Muriel Fitzgerald was released from Women's Detention House No. 1 and escorted to a police vehicle waiting at the curb. The day was already hot, with temperatures forecast to climb into the mid-nineties after several days of temperate highs in the seventies and low eighties. Once inside the vehicle, the prisoner was driven north through crowded streets to the Chicago Avenue police station, where she would be questioned by Captain Ernest Mueller and several detectives.

By prior arrangement, John Wilkinson was seated in the office when she arrived. Mrs. Fitzgerald immediately ran to him and put her hands on the stricken man's shoulders. "Oh, Mr. Wilkinson, I don't know where your little girl is," she cried. "I feel so sorry for you and would do anything in the world to help you find her."

Unmoved, Wilkinson reached up and removed her hands from his shoulders.

Apparently upset by this rebuff, she turned to Captain Mueller and said, "When I [first] received word that my husband was in trouble, knowing his weakness as I do, I was positive that it was in connection with some little girl. . . ."

"Do you think your husband guilty then?" asked one of the detectives.

"What can I believe?" she exclaimed. "All evidence shows that he is guilty. [But] he needs someone to stand by him." After a pause, she reconsidered: "I cannot think of him having strength of mind enough to murder a child." She proceeded to tell them the story of her marriage—how she and Fitzgerald were wed when she was just seventeen and he was over thirty. "I knew of my husband's having trouble. My life with him has been a living hell since I discovered his weakness. . . . He is subnormal, and I have not lived with him as his wife for seven years. But I always have been kind to him, and he needs my help more than ever."

She burst into tears then. "I have been living in horror," she cried, "and dreaded this very thing would happen."[1]

But what exactly *did* happen? Throughout the interview, Muriel Fitzgerald continued to insist that her husband could not have hurt the little girl they both knew and liked. And yet, if he had not harmed her, where was she? Certainly the circumstantial evidence was mounting against the suspect. More and more accusers were coming forward with stories about the Fitzgeralds, some of them outright bizarre. A Helen Hedin of Sedgwick Street claimed that, just a week before Janet's disappearance, Fitzgerald had exposed himself to her ten-year-old daughter. According to the girl, the night watchman had stood naked in his front window, blowing kisses to her as she passed on the street below. Then a vaudeville actor known as "the Hand-cuff King" reported that a person named Fitzgerald had kidnapped his four-year-old the previous year at Benton Harbor, Michigan. The child had been returned only when the vaudeville troupe was sched-uled to leave for another town. Yet Fitzgerald continued to deny everything. "I'm not the man," he would insist, even when positively identified by eyewitnesses.[2]

Lieutenant Howe was exasperated. "In my 25 years of police experience," he told reporters at a news conference, "I never knew a suspect so cunning." But the lieutenant was still confident of a con-fession: "He is weakening," Howe said. "He is nervous and haggard and on the verge of a breakdown. I believe he will be glad to talk soon and tell what he knows."

Howe and the other interrogators had been trying numerous tactics to force the suspect to confess. They'd kept him awake now for two and a half days straight, hoping to wear down his resistance. They'd brought in an alienist (that is, a psychiatrist) to examine him. They'd even tried showing him a picture of Janet with her arms out in supplication. "Look at that picture, see those hands stretched out to you," Detective Sergeant Powers had said to him. "She is pleading. Tell me where you have hidden her body. Where did you hide it?"[3]

Investigators were having no greater luck searching for the girl. One team of police was now scouring the streets of the North Side with a borrowed pack of bloodhounds. Another was sifting through the ashes of the enormous Virginia Hotel furnace. In late afternoon, a fisherman reported seeing a child's body floating in Lake Michigan off Oak Street. "The police rode around in the water for hours while Janet's father paced the beach," the *Tribune* reported, "but there was no sign of the body."[4]

Every newspaper in town was dwelling on the sorrows of the frantic parents, filling columns with sob-sister stories of the most maudlin kind. "For two days and two nights, Mrs. Wilkinson has not taken off her clothing or tasted a morsel of food," the *Daily Journal* reported. "When she is not running up and down the lake shore with her husband, she sits in the parlor of the little flat, constantly praying. 'Just send my baby back to me,' she moans. 'That is all I will ever ask.'"

Reporters found easy poignancy in the image of Janet's favorite plaything—a much-battered doll sitting in a little red chair in a corner. The week before, Janet had complained that the doll was "losted." "I had put [the] baby doll away from her," Mrs. Wilkinson allegedly keened, "for she was such an ugly doll. No wig—it had been torn off—[and] nothing but a shabby skirt. . . . And now it's *my* baby doll who is lost."[5]

When Muriel Fitzgerald appeared at the apartment (with a police escort), reporters were there to record the scene:

> When [Mrs. Fitzgerald] entered the door, she stood a moment on the threshold, looked fondly at the mother who was lying in her bed, and then rushed over, fell on her knees, and threw her arms around the unfortunate woman's neck. The two began to weep.
>
> Mrs. Fitzgerald sobbed: "Is there anything in the world that I can do for you?"
>
> The answer she got was a sad nod of the head.
>
> The glance of the two women then fell on the chair and doll, and they became silent.[6]

Such manipulative reporting did little to quell Chicagoans' increasingly strident calls for a rapid solution to the "moron problem." And when on Friday afternoon another molestation report came in—of an attack by a fifty-year-old man on a nine-year-old girl—Deputy Chief Alcock, under enormous pressure, decided to take action. "I have ordered the arrest of all half-wits and subnormals, because they are a danger to every woman and girl in the city," he announced to reporters. "They are responsible for almost all of the attacks that are reported to the police, and they should have been rounded up long ago and sent to institutions where they can be cared for."[7]

Precisely how these "subnormals" were to be identified was not specified by the acting chief. The order, in fact, was almost certainly unconstitutional, and would probably have failed to stand up under even the permissive law enforcement standards of the day. But the citizens of Chicago, roused by the spectacle of little Janet, would not be restrained by such legal niceties. According to the *Herald and Examiner,* an aura of mistrust now hung over the entire North Side, turning every unusual occurrence into a source of suspicion. The danger to the city's children was obviously very real, and it was imperative that something—no matter how drastic—be done about it.[8]

* * *

At the *Wingfoot* inquest—which reconvened on Friday at 11 a.m., after its one-day recess—the shouting began even before the first witness was called. The coroner's jury of experts had requested to hear Captain Benjamin B. Lipsner, first Chicago superintendent of the U.S. Air Mail Service. Lipsner had allegedly spoken to injured mechanic Harry Wacker in the hospital shortly after the crash. According to rumors that had been sweeping the city for days, Wacker had made some alarming admissions to Lipsner at the time. But Goodyear's attorneys were determined that the jury would not hear this testimony until pilot Jack Boettner had given his version of events. "What this man [Lipsner] has to offer is hearsay," attorney Elias Mayer objected. "It is our idea to let Boettner tell first how the blimp was conceived and built, and then exactly what happened before and during the fire."

At this there was much squabbling among lawyers and jury members, but Coroner Hoffman was adamant. "My jury of engineers has elected to hear Lipsner," he said firmly. "He will testify now."

When Lipsner finally took the stand, it was immediately obvious why Goodyear wanted to delay his testimony. "Wacker told me that he was nervous and scared throughout the flight," Lipsner claimed. "He said that the blimp acted up from the time they started on the first trip from White City to Grant Park, and that he was mighty glad when they made the first landing. . . . He said that the motors were working badly—that they were throwing oil and sparks and that there was no water ballast in the ship."

This was damning enough, but then Lipsner went on to describe the airship's final flight: "Wacker said that Carl Weaver, one of the victims, had control of the blimp at the time of the accident, and that just before the machine went down he was continually calling [to Weaver], 'Too much gas! Too much air! This isn't right!'"

"He [also] told me," Lipsner went on, "that Boettner jumped first. He himself warned the others to jump, and after seeing Norton, the newspaper photographer, jump, Wacker slid over the side with his chute burning. He told me he reached up to extinguish the flames with his hand. . . ."

This last detail finally gave Goodyear's attorneys something to pounce on. "Fabrication!" Mayer shouted, as arguments broke out among the spectators.

"That man is a perjurer," Henry Berger interjected, "and I will personally take the burden of proving it!"

Even members of the jury lost their tempers. "Produce the evidence," one juror shouted, "and don't waste so much time!"

Amid this upset, John C. Lowery, an assistant to State's Attorney Maclay Hoyne, threatened to clear the inquest room unless everyone settled down.[9]

Order was restored after a few minutes, but Mayer wasn't finished. "Wacker isn't dead yet—he will get well," the attorney asserted. "We will have him testify to the coroner and then Lipsner will learn that Wacker calls him a liar and a crazy man!"

He turned to Major C. H. Maranville, another expert witness. "He [Lipsner] said Wacker reached up to put out the flames of his chute with his hands. Major Maranville, is that possible?"

The Major shook his head. "No, it is not. The man hangs 40 feet below the supporting surface [of the parachute]."

Thus caught in an obvious absurdity, Lipsner stood up and refused to answer any more questions. He pointed out that he was not testifying as an expert witness—that he was merely reporting what Wacker had told him. He also said that he resented the Goodyear attorneys' attacks on him. Coroner Hoffman, pounding his desk for order, agreed to excuse Lipsner for the time being, but asked that he remain available for the rest of the hearing.[10]

With the inquest room still buzzing from this dispute, Assistant

State's Attorney James O'Brien demanded that Jack Boettner be questioned next. The pilot, dressed in a light-colored suit and carefully knotted tie (while most present were in their shirtsleeves), exuded an air of unruffled coolness as he came before the juries. Answering questions in a steady, dignified voice, he testified that he had been an aviator since February 1917, and that he had never experienced a mishap of any kind before this. Proceeding systematically, he related precisely how the airship had been assembled, and described each of the three trips made that day. "We had no trouble during our flights on Monday," he said. "Everything went smoothly. The ship did not roll much on the first two trips, but it was very sensitive to control." When asked if the flights were experimental, he insisted that only the first one was, and that this initial trip had taken place entirely along the unpopulated shoreline of the lake. "After that flight," he said, "I believed the ship perfectly safe. . . . I know that the engines were working perfectly and that there were no sparks or flames thrown from them."

"When did you discover the dirigible was in trouble?" he was asked.

"About three minutes to five," he said. He described feeling a jerk on one of the suspension cables holding the gondola. That's when he looked around and saw a flame on the back of the balloon near the equator line. "I knew we didn't have a chance," he said calmly. "I said, 'Everybody jump; that's our only chance.' They went over and the gondola dove down." He insisted again that he was the last person to leave the ship, and that he remembered seeing Wacker four hundred feet below before he himself finally jumped.

When asked to explain Lipsner's contradictory testimony, Boettner said that he didn't believe Wacker had really made the statements attributed to him.[11]

As if to confuse the coroner's juries even more, the remainder of the session was devoted to an examination of several eyewitnesses

who seemed to agree on very little. Major Maranville, who claimed
to have watched the entire flight from Grant Park, asserted that the
fire had started "on the right side [of the balloon] near the rear fins."
But the next witness—Irwin A. Phillips—insisted that the fire had
started near the front, just above the blimp's nose. Several other
witnesses corroborated Phillips's account. Just about the only thing
everyone agreed on was that the flame was yellow and not blue, indicating that it was the bag that was burning and not the hydrogen gas
inside. Even so, by the end of the day's session, the two juries still had
no idea what to believe.[12]

* * *

Over at the transit parleys, negotiations were moving ever closer to
a breakdown. Emerging from a two-hour morning session, all sides
seemed grim. "I can't see that we've done a thing," surface line president Busby grumbled. Maurice Lynch, his opponent on the labor
side, agreed. "We may have something to say after our next conference this afternoon," Lynch said, "[but] just now everything is up in
the air." Even utilities commissioner Patrick J. Lucey refused to be
upbeat: "All I can say is that we haven't reached a dead wall yet."

As before, the main sticking point was the issue of the eight-hour
day. The companies and the unions disagreed vehemently on how
much a shortened workday would cost the car lines. According to
the unions, management was exaggerating the costs in order to force
through a nine-hour compromise—something that the car-men still
considered unacceptable. Talk of a possible strike vote, to be taken
on Saturday, was becoming more insistent.[13]

Some hope was offered by a personal intervention in the talks
by Governor Lowden himself. The governor, perhaps hoping to take
advantage of his rival's absence, had come up from Springfield on
Thursday evening, determined to sit down with everyone involved
and hammer out an agreement. Starting at 4 p.m. at the Blackstone

Hotel, he began a series of closed-door meetings with negotiators to hear all sides of the dispute. And although he refused to comment on the outcome of the talks, prospects were looking somewhat brighter by Friday evening. "It is understood," the *Herald and Examiner* reported, "that some progress toward conciliation was made, and for the first time there appeared a chance that an agreement might possibly be reached."

In his private communications, however, the governor was decidedly less sanguine. "Frank telephones [to say] that the streetcar situation is very bad," Mrs. Lowden wrote in her diary. Apparently, the governor had hoped to make short work of the negotiations and get away to the family farm at Sinnissippi, west of the city, for some rest and relaxation. But now he was forced to cancel those plans: "He cannot possibly come out here for the weekend," his wife lamented.[14]

Still more disturbing news was emerging from the Black Belt, where the racial tensions of early summer were showing signs of coming to a head. Carl Sandburg's reports on "the Negro Problem" had been appearing in the *Chicago Daily News* for ten days now, and the situation they described was hardly encouraging. White newspaper coverage of the Black Belt always tended to be anecdotal, focusing on individual instances of alleged black dysfunction. But Sandburg's articles were showing the problem in a different light, hinting that the true root of the troubles might have more to do with white attitudes than anything else. Though the poet was careful to point to a few areas of hope, his emphasis was on the blatant injustices that Ida Wells-Barnett had been complaining about for months—the rampant discrimination in jobs and housing, the inequalities in access to services, and the inept police response to repeated incidents of bombing and other interracial violence.

Sandburg's article in Friday's paper—"Deplore Unfounded Negro Crime Tales"—was especially blunt. Writing about the race riots that had convulsed Washington, D.C., for several days that

summer, he attributed the violent outbreaks to the prevailing atmosphere of mutual racial suspicion, showing how specious accusations of black crime against white women often served as cover for
the "ulterior purposes" of hostile white agitators. Another article
published in that same day's *Tribune,* on the other hand, focused
on black defiance and served only to intensify white paranoia. "The
American Negro encountered no color line in France," the article
claimed. "Returned to the United States, he is determined never
again to submit to race segregation in either society, business, or
politics." The reporter cited analysis in two leading French newspapers, which maintained that "the Washington riots do not represent
sporadic outbreaks," but rather were " 'feelers' to test the strength
and determination of whites and blacks, and a possible forerunner
to widespread revolt."

"The attitude of the Negro movement in America," one of the
papers had ominously suggested, "leaves it supposable that a general
Negro upheaval may develop."[15]

Clearly, this analysis could not be entirely dismissed as typical
Tribune race hysteria. Blacks across the country—especially former soldiers—were indeed showing a greater willingness to assert
their rights, and by violent means if necessary. "[Black veterans]
will never be the same again," W. E. B. DuBois had said in a speech
at Chicago's Wendell Phillips High School in May. "They are not
the same men anymore." This so-called New Negro sensibility was
marked by a rejection of the accommodationist stance espoused by
old leaders like Booker T. Washington. Of course, talk of a premed-
itated insurrection was nonsense, but as the riots in Washington,
D.C., demonstrated, blacks were no longer willing to cower in the
face of lynchings, mob attacks, and other instances of white hostility. Aggressive resistance had become common. Just a few days
earlier, in a poem published in the journal *Liberator,* Claude McKay
expressed the essence of this new defiance:

Oh, Kinsmen! We must meet the common foe;
Though far outnumbered, let us show us brave,
And for their thousand blows deal one death blow!
What though before us lies the open grave?
Like men we'll face the murderous cowardly pack,
Pressed to the wall, dying but fighting back!

To some, that "awful day" of armed conflict in Chicago that the *Broad Ax* had warned about in early May was seeming ever more plausible in July.[16]

Recognizing the dire situation in the city, the *Chicago Evening Post* made its recommendation known in a plainspoken editorial in its late edition, under an all-caps headline reading simply: "THE MAYOR SHOULD RETURN." "One way to boost Chicago is to go bronco-busting," the *Post* observed. "Another is to stay on your job when your city is threatened. . . . Mayor Thompson should not go to Cheyenne; he should turn in his tracks and come back to face his difficult and important duty at the City Hall."

But this advice was much too tardy. Big Bill and his crew were already in Wyoming, kicking up their heels in fine fashion. Dressed in a cowman's Stetson, a colorful silk shirt, and shaggy black chaps, the mayor had already led the Frontier Days parade through the Cheyenne streets, showing off his skills with a lariat. "From noon to dewy eve," wrote Charles MacArthur in the *Tribune,* "the Mayor and his Chicago boosters roped steers . . . and carried on in real Wild West style. Chicago was talked of, sung of, and boosted of as long as their voices held out, which was until about four o'clock." MacArthur, later to achieve fame as Ben Hecht's collaborator on the play *The Front Page* (and as husband of the actress Helen Hayes), was making plenty of ironic hay with the mayor's visit, using the event to comment obliquely on the politics back home: "Excitement was caused during the afternoon by the disappearance of Fred Lundin from the

grandstand before the last event," MacArthur wrote. "He was discovered beneath the stand in earnest conference with Hole-in-His-Sock,
an ancient Indian chief. In return for some lore of the northland, Mr.
Lundin was instructing the chief how to vote his tribe." MacArthur
also took delight in pointing out that Big Bill seemed particularly
adept at lassoing attractive young ladies.[17]

Whether the mayor ever heard about the chastising *Post* editorial
is unclear. Even if he had, however, he likely would have ignored it.
With the weekend at hand and their return to Chicago scheduled
for Monday morning, Thompson and his entourage saw little reason
to curtail their stay. After all, their goodwill mission, frivolous as it
may have seemed, had the highly laudable purpose of boosting their
illustrious hometown. And besides, if they were to leave now, they'd
miss the Saturday night gala and parade.

CHAPTER THIRTEEN

Saturday, July 26

"A LL CHICAGO SEEKS SOLUTION of Missing Child Mystery," the *Chicago Daily News* reported in its early-Saturday edition. The headline was hardly an exaggeration. The entire city, it seemed, was now engaged in a gruesome guessing game, appalled and yet intrigued by the ongoing Janet Wilkinson case. The *Daily Journal,* calling the girl's whereabouts "the biggest question in the minds of hundreds of thousands of Chicagoans today," outlined its four working hypotheses: that Janet had drowned in the lake; that she had been hit by an automobile whose driver then carried her away in a panic; that a lonely, childless woman had abducted her; or that Fitzgerald (or some other person "of low moral type") had murdered her.[1]

By the time the *Tribune* announced an additional $2,500 reward for a productive lead, the Chicago Avenue station was already being flooded with calls, telegrams, and letters by the hundreds. Some merely sought corroboration for one of the many wild rumors running through the city; others offered purported leads, most of which the police did their best to check out. One tip—that Janet was seen on a Chicago-bound train now en route from Benton Harbor—was taken especially seriously. John Wilkinson and a police detective rushed to the Dearborn Station to meet the train. They discovered that a young girl of Janet's age was indeed among the passengers, but it wasn't Janet.[2]

The close of business at noon made many additional volunteers available to scour the streets for any sign of the girl. As Janet's class-mates at Holy Name Cathedral School finished summer classes for the weekend, their sister superior urged them to join the search. "Don't waste your time in the playgrounds or [on] the beaches," she said. "Go look for Janet." It was a call that many adult Chicagoans also heeded, joining police and other city workers in what had now become a regionwide hunt. "Boatmen began dragging the lake for a third time at daybreak," the *Evening Post* reported. "Police and vol-unteer searchers are once more going over the double stone building at 112–114 East Superior Street. . . . Other searchers are covering every foot of the weed-grown vacant property in the neighborhood. Men from the street department are looking in sewers and catch basins near the Wilkinson home."[3]

Detectives received a shock that afternoon when a dredging tool used to probe the Virginia Hotel sewer came up filled with crushed bones. Chief of Detectives Mooney sent them over to a Dr. W. A. Evans for identification (there was no official medical examiner for Cook County until 1976, so police often had to rely on private doc-tors for such tasks). After a brief examination, however, Dr. Evans determined that they were a combination of chicken joints and the bones of "an animal far larger than a human being"—probably a cow.[4]

At the Chicago Avenue station, investigators were now question-ing Fitzgerald's coworkers, and this new testimony only strengthened their conviction that they had the perpetrator—of whatever crime—in their custody. Marie Pearson, a Virginia Hotel chambermaid, told police that Fitzgerald had once attempted "familiarities" with her. William Harris, a chef, claimed that the night watchman had nearly fallen asleep over his supper on Tuesday evening, six hours after Janet's disappearance, and that he complained of not having slept all day. Engineer W. J. Hogan claimed that Fitzgerald had mysteriously sent him from the hotel boiler room on Tuesday night on "some trivial business." When Hogan returned, Fitzgerald was still in the boiler room. The engineer had been gone long enough, police concluded, for Fitzgerald to dispose of the child's body in the furnace.

Most incriminating, however, was an incident described by Michael Kezick, a fireman at the hotel. Kezick claimed he saw a girl fitting Janet's description sitting in Fitzgerald's lap in the boiler room a few days before her disappearance. Fitzgerald tried to insist that it had been another girl—the daughter of hotel employee Florence Howe—but Kezick wouldn't back down. "No, it was Janet, I am sure."

Fitzgerald shook his head at this, making a show of "pitying the ignorance" of his accuser. "Mike," he said, "you are mistaken."

"I am not mistaken," Kezick said vehemently. "I know the [Howe] girl."[5]

The incident was typical of Fitzgerald's ever more brazen intransigence. Despite the wealth of evidence against him, the man continued to flatly deny all accusations, often adopting a tone of outraged condescension toward witnesses against him. Now facing his fourth day of round-the-clock interrogation, he apparently had yet to request a lawyer, and no attorneys had voluntarily come forward to offer their services. According to the *Evening Post,* this was unprecedented in Chicago: "Ordinarily, the arrest of a suspect in any case is followed by a rush of lawyers to the station. So brutal does this case appear, however, and so strong is the circumstantial evidence against Fitzgerald, that no offers of legal aid have been made."

At any time since his arrest, an attorney could have insisted on Fitzgerald's release, since no formal charges had yet been brought against him. That the prisoner seemed unaware of his basic rights was fortunate for police, who, in those days before Miranda warnings, were naturally in no hurry to enlighten him. Even so, Lieutenant Howe had a backup plan, should any effort be made to free him. John Wilkinson was reportedly willing to press charges based on Fitzgerald's alleged assault of Janet the previous December—

although without a victim or firsthand witness to testify against him, holding the suspect on those hearsay charges might have been problematic as well.[6]

Certainly any conscientious lawyer would have objected to the manner in which the suspect was being questioned. Forced to stay awake for days now, slapped or shouted at whenever he tried to sleep, Fitzgerald had broken down at least once in a fit of hysterical weeping. But for the most part, he was maintaining a cool, almost haughty, sometimes taunting demeanor under questioning, once even interrupting an interrogation to tease Captain Mueller about a new straw hat he was wearing. Lieutenant Howe, who must have been near weeping in frustration himself by now, was nonetheless still sure that a confession was imminent. "He is the most stubborn and one of the shrewdest men I have ever questioned," he told reporters after a morning session with the suspect. "He misrepresents about the most trivial and unimportant details, apparently just to be contrary. But I am sure he will come off his high horse before many more hours. He will have to give in."[7]

Hoping to overwhelm Fitzgerald with a rush of new accusations, Howe decided to bring in five North Side women and their daughters to see him. Each mother had recently complained about a strange man bothering her child, and authorities thought that at least one or two might recognize the prisoner. But not one of the girls identified Fitzgerald as the man who had accosted her. The tactic thus backfired on the lieutenant, further emboldening Fitzgerald in his stonewalling campaign. It also raised a disturbing question: If Fitzgerald was not the molester of these girls, who was? Just how many men were out there victimizing Chicago's children?

By late afternoon, word had gone out to police to be on the lookout for "another moron" at large in the city streets.[8]

* * *

Day four of the *Wingfoot* inquest was proving to be no less con-
founding than the previous three sessions. Yet another new expert
witness—Major John York, an officer in the army's wartime balloon
service in France—was called to testify, and he produced yet another
new theory of what had actually caused the disaster. "From an examination of the bag," he said, "I believe that the fire was a result of
friction between the fabric and the finger-shaped patches that attach
the bag to the cables supporting the car. A bumpy condition of the
air could have jiggled the car up and down and caused such friction."

Apparently noting confusion among the layman's jury, Goodyear
attorney Mayer interrupted him. "Your evidence is interesting from
a scientific standpoint," he said to the witness, "but come down to
earth and explain it so [that] this jury of businessmen will know what
you mean."

Major York flushed red and asked for a pencil and paper. He carefully drew a diagram of the connection patches and showed how air
turbulence might generate the friction he described.

"I think," an increasingly testy Coroner Hoffman said then,
"these businessmen will understand now."[9]

Perhaps the jury did grasp York's theory, but they definitely
seemed more interested in the sparking-engines scenario described so
vividly by Benjamin Lipsner the day before. When H. T. Kraft, chief
pilot for Goodyear, was called next, he was peppered with numerous
questions about the engines and their behavior on the first two flights
of the day. But Kraft maintained that he had seen no sparks during the blimp's preliminary tests, which he had conducted himself.
"You know it is possible to test a dirigible on the ground—something that cannot be done with an airplane," he pointed out. "The
motors started with the first swing of the stick [that is, the propeller]
and there was no backfire. They worked beautifully." He also argued
that sparks would not have been a danger even if the rotary engines
had created some. It was virtually impossible for exhaust emissions

to ignite the balloon gas, he insisted, since any hydrogen from the bag, being much lighter than air, would quickly rise away from the engines.[10]

Which explanation, then, should the juries accept? Clearly, no one was entirely satisfied with any of the theories offered so far. The consensus was that no finding should be made until the juries heard directly from Harry Wacker, the only survivor besides Boettner of the blimp's third flight. "I have made an effort to see Wacker," Coroner Hoffman announced, "but he was [still] too sick. . . . The jury will go to Wacker's bedside as soon as he is sufficiently well."

Taking note of complaints about the length of the inquest, Hoffman expressed his hope that Wacker's testimony would complete the evidence, meaning that the inquest could be wrapped up at the next session. With that—and since it was already after noon, the time when the jury was told they'd be released for the day—he called for an adjournment until Tuesday morning.[11]

* * *

Temperatures had already hit the low nineties when the dismissed *Wingfoot* jurors left the stifling City Hall–County Building and joined countless others streaming out of their workplaces for the start of the summer weekend. Chicago was by 1919 a modern, round-the-clock metropolis in many ways, but most city workweeks still ended at midday on Saturday, when the streets would fill with people eager to begin their day and a half of leisure. Some of them would make straight for the Ls and streetcars to head home. Others would linger downtown to run a few errands or do a little shopping at the State Street department stores. Many would gather over lunch with friends and coworkers to exchange news and discuss the week's events. Certainly there was a lot to talk about this week. Somehow, between the blimp debacle and the Janet Wilkinson case, life in the city seemed significantly more precarious than it had just one week earlier. There were also other signs of trouble ahead. Picket lines seemed to be going up everywhere; street crime was just getting worse. And would the trains and trolleys even be running by the beginning of the next workweek on Monday?

But a city is a complex thing, a nexus of countless intersecting lines of narrative, comprising a myriad number of individual interests, worries, aspirations, and struggles. So there would have been other topics of conversation on that hot afternoon. There would have been weddings and vacations to discuss, along with the usual birthdays, job woes, new automobiles, visiting relatives from out of town, and deaths of loved ones that would never make the evening papers. "All Chicago" may have been collectively preoccupied with the big news stories of the day, but "all Chicago" consisted of 2.5 million individuals who had countless other distractions of their own. Carl Sandburg, for one, had been profiled prominently in that day's *Tribune,* a bit of welcome publicity that probably took the poet's mind off the ongoing troubles in the Black Belt. Frank Lowden, deeply mired in the traction situation, doubtless had one eye on Washington, D.C., where Illinois congressman Edward Everett Denison would be booming him for president on the floor of the U.S. House of Representatives. And Emily Frankenstein's main concern that afternoon, according to her diary, was not a missing six-year-old or a fluke aviation disaster, but rather the conundrum of her fiancé's unfortunate religious beliefs. She had decided just that day that it was finally time to "say goodbye" to Jerry the next time they got together. It seemed to her that they were just too different from each other in so many ways. And though it was a difficult decision for her, she thought that it would be best for both of them just to part.[12]

Yet it's not unreasonable to assume that the rising sense of menace in the city was being felt by everyone, if only as a background to their more personal dramas. The events of the past week, after all, were unsettling even by the standards of Chicago, no stranger to strife and unrest even in the best of times. If a city is an organism, capable of sickness and of health, then Chicago was showing some alarming symptoms of illness lately.

And by the end of the lunch hour, there would be yet another alarming development to talk about.

At twelve forty-five, two women leaving their city hall office stopped at an open window on the seventh-floor corridor, "trying to catch a breath of cool air." Glancing upward, they saw a large, coatless man stepping out of another window on the eleventh floor of the building. As they watched, the man stood for a moment on the ledge, set his feet, and then jumped. "I saw the body flash down," one of the women later said, "and then I heard the crash."

The crash was the sound of the man falling through the skylight of the city collector's office below. There was a wire cage protecting the skylight, but the body passed right through the mesh and continued falling. Amid a shower of glass, the body hit the top of the clerk's cage, rolled off, dropped to a desk, rolled again, and then hit the floor facedown.

For the people working in the office, the spectacle must have been an alarming echo of the *Wingfoot* event five days before. Two janitors cleaning the room had in fact started running the moment they heard the crash of the skylight, apparently fearful of another plummeting firebomb. A special policeman assigned to the office, however, had the presence of mind to remain. When the body had come to rest on the floor, he approached it and turned it over, but the face was too battered to recognize.[13]

The two witnesses on the seventh floor had immediately run to the office of Coroner Hoffman, who was still finishing up work after the day's inquest session. When they reported what they had seen, Hoffman and Health Commissioner John Dill Robertson rushed to the collector's office. They, too, were unable to identify the victim by sight, but a key ring in a trouser pocket established his identity. It was Judge Harry P. Dolan, an associate justice of the Municipal Court.

When word reached the eleventh floor, the judge's coworkers were incredulous. "I went to the judge's courtroom shortly after noon to get him to go over to the Illinois Athletic Club with me," attorney Eugene O'Reilly later said. "He was on the bench when I entered, but he beckoned me to come up, and he asked me what I wanted. I told him and he said, 'No, I don't think I can go over. You'd better go yourself.'"

O'Reilly decided to wait for the judge anyway. He sat in the courtroom while Dolan finished his case—that of two boys accused of stealing and then wrecking an automobile. After letting the boys off easily, as was his wont, the judge went to his chambers, presumably to take care of a few last details before joining O'Reilly for lunch at the club. But he didn't come out for some time.

"After a few minutes, I and the bailiff decided we would go in and see what was detaining the judge," O'Reilly said. "The room was empty. He had taken off his coat and left it on the coat tree. His white Panama hat and $50 were on the table."

At first, no one could believe that the fall was a suicide. Friends and associates discounted the witnesses' statement that the judge had paused on the ledge and voluntarily jumped. They claimed instead that he had probably been overcome by the heat and fainted while standing at the window. Judge Dolan, they pointed out, was a highly regarded jurist in the Municipal Court, "a sort of father to the boys of Chicago" who had been prominent in the fight to reform the court's handling of youthful offenders. "I can account for no reason for this act," one person close to him said afterward.

But as other information emerged, it began to look more likely that Dolan was a suicide. Back in April, the judge had suffered a nervous breakdown, apparently as a result of an attack of Spanish influenza. At the time, he had allegedly remarked to friends that he "saw nothing more in life to live for." But a two-month stay at

Chicago after World War I stood at a pivotal moment in its evolution, struggling to accommodate a vastly diverse population and invent for itself a new, uniquely modern identity. The man entrusted with leadership of the city through this critical time was its irrepressible and highly controversial Republican mayor, William Hale Thompson (standing).

Chicago skyline ca. 1925

A former athlete and self-styled cowboy, Thompson was nothing if not colorful. Regarded by some as a blustering demagogue, he was to many others a genuine hero, hailed as "the People's David" or "Big Bill the Builder"— the one man who could corral Chicago's warring factions and lead the way to a "Greater Chicago."

The brain behind the Thompson phenomenon was the notorious Fred Lundin, known to insiders as "the Mayor's Mephistopheles." Masking his ambitions behind an eccentric milquetoast persona, Lundin hoped to use his protégé's popularity to build a political machine to rival New York's Tammany Hall.

Many powerful enemies stood in the way of Lundin's plans. Among them were the publishers of the city's two most influential newspapers—Robert R. McCormick of the Chicago Tribune *(left) and Victor F. Lawson of the* Chicago Daily News *(right).*

The most powerful enemy of the Thompson-Lundin organization, however, was Frank O. Lowden, the Republican governor of Illinois. A former ally of the mayor, he was now determined to see control of the city wrested from an administration he considered hopelessly corrupt.

July 1919 proved to be a turning point in this conflict, as the city was hit by an unprecedented eruption of violence, technological disaster, and sordid crime. The crisis began with the bizarre crash of the airship Wingfoot Express.

BLIMP HORROR

The blimp caught fire in flight and crashed through the skylight of the Illinois Trust and Savings Bank in the heart of the Loop, killing thirteen and injuring dozens more in what is regarded as the country's first major aviation disaster.

ALL CHICAGO SEEKS SOLUTION OF MISSING CHILD MYSTERY

MISSING GIRL AND HER PLAYMATE

Six Year Old Child, Who Disappeared at Rush Street and Chicago Avenue.

$2,500 for Janet!

To aid in relieving the suspense of her parents and friends,

The Chicago Tribune

will pay

$2,500.00

for exclusive information leading to the discovery of Janet Wilkinson and the solution of the mystery of her disappearance.

The very next day, six-year-old Janet Wilkinson went missing on Chicago's North Side. For days, the city was consumed by the mystery of the child's disappearance. When suspicion was cast on a seemingly innocuous friend of the family, Chicagoans were appalled, leading many to wonder whether their own neighbors could be trusted.

STRIKE IS ON; CARS STOP!
20 SLAIN IN RACE RIOTS

But the real chaos set in a few days later, when a racial incident at a crowded South Side beach spiraled into one of the worst race riots in American history. The bloodshed intensified when, two days into the riot, a transit strike paralyzed the city, forcing hundreds of thousands of commuting workers onto the dangerous streets.

Calls for the National Guard to restore order ultimately forced the mayor and the governor into a confrontation that would have far-reaching consequences for the city's future.

Chicago Historical Society: DN-0070258   Library of Congress

Caught up in the summer crisis were numerous Chicagoans of greater or lesser fame. Carl Sandburg (left) reported on the riot for the Chicago Daily News. *Ring Lardner (right) was a columnist for the* Tribune.

Tuesday June 11, 1918

a little before noon, Jerry came over. He brought me his golf clubs to use while he's gone. We were going downtown for lunch and afterward Jerry had some things to do. Before we left, I sewed a sergeant ensignia on his sleeve. He is expecting to be made a sergeant any day and had his old one with him.

We went to Grant Dewey's first and had our picture taken together. It was a notion, but we were happy - and it was only for ourselves. Mr. Dewey teased us though.

We took the 47th St. car to St. and then went down - town. And

University of Chicago   Chicago Historical Society: i36135

Activist Ida Wells-Barnett (left) worked to help the victims of the rioting in the city's Black Belt. And young Emily Frankenstein (right), seen here with her fiancé, Jerry Lapiner, recorded the unfolding events in her diary.

The effect of the 1919 crisis was to leave Chicago a chastened but, in many ways, a stronger city. While dreams of implementing architect Daniel Burnham's wildly ambitious Chicago Plan were never fully realized, the city did see remarkable urban improvements in the 1920s.

Chicago Historical Society: i39070_6t

Today, showpieces such as the Magnificent Mile of Michigan Avenue make Chicago perhaps the most architecturally distinguished city in the Americas—in large part thanks to the leadership, however corrupt, of Big Bill Thompson.

Chicago Historical Society: i39748

a Wisconsin sanitarium had restored him to good health. In June, he had apparently felt well enough to play catcher for the judges' team in the annual Judges vs. Lawyers charity baseball game, raising money for the *Tribune*'s Algonquin Hospital fund (Clarence Darrow played first base for the lawyers, with State's Attorney Hoyne on third). His friends believed that he had completely recovered. "He seemed jolly and carefree," O'Reilly insisted.[14]

For most Chicagoans, then, the judge's suicide was just one more mystery, one more ghastly and inexplicable tragedy to augment the already pervasive sense of chaos in the city. Something seemed fundamentally wrong, and who was working to steer Chicago through this crisis? The mayor was absent, the police appeared helpless, even the governor seemed incapable of taming the disorder. And now the city's distinguished judges were jumping out of downtown windows. This was supposed to be "Chicago's greatest year," and yet the city now seemed in danger of spinning entirely out of control.

At 4 p.m., temperatures peaked at ninety-five degrees, with more heat forecast for the next few days. The early editions of the evening newspapers were just hitting the streets, and they contained more bad news about the transit negotiations. Fed up with what they called a "gross breach of confidence" on the part of the car companies, the unions had bolted from the official talks that afternoon. "Negotiations are over," the president of the streetcar employees had declared, backed up by six other union leaders. "We are going into conference now to draw up a statement explaining our position."

The *Evening Post* was fatalistic: "Chicago is in for a streetcar strike," the paper reported. "It may last two days; it may last longer. But it's coming."[15]

* * *

Late that night, after another unsuccessful interrogation in Captain Mueller's office, Lieutenant Howe decided that the time had come to push Thomas Fitzgerald to the limit. Along with two other police lieutenants and several reporters from the *Tribune* and the *Herald and Examiner,* Howe planned out an elaborate overnight program of ruses, psychological assaults, and other interrogation tactics designed to get the already sleepless and overwrought prisoner to crack. This so-called fourth-degree interrogation, described in hour-by-hour detail in a subsequent edition of the *Tribune,* began at midnight with five men in Fitzgerald's cell, all of them pummeling him with questions. And for the next eight hours, police refused to ease up on him, saying that they wouldn't let him rest unless and until he confessed to the crime they all knew he had committed.

They tried everything. They took his glasses away so he couldn't see. They had a policeman dress up as a priest to counsel him and urge a private confession of his sins. They had another policeman pose as a relative of the missing girl and plead with him to end the family's agony. A doctor came in to examine him (Fitzgerald complained of a weak heart) and then left, looking worried but not saying a word. Once (bizarrely) they even stood the suspect before a table covered with dozens of small plaster doll hands posed in pleading gestures. For hours on end, they shouted at him, whispered soothingly to him, invoked his own mother's name, and slapped him when he tried to sleep. But nothing would work. Fitzgerald would just sit there grasping his head in his hands, complaining about the bright lights. "Sleep, sleep, sleep," he moaned at one point. "I wish to sleep. Please let me alone."

"Tell me where the body is," one of the interrogators told him, "and you can sleep."

"I don't know! Honest to God, I don't know!"

Finally, around dawn, they decided to try something they hadn't tried before—they left Fitzgerald entirely alone. They exited the cell and went upstairs to the main floor of the station house, locking the cell behind them. Whether they put Fitzgerald in restraints beforehand is unrecorded. Presumably they did, for he was certainly a suicide risk. But he sat alone with his thoughts for some time.

At around 8 a.m., one of the reporters, Harry Romanov of the *Herald and Examiner,* went downstairs again and walked up to the cell. "The faint sound of tolling church bells reached the sunless cell room," Romanov later wrote. "It was the Sabbath and by chance Fitzgerald's 39th birthday. He was sitting in a corner of the cell with his head in his hands and elbows on his knees. He was reflecting. Now that he could have slept, sleep would not come."

"Well?" the reporter asked. "Ready to talk?"

Fitzgerald looked up at him. "Send down Mr. Howe," he said.

The lieutenant, exhausted by the all-night grilling, was upstairs nodding over some routine paperwork. He was visibly emotional when the reporter told him that Fitzgerald was apparently prepared to confess. More than anyone else involved in the investigation, Howe had taken an obsessive personal interest in the case, trying to befriend the prisoner and earn his trust, working long hours to extract a confession he had known for days was inevitable. And now, apparently, that confession was finally going to come. He took a moment to compose himself before rushing down to the cell.

"Lieutenant Howe," Fitzgerald said calmly, stopping to draw a deep breath. "You've been the only friend I've had. I wouldn't tell anyone else, but I think I'll tell you." He hesitated again and peered into the lieutenant's eyes. "I'm afraid you'll think me a horrible man."

"No, I won't, Fitzgerald," Howe said. "What I'll think is what I've thought all the way through this case—that you have a diseased mind." He paused and said: "Tell me the truth, my man."

Fitzgerald lowered his eyes. Then, at exactly 8:13 a.m., he finally told the truth: "I did it," he said. "I killed her."[16]

CHAPTER FOURTEEN

Sunday Morning, July 27

I WAS SITTING in the window [at home] at 10 minutes after 12 on Tuesday," Fitzgerald began, "when I saw Janet coming towards the building."

Howe listened in silence, alone with Fitzgerald in the hot, cramped jail cell. Later, the prisoner's words would be recorded by an official police stenographer before a roomful of men. But Howe must have known that any sudden call for witnesses might cause the prisoner to balk yet again, and so he let him speak. For now, the lieutenant just needed to hear what had happened.

"When she came up the stairs to the landing," Fitzgerald continued. "[I was waiting] at my doorway. I said to her, 'Dolly, would you like some candy?'"

The child had paused on the landing then. Apparently, she was tempted. As hackneyed and transparent as the offer might sound to modern ears, it must have seemed enticing to Janet. But the girl would have remembered her parents' warning not to go near this man.

Fitzgerald, however, didn't give her time to refuse. "I picked her up in my arms," he said, "and carried her into my apartment."

He wasn't prepared for what came next: "She started to scream. [And] before I knew it or realized what I was doing, I grabbed her by the throat and choked her to death."

It was over very quickly. When he understood what he had done, Fitzgerald, still in his bathrobe, put the child down on his bed and quickly dressed. Then he picked her up again and carried her to the door of his apartment. After checking to make sure no other tenant was in the stairwell, he took Janet's body down the stairs to the basement—"where I buried it under a pile of coal."[1]

This was all Howe needed to hear. Any uncertainty was gone now. The child was dead, and he had the man who did it. He notified the other interrogators, sent word to Deputy Chief Alcock, and brought the prisoner upstairs to dictate his official sworn confession. The statement was written out in longhand and then signed by Fitzgerald and witnessed by Howe, Detective Sergeants Quinn and Powers, *Tribune* city editor Perley H. Boone, and W. C. Howey, managing editor of the *Herald and Examiner.*

At 9:15, Deputy Chief Alcock arrived at the station. He examined the written confession and then he, Lieutenant Howe, and a guard of detectives and reporters took Fitzgerald over to the duplex building on East Superior Street. In the basement, sanitation workers and police were still sifting through the enormous pile of coal stored there. Fitzgerald walked over to one corner of the basement where a rusty iron chimney stuck out of the coal pile near the wall. "She's over there," he said, pointing to a narrow, coal-filled space between the chimney and the wall. Somehow, over days of searching, the workers hadn't looked in this space, perhaps because they regarded it as too small to contain a body.

"Do you want to lift her out?" Detective Sergeant Powers asked him.

Fitzgerald acquiesced, but when he bent over, the pale, exhausted prisoner found he couldn't do it. Two of the sanitation workers came up behind him. "The head is here," he said, showing them where to dig. "And the feet are over there."

The two men started shoveling away the coal, but Deputy Chief Alcock told them to use their hands. Understanding, they threw aside their shovels and began gently pulling away the dusty black lumps. In a few minutes, they had uncovered a small figure wrapped in white cloth. It was wedged so tightly into the narrow space, however, that they finally had to use a two-by-four to pry the chimney away from the wall, exposing the small, blackened corpse of Janet Wilkinson.

"I can't stand it," Fitzgerald said, turning away.

They lifted the body from the coal pile and placed it on a stretcher they had brought over from the police station. Then they carried it up the stairs and out to the street, where a police ambulance was waiting to take it away.[2]

An angry crowd was already gathering around the entrance to the building. The newspaper reporters assigned to the case—who had been given a level of access to the investigation unimaginable today—had sent word of the confession to their city desks the moment it was made, and the *Tribune* had managed to put an extra on the streets by 9:15. Now, at 10:05, most of Fitzgerald's neighbors had already heard about his confession, and they were apparently ready to take action. When Fitzgerald was brought to the front vestibule, the crowd grew restive. "Lynch him!" a few men shouted. "String him up!"[3]

Fitzgerald recoiled and cowered in the doorway. It seemed possible that members of the crowd might indeed take the law into their own hands. Because of some confusion in arrangements, no police vehicle was waiting to take Fitzgerald back to the police station. "The crowd seemed to sense this fact," one reporter from the *Herald and Examiner* later wrote, describing the scene. "It surged toward the building's entrance. . . . A dozen uniformed policemen appeared powerless to stem the tide of enraged humanity."

Fortunately, a number of plainclothes police arrived at that moment. "They elbowed their way through the crowd, knocking men, women, and even children right and left. With the reinforced guard now before the doorway, clubs and revolvers brandished menacingly, the crowd withdrew to the street."

One policeman had commandeered a taxicab and brought it around to the duplex apartment. When it got to within ten feet of the curb, Fitzgerald, surrounded by thirty policeman and detectives, was led from the entrance of the building.

"The howls of the multitude burst forth anew as the slayer came down the two steps from the front doorway to the sidewalk," the paper reported. "Fitzgerald made no attempt to conceal his fear. His body shook visibly. His eyes were shut tight, as though he feared being struck down by missiles. He held a handkerchief tightly against his mouth and nose."

What followed was a near riot. Fitzgerald was pushed into the back of the cab, but then the crowd swarmed the vehicle. Some reached in through the open windows on the opposite side to grab at the prisoner, who was now sprawled across the backseat. Detectives climbed over him and tried to beat away the arms and fists. One of the detectives barked an order to drive away. The cabbie sounded the horn. The crowd in front scattered as the taxi shot forward. "Amid parting hoots, shouts of dismay, and shrieks of women and children, Fitzgerald was borne away back to his cell."[4]

Another mob was waiting at the Chicago Avenue station when they arrived, but Fitzgerald's police guard whisked him into the building before any spontaneous outbreak of violence could develop. Even so, Captain Mueller called for a hundred reserves from the city's corps of traffic policemen. Some members of the mob were carrying "ill-concealed weapons," so Mueller had police cordon off the area around the station. When the time came for Fitzgerald to make his official statement to the state's attorney, he was spirited through a rear entrance and rushed in a waiting automobile to the Criminal Court Building. There, Assistant State's Attorney M. F. Sullivan questioned him at length. Little new information emerged in this interrogation, though a few inconsistencies in the evidence were cleared up. Fitzgerald was described as "cool" and "a picture of control" throughout the process, though he was apparently more nervous than he let on. "Don't let them hang me, will you, Mr. Howe?" he asked nervously at the end of the interrogation. "Have them send me to some insane asylum?" The lieutenant didn't answer.

But State's Attorney Hoyne had other plans for Fitzgerald. He promptly turned over principal responsibility for the case to prosecutor James O'Brien—a man known around the Criminal Court Building as "Ropes" O'Brien, for his enthusiastic (and usually successful) pursuit of the death penalty in homicide cases. Hoyne promised that once Coroner Hoffman had completed his inquest in the case, expected to happen tomorrow, the pace of justice would be swift.[5]

Such reassurances, however, were not enough for many of those out on the streets. Cries for summary government action against Fitzgerald and other sexual predators went up throughout the city. "Acting Chief Alcock already has issued orders that defectives be rounded up and placed in custody," the *Evening Post* reported, "[but] civic organizations and social workers are demanding action more comprehensive than that. The City Council and the state legislature will be asked to pass laws dealing with the subject." Alcock himself underlined the urgency of the need for such legislation. "This case," he announced at an afternoon press conference, "should cause the people of Chicago to demand a special session of the legislature. As long as there are morons running loose, such frightful crimes are bound to occur."

It was not an utterance designed to calm the crowds of angry and frightened parents gathering throughout the city, intent on revenge.[6]

CHAPTER FIFTEEN

Sunday Afternoon, July 27

MIDAFTERNOON ON SUNDAY, as news of Fitzgerald's confession filtered through the sweltering city, five teenage boys from the Black Belt decided to grab their bathing suits, hop a passing produce truck, and take a ride to the beach. Temperatures were already reaching ninety-six degrees, and the boys knew a special place on the lakeshore where they could escape the heat without their parents finding out about it. Just offshore near the foot of Twenty-sixth Street was a little island they called "the Hot and Cold"—named for the contrasting effluents of a brewery and an icehouse nearby. It was an ideal playground. Located roughly halfway between the crowded Twenty-fifth Street beach (touted by one black weekly as the race's answer to Atlantic City) and the equally crowded white beach at Twenty-ninth, the island was private and unsupervised by adults.

When the truck slowed to cross the streetcar tracks at Wabash and Twenty-sixth Street, the boys hopped off and headed straight east toward the lake. They didn't linger, for this was the territory of an Irish gang that had thrown stones at them on several occasions in the past. Today, however, the boys were able to travel unmolested. Before long, they crossed the Illinois Central tracks and made their way around the Keeley Brewery to the shore. Quickly changing into their bathing suits, they waded across the shallows to the Hot and Cold. Here they'd hidden a large homemade raft built from logs and railroad ties scavenged in the area. According to one of the boys—

a fourteen-year-old named John Harris—they liked to attach a rope to the raft and tow it out into the deep water, where they could practice diving and underwater swimming while having the makeshift lifeboat to hold on to if they got tired. Today their goal was to tie up at a post standing in the water several hundred feet offshore. And so, at about two o'clock, the boys pushed off from the island and began steering the raft eastward and southward into the lake.[1]

What the boys did not know was that a fight was developing at this very moment at the Twenty-ninth Street beach a few blocks south. Beaches in Chicago were not officially segregated in 1919, but there was a tacit understanding that the area around Twenty-ninth Street, just south of a manmade breakwater, was for whites and whites only. So when two black couples appeared on the beach and attempted to enter the water, they were turned away by several angry white bathers. The couples left, but returned sometime later, accompanied by a number of friends. Again they were confronted by white bathers. Tempers flared in the searing afternoon heat, and the situation deteriorated rapidly. Curses and arguments soon led to shoving, fistfights, and rock throwing.[2]

As this was going on, the raft bearing the five teenagers floated past the breakwater, crossing an invisible line marking the boundary of the white bathing area. A young man standing on the breakwater—later identified as George Stauber—saw them and began hurling stones at the raft. At first, the boys thought he was playing a game, and they joyfully dodged the incoming missiles. But then they realized that this was not intended as fun. According to John Harris, Stauber's next rock struck his friend Eugene Williams on the forehead, and the boy slipped off the raft and into the water. When he didn't resurface, Harris dived in after him. Eugene "grabbed my right ankle," Harris later said, "and, hell, I got scared. I shook him off." Gasping for air, Harris surfaced and swam out of his friend's reach. "You could see blood coming up [in the water]," he said, "and the [other] fellows were all excited." Harris returned to the raft just in time to see Stauber running from the breakwater back to the beach.

Panicking, the boys realized they needed help. "Let's get the lifeguard," Harris shouted. He pushed off from the raft again and, though he wasn't a strong swimmer, managed to dog-paddle the forty feet back to shore. He ran to the Twenty-fifth Street beach and found the head lifeguard, who "blew his whistle and sent a boat around" to look for the boy. But the rescue came too late. After about a half hour of searching, they found Eugene's limp body in the shallows.

In the meantime, Harris and the other boys had come back to the Twenty-ninth Street beach with a black policeman. Various groups were still fighting, but the boys managed to point out George Stauber, the man they claimed had thrown stones at their raft. When the policeman moved to take Stauber into custody, a white colleague—Officer Daniel Callahan—allegedly stepped in to prevent the arrest. The two officers argued, and then, to make matters worse, Callahan proceeded to arrest one of the black combatants. Incensed, the black crowd set upon Stauber, beating him severely, and, according to one report, also began menacing Officer Callahan, who ran to a nearby drugstore to phone for backup.[3]

By now, a crowd of some one thousand people of both races had gathered at the foot of Twenty-ninth Street, roused by exaggerated rumors about what had just happened on the beach. One story held that a white swimmer had drowned after being hit by a rock thrown by a black man. Another claimed that Officer Callahan had actively prevented the rescue of Eugene Williams, even holding a gun on the black crowd to keep them from the water while the boy drowned. The fact that several white bathers had actually assisted in the search for Eugene Williams was lost in the swirl of ugly hearsay. Given the toxic racial atmosphere in the city after months of bombings and other incidents, each race was clearly willing to believe anything of the other, no matter how brutal, and so escalation of the conflict seemed inevitable.[4]

Before long, two patrol wagons pulled up at the chaotic scene at the foot of Twenty-ninth Street. As police emerged from the vehicles, shots were fired from one of the black crowds. One bullet hit policeman John O'Brien in the left arm. The crowd scattered immediately, but a black policeman named Jesse Igoe returned fire, fatally wounding the shooter—James Crawford—in the abdomen. O'Brien also shot at the retreating crowd, hitting two more black men.

From there, the battle spilled rapidly out into the streets of the South Side. Police followed rioters westward from Cottage Grove Avenue, and as the individual combatants fanned out through the neighborhoods ahead of their pursuers, they drew more and more people into the sunbaked streets, ready to do battle. There was more shooting, rock throwing, and several stabbings. A white fireman was pulled from a passing engine and beaten. A man leaning out his window to watch a street brawl was hit in the head by a stray bullet. After fifteen minutes, the original beach mob had been entirely dispersed, leaving forty rioters and several policemen injured. But now new skirmishes were erupting in other areas in and around the Black Belt. By 5 p.m., according to the *Tribune,* "Cottage Grove Avenue and State Street from 29th south to 35th were bubbling cauldrons of action." Deputy Chief Alcock, hearing reports of the spreading violence, sent out a call to every station in the city to rush all available officers to the South Side.[5]

News was spreading just as fast through the white neighborhoods farther inland from the lake. In the blocks west of Wentworth Avenue, just beyond the western boundary of the Black Belt, calls for retaliation were finding especially fertile ground. This area was the territory of many of the city's so-called athletic clubs—the gangs of young white toughs who had been responsible for many of the racial attacks in the parks earlier in the summer. Still spoiling for a fight, these clubs—which bore names like "Our Flag," "Ragen's Colts," and "The Hamburgs" (whose membership included a seventeen-year-old Irish boy named Richard J. Daley)—found in the beach incident just the excuse they needed to start a rampage. Arming themselves with baseball bats, knives, revolvers, iron bars, hammers, and bricks, they poured out of their homes and clubhouses in search of any black person who made the mistake of being seen beyond the borders of the Black Belt.[6]

As evening fell, Chicago's South Side became a battlefield. Police and white and black mobs clashed at Prairie Avenue and Thirty-first Street, at State and Thirty-fifth, and at Thirty-seventh and Cottage Grove. On Thirty-ninth Street, crowds of whites took potshots at blacks on streetcars, wounding one man in the groin. Another black man was pummeled with clubs as he waited for a car on Halsted. Throughout the evening, hundreds of mounted police stormed up and down the avenues, attempting to disperse the warring mobs, but with only limited success. A confrontation quelled on one corner would only reignite on another two or three blocks away. Few arrests were made, as police concentrated on getting the wounded to hospitals, letting their attackers and any witnesses slip away to take up the fight elsewhere.

The streets of the South Side echoed with shouts and gunfire for several hours more. But as Sunday night turned into Monday morning, the fighting waned, and relative calm returned. The mounted police remained on duty into the early-morning hours to prevent any further disturbances, while South Side hospitals worked overtime to care for the injured. Citizens throughout the city could even go to bed that night hoping that the worst was over, that the day's rioting would turn out to be just a onetime spasm of violence, something brought on by the heat and by the city's numerous recent stresses. Certainly the day's toll was bad enough: two black men dead (including Eugene Williams), fifty whites and blacks seriously injured, and scores more suffering minor cuts and bruises. But with a new week beginning tomorrow, many hoped that the hostilities would somehow be put aside and Chicago would get back to work as usual.

By 3 a.m. the streets of the South Side were quiet once more. The owl cars made their way unmolested up and down the deserted avenues. The usual skeleton crew of drunkards, streetwalkers, and homeless people resumed their stations on corners and in empty lots. Behind a million windows—open to catch any breath of a nighttime breeze—Chicago slept uneasily, waiting for morning.[7]

CHAPTER SIXTEEN

Monday, July 28

A T EIGHT-FIFTEEN on an already sultry Monday morning, the special train carrying Mayor William Hale Thompson and his associates lumbered into Chicago's Union Station on the city's West Side. Dozens of officials and reporters were already milling around the train shed as the clanging, huffing engine came to a stop at the end of the platform. The mayor himself—looking fatigued and disheveled from the long journey—was the first to alight from the train, and he was immediately besieged by reporters.

"What are you going to do about the South Side race riots?" one of them shouted out.

The mayor, incommunicado since the train had left Omaha late the previous afternoon, seemed surprised. "I haven't heard about them yet," he admitted.

Various reporters filled him in on the details.

"Sounds serious," Thompson said, clearly unprepared to deal with this unpleasant news. In answer, he resorted to political boilerplate: "Conditions in that district must be carefully studied," he said, "to get at the cause of the trouble."

Another reporter asked, "What are you going to do about the Fitzgerald case?"

On this topic the mayor was better informed. In fact, while in Cheyenne he had sent a telegram to Deputy Chief Alcock directing him to make the case the police department's top priority. "My heart bleeds for the sorrowing parents," Big Bill intoned, "[but] I must let the law take its course. I understand the man has confessed and has been booked on a murder charge, so I don't see [that there's] anything I can do. I'll find out today, though."[1]

Arguably the worst development to greet the mayor, however—at least from a political perspective—concerned the transit situation. Thompson learned to his chagrin that Governor Lowden had been demonstrating consummate brinksmanship in the time since negotiations broke down on Saturday, furiously arranging separate Sunday meetings with company and union representatives to force both sides back to the bargaining table. "The general situation, gentlemen," Lowden had told the negotiators late on Sunday, "is far too serious for a car strike to take place. We have a generally disturbed industrial condition; other strikes are threatened, while the race riots on the South Side make it imperative that transportation be continued. It is a matter of public safety."

The appeal seemed to work. Thanks to these tireless efforts by the governor—whose work, according to the *Chicago Daily News,* "cannot be too highly praised"—both sides had by late Sunday agreed to give ground on some of the crucial issues separating them. More meetings were scheduled for Monday, but it was believed that union representatives would have an acceptable compromise plan to present to their men at a mass meeting on Monday night. After days of on-again, off-again strike threats, all sides were now confident that at least this one crisis in the city would be averted. For the governor, such an outcome would be a distinct boon—the perfect public-relations coup with which to launch his nascent presidential bid. The fact that it all occurred while the mayor of Chicago was off roping steers and pretty ladies in Cheyenne could only make Lowden look that much better. In fact, the governor was so certain of success that he'd decided to leave town before the vote Monday evening to give a long-scheduled speech in Lincoln, Nebraska.[2]

Awash in all of this bad news, the mayor and his men left the station and proceeded to city hall, hoping to reestablish some semblance of authority over the city. Reports coming in from the South Side all morning were mixed. By noon, only scattered violence had been reported in the riot areas, but those familiar with the situation were not optimistic. Captain Michael Gallery, an experienced South Side police officer, informed the mayor and Chief Garrity that the local force—numbering fewer than 3,500 men—would simply be overwhelmed by the violence and that the state militia should immediately be brought in. "Unless the militia is called and the entire South Side put under martial law," Gallery told them, "the race riots in Chicago will make those of East St. Louis [in 1917] look inconsequential by comparison." State's Attorney Hoyne, speaking to the press, was also calling for deployment of the militia, which by law would require Mayor Thompson to make a formal request for troops from the governor of Illinois.[3]

But Chief Garrity was not convinced. He warned the mayor that sending inexperienced militia troops into the fray could just add to the death and disorder (as it had in fact done in East St. Louis), and that the police didn't need their help. Thompson proved receptive to this latter argument. With one eye as ever on the politics of the situation, he and Lundin were understandably reluctant to be perceived as needing outside assistance to control their city—especially if that help came from Governor Lowden.

The issue of the state militia, moreover, was a particularly sore topic between the mayor and the governor. Once before—back in September 1917—the two men had clashed over the deployment of militia troops in the city, and the confrontation had come very close to ending in outright violence. The episode had started with a decision by Thompson to permit a public meeting of a controversial pacifist group called the People's Council for Democracy and Peace. Big Bill, who was at the time hoping to win support among Chicago's antiwar elements, claimed that he had no legal right to bar a peaceful assembly of law-abiding American citizens; the governor strenuously disagreed. "Win the War Lowden," as Thompson's enemy was being called, ordered then police chief Herman Schuettler to close down the meeting, which had just convened at the West Side Auditorium. The chief obeyed, but that night an angry Thompson countermanded the governor's order, instructing Schuettler not to interfere with the council's plans. From there, matters had deteriorated. Refusing to back down, Lowden ordered the state militia to Chicago by special train to enforce his original order. A contingent of 250 militiamen arrived at Union Station at 9:20 p.m. on Sunday, September 2. In the meantime, Chief Schuettler had mobilized a thousand Chicago police officers "in case rioting should break out between the Mayor's backers and the supporters of the government."

Lowden himself arrived in Chicago on Monday morning. The People's Council, he announced to a crowd of supporters, was "a treasonable conspiracy." "Freedom of speech will be respected," he opined, "but will not be permitted in Illinois to be used as a cloak for treason."

Thompson was livid. The meeting would go forward, he announced, and it would be up to the courts to decide on the legality of the governor's attempt to use militia troops to interfere in city affairs.

In the end, there was no great battle between police and militiamen on the streets of Chicago. The People's Council quickly met again on Monday and officially adjourned before anything more could be done to stop them. Lowden and his militia—without a meeting to shut down—eventually went back to Springfield, leaving Thompson with a rebellious city council, an enraged press, and yet another court case to challenge his political survival skills. But the episode had only deepened the already severe animus between the two chief executives. And now, less than two years later, the thought of asking the governor to send this same militia into the streets of Chicago was hardly one that Thompson was eager to entertain.

So Big Bill decided to defy Captain Gallery's advice and let the Chicago police continue handling the situation unaided. That afternoon, the mayor and his police chief announced that every officer in the city would be put on reserve for duty in the riot zone. Outlining a plan to physically surround and protect the Black Belt from any marauding mobs, Chief Garrity vowed that "every resource of the police force will be used to put an end to the violence—even if it becomes necessary to fill every jail in Chicago."[4]

On the city's North Side, meanwhile, the ire of a different kind of mob was focused on one man—Thomas Fitzgerald, now on a suicide watch in his cell at the Chicago Avenue station. Because of the menacing crowds, the coroner's inquest was being conducted at the police station. With ill-wishers thronging Chicago Avenue from Clark to LaSalle (and overflow crowds running up and down Clark Street for half a block), police didn't want to hazard transporting Fitzgerald to the County Building in the Loop, where inquests were normally held. Even so, it took an entire cordon of police to keep the mobs back and allow city and county officials to enter the station. And as the inquest progressed, the scene on the street was turning increasingly ugly. "Send him out here and we'll hang him for you!" one man shouted, loud enough to be heard by the prisoner inside. Several officers were sent into the crowd to check for guns and other weapons. "You can never tell what will happen," one department veteran warned. "The people seem pretty sore."[5]

The session inside was fortunately brief. Deputy Chief Alcock, back to his subordinate role now that Chief Garrity had returned, laid before the jury the signed confession, which was read aloud by the deputy coroner while Fitzgerald listened, slumped in his chair. According to the *Evening Post,* the prisoner seemed overwrought and edgy. "The nonchalance with which he had gone through the arraignment earlier in the day was gone. He hung his head, and his hands and face twitched nervously."

After the reading of the confession, Coroner Hoffman ordered the prisoner to stand. "Is this your signature?" he asked, pointing to the scrawl at the bottom of the document.

Fitzgerald mumbled a feeble yes.

Hoffman asked him to explain the autopsy results, which showed that Janet's jaw had been fractured, breaking several teeth.

"I didn't do anything to her teeth," Fitzgerald insisted. "I don't know anything about that."

It was a detail that would never be adequately explained, though the damage probably occurred after death, when Fitzgerald was disposing of the body in the coal pile. The injury was, in any event, immaterial to the prosecution of the case. The jury retired and within minutes returned with its verdict—that Janet Wilkinson had come to her death "through acts of violence committed by Thomas Fitzgerald."

The prisoner listened to the verdict in silence and then was led stumbling back to his cell.[6]

"We shall place Fitzgerald on trial as speedily as possible," State's Attorney Hoyne told reporters afterward. Though the Criminal Court justices were all currently on vacation, it was hoped that the trial could take place within thirty days. Judge Robert E. Crowe, chief justice of the court, said that as soon as the state and defense had prepared their case, he would make sure that a judge was available to hear it, even if he had to act as trial judge himself.[7]

As for a possible insanity plea, officials were quick to discourage any such attempt. "He certainly knew what he was about," said prosecutor O'Brien, who had shown up at the proceedings wearing his red hanging tie. "He may be a degenerate, but he must pay for his crime." Dr. W. A. Evans, the physician who had earlier identified the bones found in the Virginia Hotel sewer, concurred. "Fitzgerald may be a moron," he wrote in an article for the *Tribune,* "but the fact that he is a pedophile or any other variety of sexual pervert or invert does not prove him feeble-minded. Some sexual perverts are feeble-minded but perhaps more are not."[8]

The call by Deputy Chief Alcock for the incarceration of all potential pedophiles was now finding widespread support in the city. An article in Monday's *Tribune* revealed that no fewer than twenty-five child molestations had been reported in Chicago since the beginning of the year, including two that had occurred just in the days since Janet's disappearance. The number of unreported incidents could only be guessed at. One official put the number as high as two hundred cases per year in Chicago alone. "There is but one solution to the whole problem," said Judge Harry Olson, the Republican jurist who had run against Thompson in the February primary. "We must have national legislation based on scientific lines. . . . The reason that Fitzgerald killed that little girl is that he had no feeling. He is clearly a victim of *dementia praecox* and has through injury or heredity been injured in his emotional centers. It meant nothing to him to squeeze the life out of that tiny body." To Olson, the solution was simple—incarceration of all such men in farm colonies *before* they had a chance to commit crimes against children.[9]

That afternoon, the throngs around the Wilkinsons' apartment house went suddenly quiet when a hearse turned onto the street and slowly pulled up at the curb. A way was cleared on the sidewalk as two men removed Janet's casket from the back of the vehicle. While hundreds of grim-faced spectators looked on, the men carried the small white box up the stairs, through the crepe-hung doorway, and into the building for the wake.

The closed casket would remain in the Wilkinsons' apartment overnight, standing in a corner of the parlor, surrounded by flowers, with tall candles set at each end. Over the course of the afternoon and evening, dozens of relatives and friends—including many of Janet's schoolmates—would come to pray with the grieving family and say their good-byes to the dead girl. The funeral would be held at the nearby Holy Name Cathedral at 10 a.m. on Tuesday. Some of the mourners—including many strangers standing in the street who had never even seen the girl when she was alive—would remain there all through the night.[10]

* * *

On the South Side, the serious violence began again in late afternoon, in the neighborhoods around the stockyards district. At around 3 p.m., gangs of white youths began patrolling the main thorough-fares just outside the yards and surrounding factories, waiting for the end-of-the-day shifts. The gangs knew that black workers would be easy prey here. In order to reach their homes due east in the Black Belt, departing workers would have to cross the intervening white neighborhoods. Whether they traveled by streetcar or on foot, they would be vulnerable.

The attacks started the moment workers left the safety of their workplaces. Crowds of white men descended on them, beating them with clubs, bricks, and hammers. Some blacks escaped the initial assaults and were chased for blocks. Oscar Dozier, a laborer at the Great Western Smelting and Refining Company, was spotted climb-ing over a fence to avoid going out the main entrance to the factory. Soon he was being pursued by a mob of several hundred screaming white men. They followed him west on Thirty-ninth Street, throw-ing stones as they ran. Just before reaching Wallace Avenue, Dozier fell. The mob was instantly upon him. When discovered by police several minutes later, Dozier was dead, with massive contusions and a two-inch knife wound in his chest.[11]

Streetcars provided no safety whatever. Cars would be stopped by the mobs, who would yank the trolley assemblies from the over-head wires, immobilizing the cars and allowing rioters to attack their trapped black passengers at will. One crowd of 300 to 400 whites, including some children, stopped a Forty-seventh Street car in just this way after seeing several blacks inside. The white passengers got off, allowing several dozen rioters to climb aboard and start beating the five black men who remained. The five managed to get out of the car through the windows, but they were chased in all directions. One of them—John Mills—was hit in the back with a brick and knocked over. Before Mills could get up and continue running, a white youth overtook him and hit him in the head with a two-by-four, fracturing his skull. The other four black passengers were also brutally beaten, though none fatally.

Other similar incidents occurred on streetcars at Forty-seventh and Halsted, at Root Street and Wentworth Avenue, even as far away as Forty-sixth and Cottage Grove, east of the Black Belt. One car on the Thirty-ninth Street line was stopped when a stalled truck was discovered blocking the tracks. Several white men, who had apparently parked the truck there for this very purpose, forced their way into the car and began pummeling several black passengers with iron bars. Escaping from the car, the victims attempted to run east to Halsted, where several officers were stationed. Most managed to get away, but one, Henry Goodman, was tackled on the street and beaten so badly that he would die several days later.[12]

Just what the Chicago police were doing to prevent this mayhem is not entirely clear. With most of the force on duty in the Black Belt, police coverage in the white neighborhoods to the west was sparse. But even those officers who were present seemed remarkably ineffective. In some cases, their apparent passivity may have been intentional. The neighborhoods' "athletic clubs," widely regarded as the active instigators of most of the mob violence here on their own turf, were typically well connected with local politicians and enjoyed a kind of de facto police protection; much evidence exists that patrolmen from the Yards station "were all fixed and told to lay off on club members." Whatever the explanation, gangs seemed able to operate with little danger of being arrested or even having their rampages curtailed by police interference. Significantly, one of the few arrests made as a result of these Monday streetcar raids was of a black man, Joseph Scott, who defended himself on an Ashland Boulevard streetcar by fatally stabbing his white attacker, Nicholas Kleinmark, with a pocketknife.[13]

But Kleinmark was hardly the only white casualty in Monday evening's rioting. In the Black Belt, where violence broke out shortly after the disturbances in the stockyards district began, blacks were defending themselves—and, in some cases, attacking unprovoked—with a vehemence unheard of in any previous American race riot. In late afternoon, an armed mob of some three hundred to four hundred gathered at the intersection of Thirty-fifth and State Street, prepared to repulse a rumored invasion of the Black Belt by "an army of whites." Any lone white man seen in the district was attacked mercilessly. Casmere Lazzeroni, a sixty-year-old Italian peddler, turned his banana wagon onto State Street at about 5 p.m. and found himself in the middle of an angry mob. As he tried to escape, four black youths chased him down the avenue, throwing stones until they managed to grab hold of the wagon, climb onto it, and stab the man to death with pocketknives. Shortly thereafter, Eugene Temple, the owner of a State Street laundry—a business that employed many blacks from the neighborhood—was jumped by three men while getting into an automobile with his wife and another young woman. His assailants robbed him and stabbed him to death before disappearing into the crowds, all while the two women watched in horror.[14]

As evening approached, carloads of armed whites began making forays into the Black Belt, speeding down the avenues and firing at random into crowds. In response, black gunmen took up positions on roofs, fire escapes, and upper-floor windows to shoot back. Sometimes the masses on the street were thick enough to stop the passing automobiles, so that their occupants could be pulled out of the vehicles and beaten or stabbed. Other cars were fired on by snipers—whether or not they had obvious hostile intent. Police were also targets. Journalist Edward Dean Sullivan, touring the area in a motorcycle sidecar for the *Herald and Examiner,* watched as a patrolman was shot right in front of him by a sniper. As the man fell to his knees on the sidewalk, Sullivan's driver suddenly returned fire (the reporter didn't even know he was armed) and then turned the motorcycle into an alley.

"Instantly [we] discovered it was the wrong alley," Sullivan later wrote. "About twenty Negroes—waving, cursing, and obviously drunk—were to be seen about halfway down the alley-course before us. One, with his back toward us, fired a shot in the air. They discovered us even as my driver, swinging the car backwards, whirled out of the alley, turned abruptly, and started back up State Street."

As they sped away from the trouble, Sullivan saw another sniper taking aim at them from a rooftop. Someone then hurled a shovel head at them, but the driver managed to veer around it as it clanged to the pavement in front of them. Finally, they reached a group of police at Twenty-fifth Street. Sullivan reported the downed patrolman, but officers claimed they already knew all about it. "Take my advice," a police captain told him. "Get that machine out of here as fast as you can."

Sullivan and his driver were more than willing to obey.[15]

The Thirty-fifth Street crowd had by 8 p.m. grown to number several thousand and now extended east to Wabash Avenue, where armed blacks were skirmishing with a contingent of sixty to one hundred policemen on foot and a dozen more on horseback. Rumors had been circulating for hours that a white man had shot a boy on the street from the fourth-story window of the Angelus, a mostly white apartment house on the corner. Police had searched the building and failed to produce either a weapon or a gunman, but the mob wasn't satisfied and threatened to storm the building. The standoff grew increasingly antagonistic until, shortly after eight, a brick flew from somewhere in the crowd and hit a policeman. The badly outnumbered officers closed ranks and suddenly began shooting back with their revolvers. Chaos resulted as panicky rioters scrambled to get out of the intersection. The gunfire went on for almost ten minutes. Two men were shot and killed as they tried to escape into the entrance of the Angelus. More shots killed one man and wounded several others who tried to take shelter behind a trestle of the L tracks. Then gunfire erupted down the block at State Street. Rioters began shooting at a mounted policeman, who returned fire. Fleeing crowds left behind more wounded and a fourth man dead.[16]

Any semblance of law and order in the Black Belt had by now evaporated. Police headquarters at the Stanton Avenue station was flooded with riot calls from all points in the district and beyond. Ever-larger white gangs were reported to be marching into the contested border neighborhoods and beating any blacks they could find. Often police would rush to the scene of an incident only to find abandoned victims bleeding, unconscious, and/or dying in the streets.[17]

Back at city hall, Mayor Thompson was facing pressure from all sides to take extraordinary measures to control the mayhem. Several aldermen from the city council urged him to suspend search-and-seizure laws in the Black Belt so that police could confiscate rumored weapons caches. Thompson, always conscious of his black support base, refused. He did order the mandatory closing of all South Side pool halls, saloons (now serving only near beer, at least in theory), and other gathering places. But for most of the day on Monday, he and his administration tried to downplay the situation on the South Side. Comptroller George Harding, after touring the riot districts, insisted that accounts of rampant bloodshed had been exaggerated, and that no special action was required. "I think that if the police department does its duty, the outbreaks will not be serious."[18]

As more and more reports of the evening's escalating violence reached city hall, however, Thompson realized that police might soon be overwhelmed. Acceding only partially to calls from the newspapers and civic leaders to send in the militia, he reluctantly telegraphed Lieutenant Governor John G. Oglesby in Springfield, requesting that the troops be mobilized but only held "in readiness in one of our armories, to make them quickly available for the enforcement of the law when the necessity demands it." Over the next few hours, 3,500 troops—from the Illinois National Guard and the Illinois Reserve Militia—were sent to the city. Even as the violence raged, however, the mayor refused to deploy them on the streets. Instead, they were forced to merely stand by, waiting for an order to act.[19]

Some of the militia troops had been eagerly awaiting the call since the beginning of the violence and were frustrated by the mayor's decision. Sterling Morton, thirty-three-year-old scion of the Morton Salt family, was an officer with the First Regiment of the Illinois Reserve Militia. Refused on physical grounds for overseas service during the war, he had instead joined a militia training unit, part of a volunteer domestic security force set up by Governor Lowden after regular National Guard regiments were sent to fight abroad. Keen to do his part, Morton had trained hard, drilling with other volunteers (in donated uniforms and using rifles with no ammunition) at the Municipal Pier through the frigid winter of 1917–18. After the Armistice was signed in November 1918, many of the other troops quit, but Morton, realizing that the need for a reserve militia "was even greater now that the controls and restraints imposed by the war were lifted," stayed on. Eventually, his diminished unit was combined with several others to become M Company of the First Regiment. Just a few weeks before the outbreak of the riot, they had been sent to nearby Camp Logan for a week of intensive training, and now the men were more than prepared to restore order on the streets.[20]

For Morton, a member of one of the city's most prominent families, the spectacle of a Chicago at war with itself must have been particularly painful. Grandson of J. Sterling Morton (Grover Cleveland's secretary of agriculture and the creator of Arbor Day) and son of Joy Morton (founder of the famous Chicago salt company), he had been born and raised in the city and had quickly become a young lion in its commercial and political elite. In 1910 he had married Sophia Preston Owsley—the granddaughter of Thompson's Democratic predecessor as mayor, Carter H. Harrison—and began working for the family business. Four years later, when the company decided it needed a new logo, it was Sterling Morton who chose the now-ubiquitous drawing of the girl with an umbrella spilling salt ("When It Rains, It Pours"), because the girl made him think of his three-year-old daughter, Suzette. Since then, he had left Morton Salt to become president of the Morkrum Company, a firm that made automatic printing telegraph machines. But while he might have been a chief executive in the office, in the Illinois Reserve Militia he was still a lowly adjutant, and so he had to wait for orders from his superiors just like any other militiaman.[21]

The waiting on Monday had been maddening. Morton had seen the crowds around the Twenty-ninth Street beach on Sunday evening, when he was returning by train from a company picnic south of the city, but he hadn't known what it was all about until he saw the next morning's papers. Shocked by what he read, he left the office immediately and reported to Colonel Lorenzen, his superior officer, for duty. By four-thirty in the afternoon, however, no call for the militia had come, so the colonel sent Morton and the rest of the men home. That was just two hours before Mayor Thompson sent out his request for the troops to be held "in readiness." Contacted at home, Morton quickly bolted some dinner and drove back downtown to the mobilization point at Michigan Avenue and Van Buren Street in the Loop.

The scene there was hopelessly disorganized. Some of the militiamen had mistakenly been told to gather at the Old Eighth Regiment

Armory, and so were heading unarmed and in small groups straight into the riot zone—a sure recipe for disaster. Even those troops who gathered at the correct place in the Loop, while equipped with rifles and bayonets, had no ammunition. Frustrated, Colonel Lorenzen instructed Morton to commandeer a Yellow Cab and retrieve some cases of ammunition that were being stored at a South Side office building. Then he was to proceed farther south to the L station at Fortieth Street and Indiana Avenue to deliver some of the ammunition to Major Macey, who was in charge of another force of men down there. On the way, Morton was to pick up or redirect any straying militiamen he encountered heading for the Old Eighth Armory.[22]

Finding a cab was a task in itself. Morton tried to get one outside the Chicago Club, but the taxi starter there told him that no cabs were being sent south of Twelfth Street because of the rioting. Finally, one driver came up to him. "Get in my cab," he said. "It's just around the corner and I will take you anywhere you want to go."

They headed into the riot zone. Morton was armed with just a .45 (the driver also had a small pistol), and when he saw what was going on in the streets, he felt outgunned. "I saw sights that I never shall forget," he later wrote to his cousin. Gunfights raged between rioters and police, and once, after seeing a man firing from a narrow passageway between two buildings, Morton shot back at him, though this was arguably against orders. On Thirty-fifth Street, they picked up a wandering militia private who at least had a rifle; Morton issued him some cartridges and felt a little safer.

Even after they got to the L station and delivered the ammunition, however, they were not out of danger. As Morton spoke with Majors Macey and Parker at the street-level entrance to the station, a car came careening around the corner and several shots were fired from inside. No one was hit, but Macey and Parker wisely decided that they should perhaps continue their discussion on the station platform at track level, well above the street.

It was to be all the action Morton saw that night. Though he and the other militiamen waited eagerly for the command to engage with the rioters, none ever came. Finally, he was ordered to collect the roughly one hundred men who had gathered at the L station, issue them ammunition, and then march them in columns to the Seventh Regiment Armory near the White Sox ballpark. It was a journey of about a mile, and it went off without incident, the men marching with fixed bayonets as the faithful Yellow Cab accompanied them (the driver's meter running all the time). At the armory, there was no commissary or sleeping facilities, so the men were forced to simply bed down on the drill floor and hope that the order sending them into action would come tomorrow.[23]

It was a wrenching situation, for the violence in and around the Black Belt only got worse as the evening progressed. "The South Side is a seething cauldron of hate," the *Evening Post* reported in its late edition. And the police, if anything, seemed to be making matters worse. Long-standing hostility between blacks and the largely Irish-American police force was manifesting itself in grisly confrontations throughout the riot districts. Horace Jennings, a black man lying wounded on a street after an encounter with a white mob, was approached by a patrolman who he thought was going to help him. "Where's your gun, you black son of a bitch?" the officer allegedly snarled. "You damn niggers are raising hell." The officer then hit Jennings over the head with a nightstick, knocking him unconscious.[24]

This was not an isolated event. According to many witnesses, police were often "grossly unfair" in their conduct toward the rioters, frequently arresting black victims while letting their white assailants go free. Some police stood by idly even as blacks were beaten by mobs a few yards away. Nor was this kind of blatant bias entirely one-sided. In the warlike atmosphere that had developed on the South Side, many blacks regarded any white person in uniform,

regardless of his actions, as an enemy and therefore a legitimate target for their bricks, stones, and bullets.[25]

As in any war situation, there was no such thing as an innocent
bystander. In her diary, Emily Frankenstein wrote anxiously of her
father's near escape when, returning from a house call at the Vincennes Hotel on Monday evening, he found himself in the midst of
the clashing mobs on Thirty-fifth Street. One man was shot in the
stomach by a stray bullet while sitting at the dinner table in his Wentworth Avenue apartment. In one street brawl, a passing reporter for
the *Defender*, Lucius C. Harper, had to dive to the ground and play
dead while police bullets whizzed past his head and shattered glass
fell all around him. A man behind him was shot in the neck and fell
over the reporter's prone body. "Blood from the fatal wound trick-
led down the pavement until it reached me," Harper wrote, "but I
dreaded making a move."[26]

The anarchy on the South Side continued well past midnight and
into the early-morning hours. By 3 a.m., the day's death toll had
reached 17, with an additional 172 wounded—far higher than the
totals for the first day of the riot. But the worst chaos was yet to
come. Contrary to all expectations, the late-night meeting of the
transit workers, which had been held despite the widespread violence, had ended disastrously. Defying their leaders, union members
had rejected the compromise wage plan that Governor Lowden had
worked so hard to broker. Instead, the membership voted to declare
an immediate system-wide strike. So at 4 a.m. on Tuesday morning,
every streetcar and elevated train in Chicago ground to a stop, leaving the city paralyzed at its most vulnerable moment.[27]

CHAPTER SEVENTEEN

Tuesday, July 29

THE EXODUS STARTED before dawn. With all mass transit except the suburban steam lines idled by the strike, hundreds of thousands of Chicago workers had to get to work on Tuesday morning by whatever means they could find. Desperate for transportation, commuters were hitching rides on laundry vans, bicycles, produce trucks, ice wagons, furniture drays, specially chartered riverboats, and virtually anything else that moved. Long-disused surreys and buggies were brought out of storage; old cab horses were recalled from retirement; flatbed trucks were refitted with kitchen chairs to be reborn as jitneys. Price gouging was rampant. "I stood up in a truck all the way from Garfield Park and paid 15 cents for it," a female clerk complained to a reporter, "but I'm here." One boy on the West Side apparently mistook the motley procession of vehicles for a circus parade. "Oh mother, here comes the lion's cage," he allegedly cried, pointing to a department store truck carting a load of exasperated women to their jobs.

In the Loop, the traffic jams were epic. With no one to control the flow of vehicles, the result was chaos in the streets. "Never in the history of the city has such a condition prevailed," one traffic official announced. "Every one of 175 crossing policemen and 75 mounted policemen are detailed to the South Side race riots. Even the Chicago police reserve has been pressed into riot duty. The situation is entirely in the hands of the public. The people must be tolerant."[1]

At least half a million other commuters, afraid to venture into the streets, just stayed home. Virtually no one—black or white—showed up for work at the stockyards. Twelve hundred black municipal employees were officially urged to stay off the job. This proved to be a wise move, for the night's racial violence did not taper off at first light, as it had on Monday. The *Evening Post* described the mayhem: "Snipers, white as well as black; mobs armed with stones and bricks; arson gangs—all these have been active since daybreak in the face of the police department's utmost efforts to maintain order." Some workers who did decide to report to work paid with their lives. Edward W. Jackson, heading on foot to his morning shift at a South Side factory, was beaten to death at Fortieth and Halsted by a group of five white men. Walter Parejko and Josef Maminaki, laborers for the Grand Trunk Railway, were shot by three black youths in front of a Dearborn Street store. Thanks to the beefed-up police presence in the Black Belt, the huge mobs that had proven so unmanageable on Monday night were successfully dispersed on Tuesday, but smaller, more mobile groups were still on the rampage. One report cited a group of twelve armed black soldiers—all former members of the Old Eighth Division—prowling the South Side, shooting at any white faces they saw. The overall outlook was grim. "This is the most serious problem that has ever confronted the police department in Chicago," Deputy Chief Alcock told his men at the Stanton Avenue station that morning. "We need all the determination we can muster."[2]

The most ominous development of the morning was the spread of the violence beyond the confines of the South Side. With over four-fifths of the police force on duty in and around the Black Belt, much of the rest of the city was virtually unprotected. According to one estimate, the entire Loop district on Tuesday morning was being patrolled by a total of three officers and one sergeant. Rioters were quick to take advantage of the situation. Early on Tuesday, several white mobs, turned back from the Black Belt by police, headed north and began terrorizing the downtown business district, pulling black workers from railroad stations, restaurants, and factories and beating them on the streets. A group of five hundred, including many soldiers and sailors, stormed the Palmer House—one of the most luxurious hotels in the city—hoping to take its black kitchen employees. By noon, two black men had been killed—one shot, one stabbed—as they tried to escape the marauding mobs through traffic-choked streets, while hundreds of shocked bystanders looked on.[3]

For many, these Loop raids were finally bringing home the extent to which the city was out of control. "The race riots are spreading," Governor Lowden's wife wrote in her diary that day, "and a situation of incredible horror may develop at any moment!" Many business owners in the Loop, appalled that the riot had come to their own doorsteps, were now calling for the imposition of martial law.[4]

At midday, Mayor Thompson and Governor Lowden held a meeting at the Blackstone Hotel to discuss the situation. The governor had already been on his way to Nebraska when a telegram reached him en route, bearing news of the strike vote and the worsening of the riots. Taken by surprise, he had gotten off his train in Burlington, Iowa, and commandeered a special train back to Chicago, arriving at 5:30 a.m. Now he was urging cooperation "at all levels of government" to address the crisis. "I cannot say who is responsible for this situation," he told reporters before the meeting, "[but] it is here. . . . If we all keep our heads and cooperate, we will handle the situation, as a large majority of the people stand for law and order."[5]

Exactly what occurred in the undoubtedly tense meeting between these two foes is unknown. According to newspaper reports, the mayor and the governor were given an upbeat assessment of the situation by Brigadier General Frank S. Dickson, head of the militia, and Charles Fitzmorris, Thompson's private secretary, who together had toured the riot districts that morning. This report seemed to give both chief executives the excuse they needed to avoid a confrontation on the issue of the National Guard. Thompson was clearly reluctant to cede control of the city by calling in the troops, and Lowden was just as clearly reluctant to clash with the man who would head the Illinois delegation at the upcoming Republican National Convention. And so they decided to hold off on any deployment of troops, at least for the moment. Four regiments of the militia thus remained idle at armories across the city as, just outside, the killing in the streets went on.[6]

At a news conference after their meeting, both men expressed optimism that the worst of the crisis was over. "Mayor Thompson and I are cooperating heartily and shall continue to do so," the governor announced. "We will keep in touch with each other in order that all forces of law and order may be brought to bear on this situation."

Turning to General Dickson, the governor said, "Now, General, tell these gentlemen of the press what you found."

"We found the situation much improved," Dickson replied. "The commanding officers reported a great change in feeling since last night and an improved outlook and disposition on the part of the people generally. All the commanding officers we talked with felt they had the situation well in hand, and did not anticipate any recurrence of the deplorable events of last night."

"Will you keep the troops under arms at the armories?" one reporter asked the governor.

"Certainly," he replied. "We will take no chances and be prepared for any event."

Mayor Thompson, apparently dismayed that Lowden was getting all of the attention, stepped in at this point. "There is one thought that I want," he blurted. "I want to see that all the citizens of Chicago get thorough protection and a square deal all around—"

"That is absolutely right," the governor said, interrupting him right back.

The conference broke up soon after, with the two "heartily cooperating" chief executives heading back to their separate command posts at city hall and the Blackstone Hotel. As reporters prepared to leave, Chief Garrity told them that there was nothing to worry about. "Things are quieting down steadily," he said. "The police have [the situation] as well in hand as it could possibly be."[7]

But the absurdity of this last statement became more and more obvious as the day progressed. At around noon, even as the city and state officials were uttering their reassurances, 150 black prisoners started a melee at the county jail. The prisoners had been exercising in the jail's interior bull pen when a guard opened the door to allow two inmates to see their lawyers in the visiting room. Scores of prisoners instantly rushed the door, knocking over the guard and escaping into the corridor outside. They proceeded to run rampant through the jail. Some tried to force their way through doors leading to the street. Others ran to an older part of the jail where white prisoners were being held. They smashed cots and tables in the cell blocks and used the splintered debris as clubs to attack guards and other prisoners. Two hundred policemen, guards, deputy sheriffs, and detectives responded to an emergency call. They managed to round up the rioting inmates and force them back into the bull pen. Told to go back to their cells, the men refused, leading to a tense standoff. Detective Sergeant Edward Powers—who had been in the nearby office of the state's attorney, discussing the Fitzgerald case—appealed to them to disperse quietly, but still they refused to go. Then jailer Will T. Davis appeared and took command. "Look here," he said, "I'm not going to give you more than a minute or two to make up your minds. I've got 200 armed men behind me, and I can turn them loose on you—or you can go to your cells in peace. Use your own judgment, but you must make up your minds pretty quick."

The ultimatum worked. The men—hesitantly at first—began throwing down their clubs and returning to their cells. The incident ended with no shots being fired.[8]

The mayhem on the streets proved to be more intractable. Aside from a slight lull in the hottest midafternoon hours, violence raged throughout the day, at one point leading police to cordon off city hall itself with a contingent of sixty armed detectives to protect against a rumored mob assault. Rumors, in fact, were now becoming a major engine of the continuing strife, and one of the main perpetrators was the so-called responsible press. No story was too outrageous or too far-fetched to be considered off base by the newspapers—that a black man had been hanged from a building on Madison Street; that anywhere from four to more than one hundred blacks had been slain and thrown into the Chicago River and "Bubbly Creek" (a heavily polluted tributary that ran near the stockyards); that a white woman had been attacked and mutilated on State Street; that a white child had been kidnapped and dismembered by a black mob. One of the worst stories was printed in the *Chicago Defender,* which reported as fact an incident in which a mob allegedly attacked and killed a black woman and her baby, cutting off the woman's breasts and dashing the baby's brains out against a telephone pole.[9]

None of these stories was true—no women or young children were ever killed during the riot, and very few were even injured—but such reports had the effect of inflaming rioters of both races to ever greater acts of violence. Some newspapers took to listing casualties in the form of a two-column scorecard, one column labeled "WHITE" and the other "NEGROES," inspiring attempts by rioters to "even the score." The tallies themselves were often wildly inaccurate. Two major newspapers reported that 155 whites and 151 blacks had been injured by the third day of the rioting; the actual figures were 136 whites and 263 blacks. To read some newspaper reports—especially those in the *Tribune*—one would assume that 80 percent of the rioting was being perpetrated by blacks. The tenor of the reporting was also tailored to race. White bodies were "bullet-ridden" even when they had only a single bullet wound; black perpetrators were identified by race far more often than their white counterparts.[10]

Police seemed only to be heightening the hysteria. One officer claimed on Tuesday that seventy-five of his fellow policemen had been killed—an absurdly inflated number. Several police captains reportedly ran down a South Side street warning residents that a massive black invasion was imminent: "For God's sake, arm [yourselves]. They are coming; we can't hold them!" Arrest rates for white and black rioters were grossly disproportionate to the actual numbers of perpetrators of each race. Roughly twice as many blacks as whites were being apprehended for violent assaults, yet only half as many whites as blacks were being killed and injured on the streets, suggesting that the arrest rate for black rioters was far higher than that for whites. In one incident, about a dozen men were arrested for carrying concealed weapons. The blacks were held in jail while the whites (including one black man fair-skinned enough to be mistaken for white) were released and given back their ammunition with the comment "You'll probably need this before the night is over."[11]

The rioting continued to spread throughout the city all day, with some of Tuesday's worst incidents occurring well beyond the confines of the South Side. On the North Side, a gunfight broke out when a group of Sicilians besieged a Division Street apartment house filled with one hundred black men, women, and children ("pickaninnies," as the *Tribune* called them). Several white crowds in the Gold Coast neighborhood were taking potshots at pedestrians and threatening violence against the black household staff of wealthy residents. In one West Side neighborhood, a black cyclist named Joseph Lovings was knocked from his bike and chased by a mob through the alleys around Taylor Street. He hid in a basement but was soon found and dragged out to the street. The mob then "riddled his body with bullets, stabbed him, and beat him." Most newspapers reported that his body had then been saturated with gasoline and set aflame, though this was later proved false. Even so, it was perhaps the most savage assault of the riot so far, and the fact that it occurred on the Italian West Side indicates that the racial animosity in Chicago was hardly confined to just a few neighborhoods or ethnic groups.[12]

To Ida Wells-Barnett, the spectacle of violence in her adopted city had become horribly reminiscent of the southern lynchings she had crusaded against her entire life. Ever since the start of the riot on Sunday, she had been active in the streets of the Black Belt ("while all sensible people, including her husband and children, stayed indoors," as one of her biographers put it). On Monday, she had met with a group of African American ministers to organize the Olivet Protective Association and demand action from the city; she had also been interviewing riot victims in her Grand Boulevard home, preparing for the inevitable investigation that would follow. In an article printed on the front page of the July 29 *Daily Journal,* she excoriated the city and its leaders and called for the immediate creation of a biracial committee to address the violence. "Free Chicago stands today humble before the world," she wrote. "Lawless mobs roam our streets. They kill inoffensive citizens and no notice is taken. They are Negroes—they are only Negroes—and it doesn't matter."

Chicago, she wrote, "is weak and helpless before the mob. Notwithstanding our boasted democracy, lynch law is king."[13]

Wells-Barnett was not alone in her outrage. Similar cries were coming from all quarters, and much of the condemnation was centering—either explicitly or by implication—on Mayor Thompson. The *Broad Ax,* a black weekly, was blaming the current violence on the mayor's refusal to deal with the racially motivated bombings that had plagued the city all year, citing his refusal to see Wells-Barnett and her committee back in June. Victor Lawson's *Daily News,* finally finding an issue that might have some traction against the paper's perpetual enemy, accused the Thompson administration of playing politics instead of addressing a grave situation that had long been foreseen. "Though the City Hall crowd intensively cultivates the colored vote," the *News* editorialized in Tuesday's edition, "it seems able to harvest only a crop of race riots."[14]

Many Chicagoans also found evidence of municipal failure in the Janet Wilkinson tragedy. According to several commentaries in the newspapers, the mayor and his police department, despite repeated warnings of trouble, had simply ignored the festering problem of sexual deviants, failing to lock up "known offenders" in their midst. The result was widespread predation on the weakest members of the urban population—its children. "The cruel and revolting murder which has stunned the city will repeat itself," the *Evening Post* warned in an editorial. "We have other Fitzgeralds; we have other little Janet Wilkinsons."[15]

That afternoon, Janet herself was finally laid to rest. "Vast Throng Weeps at Slain Girl's Bier" read the headline in the late edition of the *Daily News*. Thousands of sympathizers gathered in and around Holy Name Cathedral for the funeral, even as the North Side rioting raged nearby. "Let this child's death be a lesson to all," the Reverend Joseph Phelan told the packed cathedral in his eulogy. "We must be ever vigilant." John Wilkinson also spoke. "If this great wave of anger at Janet's murderer that has swept the city results in the cleaning out of these unspeakable scoundrels," he said, "Janet's mother and I will feel that our baby girl has not died in vain. I urge Chicago fathers to watch the men feeding their little girls candy and giving them pennies. If they are of Fitzgerald's type, smash them on the spot."[16]

After the service and the singing of a "Mass of the Angels," Janet's coffin was carried out of the church by six of the girl's schoolmates. As the cathedral bells tolled, the coffin was put into a hearse and then carried to Calvary Cemetery, overlooking the lake in suburban Evanston, north of the city. There, not far from the grave where Judge Harry Dolan had been buried just a few hours earlier, she was interred in the family plot before another vast crowd of mourners.[17]

Just how so many people got to the funeral and burial sites was a mystery to the newspapers, since the transit strike was still creating all kinds of transportation havoc in the city and its suburbs. Rumors that the companies would try to run the cars with strikebreakers were vehemently denied by company officials, but neither side was backing down in the negotiations. "The fire will have to die out of the men before they will go back to work now," said union leader W. S. McClenathan. "We will not make any move until somebody comes to us with a proposition that will satisfy the men." The management of the transit companies was just as adamant. "The compromise was liberal and should have been accepted," Leonard Busby of the surface lines insisted. "The majority of our employees do not endorse the walkout. The meeting last night, at which the strike was called without notice to the public, was dominated by irresponsibles. We believe the car-riding public prefers to endure the temporary inconvenience of a strike rather than submit to unreasonable and arbitrary demands."[18]

Mayor Thompson, undoubtedly relishing reports that Lowden's proposal had been "hooted down" at the previous night's union meeting, professed mock bewilderment at the deadlock. "From the afternoon newspapers, I had believed that Governor Lowden had succeeded in settling the streetcar and elevated situation," he said at city hall. "I was therefore considerably surprised to learn that a strike had been called." Asked by a reporter if he felt ignored in the negotiations, Big Bill reverted to the third person: "It makes no difference if they ignored the Mayor or not," he said. "The Mayor intends to do everything he possibly can in the interests of the people."[19]

This last comment was particularly disingenuous, given the mayor's blatant disregard of the public interest in his refusal to call in the militia. As dusk approached and the city prepared for another night of violence, even the transit strike was turning ugly, with strikers setting fire to an abandoned streetcar and jeering the firemen who came to put it out. And yet the city's elected officials seemed intent on playing politics just the same. Late in the day, Thompson's constant nemesis, State's Attorney Hoyne, a Democrat, tried to form an alliance with the Republican governor, going to the Blackstone Hotel to urge deployment of the militia even without a formal request from the mayor. But Lowden—despite the fact that he had done just that in the People's Council incident in 1917—continued to claim that his hands were tied. He did ask General Dickson to put two more regiments on call—increasing the number of idle militia troops in the city to six thousand—but he insisted that this was as much as he could do.[20]

At the Seventh Regiment Armory near Comiskey Park, news of the order for more troops was apparently misinterpreted by the militiamen as the long-awaited call to action. According to Sterling Morton, "everyone cheered themselves hoarse" when they heard the rumors, elated at the prospect of finally being able to get out and do something to save the city from itself. But eventually the stories were quashed and disappointment set in again. "I did my best to put some pep into them [afterward]," Morton wrote bitterly to his cousin some days later. But his efforts apparently didn't do much good. And certainly the frustration of the troops was understandable. "For political reasons," Morton concluded, "we were kept in the armory."[21]

As night set in, the violence on the South Side reached another crescendo. Fewer people died than on Monday night, but the number of nonfatal shootings, particularly of police, spiked dramatically. Rioters had shot out many of the streetlights on the South Side, which meant that much of the fighting was occurring in near-total darkness. At Provident Hospital, a mainly black institution, rumors that two white victims were being treated inside led to an angry shootout on the street that left three police officers wounded. Another melee nearby, in which hundreds of shots were fired from dark houses up and down State Street, left thirty people lying in the street. And for the first time since the start of the riot, widespread arson was being perpetrated, mainly in the Black Belt. Entire multifamily houses were set aflame, and when police and firefighters responded, they were met with a barrage of bullets, bricks, and stones.[22]

At city hall, something of a siege mentality had set in as the mayor and his advisers tried to figure out how to restore order without admitting political defeat. At nine o'clock, General Dickson went to city hall. "Our men are all ready and we are awaiting orders from Mayor Thompson and Chief Garrity," the militia chief said. "We are ready to move the moment our aid is asked." But no such request was made. At midnight, after a conference with some of his chief aides, Mayor Thompson decided to leave matters as they were for another night. "I am going to go home," he said as he left his office. "I will not ask for the state troops before morning. I will await developments." In a move clearly aimed at putting his enemy on the spot, however, he had his assistant corporation counsel, Frank Righeimer, make a statement to the press. It was the administration's opinion, Righeimer said, that Governor Lowden need not wait for the city's permission to call in the militia. "There are a half-dozen cases on record in which [a] governor, acting on his own initiative, has sent in troops to quell disturbances without the request of the mayor of the town in question," he said. In other words, if Lowden wanted to take responsibility for a potentially bloody suppression of the riot, he was welcome to do so at his own risk.[23]

The violence thus continued through a third long night. In his Maywood cottage, Carl Sandburg sat up late that night, pouring his disgust into a new poem. Earlier in the day, he had attended the daily meeting of Wells-Barnett's newly formed Olivet Protective Association. Representatives of every African American congregation in the city had been present, reporting on events in their neighborhoods and trying to decide what to do next. "I saw seven wagonloads of people arrested go past my place," one speaker said, "and they were all colored people. One might judge by this that only colored people are rioting." Sandburg had also interviewed Dr. George C. Hall of the National Urban League, who complained bitterly of the conduct of police in the riots.

The reporter had produced articles for the *Daily News* on both of these meetings, writing in the dispassionate, neutral style that was at least the ostensible goal of 1919 newspaper journalism. But tonight the poet in him wanted to express something else. The poem he wrote—"Hoodlums"—was a coarse, rhythmless outpouring of hostility, written from the perspective of a rioter. "Being a hoodlum now, you and I," the poem ended, "being all of us a world of hoodlums, let us take up the cry when the mob sluffs by on a thousand shoe soles, let us too yammer, 'Kill him! kill him!' . . . / Let us do this now . . . for our mothers . . . for our sisters and wives . . . let us kill, kill, kill—for the torsos of the women are tireless and the loins of the men are strong."

As poetry, what Sandburg wrote that night was formless, incoherent, without art or any semblance of grace. But it was a powerful indictment of the senseless anger he was seeing all around him. It was also one of the few poems in his career that he would ever mark with a date and place: "Chicago, July 29, 1919."[24]

CHAPTER EIGHTEEN

Wednesday, July 30

"FOR SOME TIME, the city has been in a turmoil," Emily Frankenstein reported in her diary for July 30. Writing for once without ever mentioning her troubles with Jerry Lapiner, Emily recounted the incredible series of events that had occurred in the city over the past ten days—the blimp crash, the Janet Wilkinson ordeal, and now the transit strike and "race war." Although she had seen little of the violence herself, her Uncle Kurt, a volunteer on guard duty at Twenty-sixth and Wabash, had described to her "the hand-to-hand fights, shooting, sniping, chasing"—much of it taking place within a few blocks of her Kenwood home. "It seems as if the city [will] never settle down to peace," she wrote. "According to rumors of undertakers' reports, nearly 500 [have been] killed."[1]

That figure was a vast exaggeration (by Wednesday, the death toll had by some counts reached "just" thirty-three), but it hints at the magnitude of the horror and incredulity being felt citywide at the continuing slaughter in the streets. An aura of anarchy seemed to be hanging over Chicago, compounded by an overwhelming sense that local authorities were unable or unwilling to take charge of the situation. The newspapers were as incensed as everyone else. "Mayor Refuses Assent to Martial Law" read the banner headline in Wednesday's *Daily Journal,* and in the *Daily News*: "Storm Mayor with Demand for Troops to Quell Race Riots."[2]

Parts of the city had by now taken on the appearance of a war zone. On the South Side, charred houses stood empty on many streets, windows broken and occupants long gone; many other homes and businesses were shuttered or rudely boarded up, while streets and sidewalks were littered with bricks, stones, and, in some places, pools of drying blood. Police lined the main avenues of the Black Belt like an occupying army, refusing to let anyone in or out. Even the downtown Loop area seemed besieged. Traffic chaos reigned again— despite four hundred volunteer crossing guards—as the transit strike entered its second day, while many businesses, restaurants, and stores remained closed, unable to operate without their black employees.[3]

At his headquarters at the Blackstone Hotel, Governor Lowden tried to maintain a facade of optimism, but the crisis was taking a toll on him. "Frank is living through the most anxious days of his life so far," his wife fretted to her diary that day. "No one knows what new trouble may develop hourly." Certainly, with the eyes of the nation now trained on Chicago, the governor knew he had to proceed very warily. That morning, State's Attorney Hoyne—doubtless to Lowden's annoyance—had gone on the record as having formally asked the governor for a declaration of martial law. But Lowden wasn't ready to hazard such a risky move. "The troops are to be had for the asking," he announced in a carefully phrased public statement. "[But] I have certain pronounced ideas on the race situation in general, and I've had experience which makes my ideas on the use of troops equally emphatic." Citing the example of East St. Louis in 1917, where the imposition of martial law seemed to exacerbate racial hostility, he said, "If we were to order out the militia for riot duty before there was vital need, we'd be aggravating matters that already are bad enough. It would mean that the day the troops were withdrawn, rioting would break out afresh. . . . I [don't] want East St. Louis to be repeated in Chicago."[4]

The logic behind this argument is elusive, but Lowden's statement did have the virtue of inoculating him in advance against any bad outcome, should the mayor make a formal request for troops. Even so, it was clear that, despite upbeat reports in the predawn hours, the police were far from being in control of the situation. That reality became clear to the governor later in the morning, when his meeting with state officials was interrupted by shouts from the street below. The governor went to the window and watched as a crowd of a hundred white males came around the corner of Congress Street in pursuit of a lone African American man. "The black was cornered in a doorway," the *New York Times* reported, "but before the mob could reach him a mounted policeman blocked the path. Using his horse as a shield, the policeman held off the mob until a patrol wagon arrived to rescue the Negro."

Before the governor had turned away from the window, however, the mob caught sight of a second black man. "There's another one," someone shouted, and then the men began pursuing their new quarry toward the Congress Street L station.[5]

Several blocks north, at his separate command headquarters in city hall, Mayor Thompson was still refusing to commit himself to an intervention by the National Guard. To be sure, support for such a move had until now been anything but unanimous among the mayor's African American supporters. Assistant corporation counsel Ed Wright, for instance, had advised Big Bill not to call in the troops, for fear that they would "line up with the lawless whites." But the continuation of violence on Tuesday night had apparently changed some minds. A delegation of black leaders—including Ida Wells-Barnett's husband, Ferdinand Barnett—visited the mayor's office on Wednesday to formally request the troops as a means of ending "the carnival of murder and assault." Thompson listened to them politely, as he did to another ad hoc committee of notables—this one consisting of Clarence Darrow, Sears president Julius Rosenwald, Carl Sandburg, and an assortment of judges and clergymen. But he insisted that the Chicago police could handle the unrest without state help.[6]

The city council, however, was more difficult to put off. At a fiery

midday session that nearly devolved into a fistfight, the city's aldermen voted overwhelmingly for the mayor to deploy the militia. Joseph
McDonough, the three-hundred-pound alderman from the mostly
Irish Fifth Ward (and an early mentor of future mayor Richard J.
Daley), was especially vehement. "You aldermen would be amazed
if you could see what is going on in our ward," McDonough said.
"Alderman [Thomas A.] Doyle and I were driving in my automobile . . . and were fired upon from a house at the corner. A block away
were a lieutenant and 20 policemen. We told them what had happened and asked them to raid the house. The lieutenant told me to tell
my troubles at the City Hall. . . ."

"At 38th Street and Steward Avenue," McDonough continued,
"a mob of Negroes assembled and threatened to march through the
white districts and wipe them out. The police made no attempt to
interfere."

Doyle had an even more chilling (and probably overblown) tale,
describing a car filled with black rioters who shot down a woman
and a little boy standing right next to him on West Thirty-fifth Street.
"I was lucky I didn't get it too," Doyle said. "As the guns spurted
fire, the muzzles looked as if they were aimed straight at me!"

Alarmed by these anecdotes, the council demanded to see Chief
Garrity, who was quickly found in his city hall office and brought
before them. Trying to calm the unruly aldermen, the chief, "sitting
in his coatsleeves, sweating profusely," insisted again that the police
had the situation well in hand, and that his morning tour of the riot
districts had revealed that "everything was quiet." Turning to Alderman McDonough, Garrity said, "I admit things in your district were
in bad shape until last night. I transferred Captain Coughlin out
and put Captain Hogan in to straighten things out, and he is getting
results. . . . If you gentlemen think I can't do it or that you can do it
better than I can, I am willing to step out and let you do it."[7]

No one took the chief up on this apparent offer to resign, but the aldermen were far from appeased. "The Chief says conditions are fine today," McDonough remarked then. "I agree they are fine today. But they weren't fine last night and they won't be fine tonight." He went on to describe—with increasing hyperbole—the mayhem in his district. "I saw bombs going off! I saw white men and women running through the streets dragging children by the hand and carrying babies in their arms. . . . The police are powerless to cope with the situation!"

"Don't you believe the militia should supplement the police?" another alderman asked Chief Garrity.

"No," the chief replied. "We would run the danger of having a lot of undependable men to work with."

But the councilmen remained skeptical. Alderman Sheldon W. Gouler said, "I want to say on my own responsibility that I believe nothing except rotten politics is preventing the calling out of troops."

More argument followed, but in the end Garrity convinced the assembled aldermen to vote funds for one thousand special temporary policemen instead of resorting to the militia. Even so, McDonough insisted that he would advise his constituents to arm themselves against a possible black invasion. "The Governor and the Mayor are not telling the public everything they know," he maintained, and warned that the city's black population was actively arming and preparing for all-out war.[8]

Such paranoia was not limited to the city council chamber. State's Attorney Maclay Hoyne, clearly not immune to the rising hysteria, was by afternoon pointing to a "secret order of Negroes" behind the unrest. "I am convinced that these riots are the result of a plan carefully laid by a certain vicious Negro element which has been encouraged by a group of City Hall politicians, both black and white." Ignoring all reliable data to the contrary, the state's attorney insisted that "from observations which I have made in the so-called Black Belt, I believe that the victims of the riot are chiefly innocent bystanders and that

the fights are provoked by the colored people rather than the whites."
At their joint press conference, Hoyne and Illinois attorney general
Edward Brundage, who had cut short a Michigan vacation in order
to race to the city, disagreed on the question of martial law (Brundage
opposed it), but they seemed in perfect accord on just what had caused
the riot. "A number of politicians, whose aim was solely to get votes,"
Brundage said, "fanned this feeling [of hostility] among the Negroes
and encouraged them in their ideas of race equality." According to
Brundage, the alleged secret cabal of black agitators "has sworn to get
three white men for every Negro who is killed."[9]

With such wildly incendiary statements coming from their state
and local officials, it was little wonder that many white Chicagoans
were demonstrating their willingness to resort to desperate measures
to solve what now seemed an intractable problem. And to its dis-
credit, the *Tribune* took the opportunity to nurture the despair. "It
is becoming more and more evident that the white and colored races
are not living in harmony in Chicago and that the tendency toward
conciliation is not sufficient to bridge the chasm," the editors claimed
in an editorial.

> If the whites and colored cannot refrain from riots
> and bloodshed and interminable violence on the bath-
> ing beaches, how long will it be before this question is
> asked: Shall there be separate bathing beaches for the
> whites and colored?
> . . . If a colored person cannot enter a street car
> without this being the signal for shooting and furore,
> how long will it be before public policy and the pro-
> tection of life and property makes necessary another
> system of transportation?
> . . . If the races are always at swords' points and
> individuals of each continually being sacrificed to the

violent feeling which exists and which it is no use to
deny, does it not follow that somewhere there must be
a rule of conduct?

That the paper stopped just short of recommending a formal Jim
Crow "rule of conduct" speaks volumes about the level of fear being
felt by a large number of white Chicagoans. As in the Janet Wilkinson
case, the response to a perceived threat from within the community
was—for all too many in the city—a desire to indiscriminately quar-
antine any and all who might potentially do them harm. Never mind
the rights guaranteed by the nation's founding documents. As one
alderman said when requesting the suspension of search-and-seizure
laws in the Black Belt, "That may be unconstitutional, but we should
not waste time over details."[10]

For his part, Mayor Thompson was finding it more expedient
to downplay the severity of the discord rather than advocate any
long-term solution to it. Now was not the time, Big Bill maintained,
"to investigate the cause of the rioting or to appoint a committee
to consider the question of preventing its recurrence." Besides, the
trouble on the South Side was, in his opinion, all but over now. "Yes,
the situation is better," he said to reporters that afternoon. "I am
glad of it, too, and feel relieved that we have gotten through without having to call the troops. I am pleased with the way things are
quieting down." After a tour of the Loop with his commissioner of
public service, the mayor was positively upbeat. "The rookie police
are doing wonderfully well," he said, "and only demonstrate my contention that Chicago people are the best on earth and Chicago spirit
the greatest on earth." According to the mayor, even the transit crisis
wasn't as hopeless as advertised. The international president of the
Amalgamated Association of Street and Electric Railway Employees,
W. D. Mahon, had arrived in town that day and was now promising
a second vote on the compromise wage offer—one that would not

be dominated by the "200 or 300 extremists" who had influenced the strike vote on Monday. City officials even hinted that the Ls and streetcars could be running again as early as Thursday.[11]

But the situation on the South Side remained critical, all sanguine utterances to the contrary. That afternoon, Coroner Hoffman, who had been forced to drop his *Wingfoot* inquest when the number of riot deaths became too overwhelming, impaneled a jury and took them to the riot district, stopping at morgues and hospitals to view the bodies of the latest victims. The jury's marked automobiles attracted mobs at every stop, though no violence erupted. But they found a new problem festering in the Black Belt: "My people have no food," one community leader complained. "Retailers in the district have run out of stocks, and outside grocery and butcher men will not send their wagons into the district." Uncollected garbage was piling up in alleys and on sidewalks, and since the unions of the icemen and milk drivers had forbidden deliveries by their members, what little food there was in the district was rapidly spoiling in the summer heat. Since few blacks had been able to get to their jobs since Saturday, moreover, many families were running out of money to buy essentials.

And now there were rumors racing through the Black Belt that Ragen's Colts and the other white clubs were preparing for an all-out confrontation that would dwarf the attacks of previous nights.[12]

"This Is Chicago's Crisis; Keep a Cool Head," the *Chicago American* urged its readers that evening:

> Chicago is facing its crisis today.
>
> In one great section of the city, law and order for the time being seem to have been flung to the four winds. White men and colored men are shooting one another down in the streets for no earthly cause except that the color of their faces differ.
>
> It is worse than a calamity, this race rioting. It

is a deadly, ghastly scourge, a dire contagion that is
sweeping through a community for no reason except
that mob violence is contagious.

It is up to the cool-headed men of Chicago to settle
the great difficulty. It is up to the serious-minded business men of the city to get together and find a *solution*
to a problem which has become so serious. . . .

There is no time to be lost. Other matters must be
put aside for the moment and a solution reached for
Chicago's greatest problem.

But cool heads seemed in short supply in Chicago just then. And
as darkness approached, signs of brewing violence were multiplying once again. General Dickson, who made several trips through
the South Side that day with Deputy Chief Alcock, returned in the
late afternoon with an ominous assessment: "The condition is very
grave," he said. "I am afraid it is even more serious now than [on]
Monday and Tuesday."[13]

And indeed, the riot calls began flooding in shortly before nightfall.
Shootings and clashes were reported in rapid succession throughout
the South Side, forcing police—most of them utterly exhausted by
now—to race from one disturbance to the next before any of them
could be entirely put down. As feared, roaming white mobs were rag-
ing through the Black Belt and contested neighborhoods adjacent to
it, setting fire to houses and shooting residents as they fled for their
lives. By ten-thirty, 112 fire alarms had been sounded, coming in at
such a pace that dispatchers could barely keep track of them. And
on Wells Street, the orgy of debasement reached its absolute nadir.
Several hundred white gang members—having shot up, ransacked,
and set fire to the black-occupied homes up and down the street—
celebrated with a riotous bacchanal. To music provided by a player
piano stolen from a black home and set up on the street, they danced

and sang in the flickering light of a dozen burning houses, drinking, firing their pistols in the air, and feeding broken furniture, toys, and clothing into the flames. It was a demonstration of mind-boggling barbarity—a spectacle from Hieronymus Bosch, played out on the streets of South Side Chicago, to the city's lasting shame.

Mayor Thompson, closeted in his city hall office, had been receiving reports on the rioting all evening, but still he would not change his mind. It seemed that nothing could persuade him to give way on the issue of the militia. Insulated from the anarchy on the streets, in thrall to what now seemed like obviously misguided political instincts, he stubbornly refused to budge. The absurdity of the situation was blatant. In the greatest crisis Chicago had faced in decades, would the city's fate be determined by the simple but profound hatred of two political enemies for each other?

But then one report came in that Thompson simply could not ignore. Although he would not go public with the specifics until the next day, the report was dire enough to convince the mayor— finally—that he had no choice. Assuming the report he had just received was accurate, if he didn't act decisively now, the city could very well plunge into something like civil war.

At about 9 p.m., Big Bill called for his secretary to take a letter. In it, he officially requested that General Dickson immediately deploy the militia troops under his command "for the protection of life and property and the preservation of law and order." At 9:15, he called the general into his office and handed him the letter. And by 10 p.m., hundreds of Illinois reserve militiamen were pouring out of armories all over the city and heading into the streets.[14]

CHAPTER NINETEEN

Thursday, July 31

RAIN BEGAN TO FALL as five armed militia regiments fanned out across the South Side of Chicago, bayonets gleaming in the drizzle. Moving with perfect discipline and (unlike the city police) operating under clear instructions and a strict chain of command, the troops quickly took up their positions in the combat zone, dispersing any lingering crowds and setting up machine guns on key corners. By the early-morning hours of Thursday, over 1,500 soldiers had been deployed, more than doubling the number of active peacekeepers on the streets. Automobiles were stopped, pedestrians and loiterers were searched, weapons and alcohol were seized. In accordance with standing instructions, troops fired their weapons only as a last resort.[1]

Sterling Morton, down at the Seventh Regiment Armory, was euphoric. All day he had been drilling his men in the parking lot adjacent to Comiskey Park, waiting impatiently for the call to action. When assembly was blown that evening, he and his men were hopeful but guarded; they cheered, but—remembering their previous false alarm—their cheers were not as loud as the night before. Then Major Macey, "in a voice you could hear all over the armory," sang out for the squads to fall in, and they knew that their time had finally come. "[A] cheer went up that raised the roof off the place," Morton later wrote, "and from that time until I pulled out with my company, about 10:30, the cheering was incessant."

Moving out of the armory, they headed toward their assigned

position at Forty-seventh and Wentworth in the Black Belt, clearing the streets as they went. "We met with no resistance," Morton later wrote to his cousin, "but heard many unflattering comments on our appearance and [our] ancestors!" Per orders, they stopped all vehicles and relieved the drivers of any weapons and liquor found in their possession. But for the most part, he was surprised by how few people were on the streets. "The rioters are a white-livered lot of cowards," he wrote. "They are all right when twenty of them jump one defenseless Negro, but when they saw the steel on the end of [our] rifles, they left P.D.Q. for parts unknown, and try as we would, we couldn't get any fight out of them."

Morton set up his company headquarters in a Greek restaurant on Wentworth Avenue and then took his men out on patrol into the surrounding neighborhoods. By his own admission, it was "a rather eerie experience." All of the streetlights had been shot out, and since most blacks had left the neighborhood by then, the soldiers found themselves patrolling nearly deserted streets, maneuvering solely by the irregular light of burning wooden houses. The streets all around them were littered with clothes and broken furniture, shattered Victrolas, and coin-box telephones that had been smashed during the looting raids of the past few days. Morton may have missed seeing action in Europe, but here were scenes reminiscent of the Argonne, right in his own hometown.[2]

Other companies in other parts of the South Side encountered greater resistance from rioters, but the violence was generally sparse overnight, the combatants subdued as much by the rain as by the show of military force. By morning, as people emerged from houses seemingly unoccupied the night before, the relief in the Black Belt was palpable. "You soldiers don't know how glad we all are you are here," a black stockyards worker said to one of the patrolling doughboys. "We wish you had come on Monday. A lot of trouble might have been avoided." Reacting to the sudden appearance of real authority in the district, members of the city's wholesale grocers' association began rushing truckloads of food into South Side neighborhoods that had been all but starved out for days. Even the police were relieved to see the troops, despite the fact that their presence constituted an admission of defeat for the local force. "Thank God!" one patrolman said when the troops appeared. "We can't stand up under this much longer." At the Cottage Grove station, another officer told a militiaman, "We are tickled to death to see you fellows come in; you have never looked so good to us before!" If nothing else, at least now there would be other targets besides policemen to draw the potshots of rooftop snipers.[3]

In fact, the soldiers did begin to draw some sniper fire. As the morning progressed, isolated skirmishes broke out between militia troops and scattered groups of rioters—in particular the white athletic clubs, which had enjoyed relatively free rein when the police were in charge. And in the stockyards district, where soldiers were attempting to escort black workers to their jobs, the mayhem erupted on Thursday morning with all of its previous intensity. In what resembled a wartime military action, scores of white stockyards workers tried to repulse the advancing legion of militiamen and black workers, engaging them in hand-to-hand combat. In the confusion, four black workers were separated from the troops, chased down, and beaten. One of them—William Dozier, an employee at Swift and Company—was struck by a white worker with a hammer. As he tried to run away, other workers bombarded him with a street broom, a shovel, and other missiles. Finally, he was hit with a brick, which killed him. His was the thirty-seventh fatality of the riot, but it was to be the last for several days. By Thursday afternoon, the militia troops had effectively restored order, and the South Side—for the first time in days—seemed genuinely under control. "Peace has been established," General Dickson proclaimed that afternoon. "There is no longer any reason why anyone, black or white, should be afraid to enter or leave the Black Belt."[4]

At city hall, Mayor Thompson—ever the master of manipulating public opinion—was busy with his own damage control efforts, forging a narrative that would satisfactorily explain his performance during the crisis. At a dramatic morning press conference, he tried to depict his reluctance to call for troops as concern for the welfare of the Black Belt. But that caution, he said, was finally outweighed by signs of an imminent threat he just couldn't disregard—namely, evidence of a massive, widespread conspiracy to set the entire South Side aflame. Citing reports from an informal intelligence network set up by city hall in the first days of the riot, he claimed that immediate and decisive action had been necessary to foil the arson plot, which involved both black and white gangs allegedly determined to burn each other's neighborhoods to the ground. "We had information last night," Thompson said, "that there was to be a general effort to start fires. . . . The information was definite and authentic and required action. The condition of buildings was such that a great conflagration would have started in no time. There had been almost no rain during the month of July and everything was as dry as tinder." According to the mayor, the threatened conflagration would have brought "death to thousands and the loss of millions in property," and would have resulted in widespread chaos "because of the frightened hordes rushing pell-mell in every direction."[5]

Big Bill, of course, was possibly exaggerating the arson threat as a way of excusing his sudden turnabout on the deployment of the militia, but the story at least seemed plausible. Numerous fires had indeed been set over the previous twenty-four hours, and in some cases arsonists had even stretched cables across streets to prevent fire engines from reaching them. But it was probably the timely rain that had done the most to keep the fires under control, and there is some evidence that pressure from the big meatpacking companies, which had been losing money every day that rioting prevented their workers from reporting for duty, may have been the truly decisive factor in Thompson's decision to finally use the militia. In any case, the mayor's emphatic justifications notwithstanding, the impression remained among many Chicagoans that Big Bill had, for political reasons, simply waited too long to solicit the governor's help. Had the troops been deployed on Monday, when they were first mobilized, much of the violence would likely have been avoided.[6]

The mayor's exculpatory maneuvering continued that afternoon at an emergency meeting of the city council. Pointing out that he had repeatedly asked the council in the past for "more policemen, more vehicle equipment, a modern signal system, and a modern police administrative system," he lodged a formal request for a permanent expansion of the police department. "In view of the existing conditions of public disorder," he intoned, "I now urge your honorable body to take steps immediately to provide for the permanent employment of 2,000 additional patrolmen. . . . The crisis through which our city has passed during the last few days has brought home to our people the fact that the 3,564 patrolmen from whom the public expects police protection in this city [are] woefully inadequate."

In an attempt to defend themselves, several of the aldermen pinned the blame on the city's reformist Bureau of Public Efficiency, whose insistence on reductions in government expenditures had tied their hands. "The finance committee has spent many nights trying to find the money for more policemen," Alderman John Anthony Richert asserted, "but the civic organizations have blocked our efforts." Alderman Anton Cermak, head of the anti-temperance United Societies, tried blaming the city's drys: "It was claimed [that] Prohibition would reduce the need for police," he said, "but we needed *more* police last month and last year, and we will need them next year." But it was the great antireformer himself—Alderman "Bathhouse John" Coughlin—who put it most bluntly: "Five years ago we were a peaceable city. Reformers spoiled it. Those were happy days. Now we're discontented and everybody knows it!" The city of Chicago, in other words, had gotten along just fine until progressive crusaders came along and started meddling in city business with their campaigns against government spending and the evils of vice, graft, and patronage.[7]

Those alleged good-government types were also doing their best to use the crisis for their own political advantage. State's Attorney Hoyne, doubtless sensing weakness in city hall, now promised an energetic prosecution and a full investigation of the politicians who allowed lawlessness to flourish in the Black Belt. The anti-Thompson newspapers were not silent, either. In an editorial entitled simply "Why?," the *Chicago Daily Journal* called for a full explanation of the decision to wait until day four of the riot to deploy the troops. In an even more caustic editorial (under the headline "War in a Great City's Streets"), Victor Lawson's *Daily News* complained: "Chicago never had a more terrible warning of the absolute necessity of setting its house in order. . . . The citizens have allowed politicians and incompetents to sow the wind, and the community is now reaping the whirlwind."

The bitterest remarks came from the *Tribune*. "Chicago is disgraced and dishonored," the World's Greatest Newspaper declaimed. "Its head is bloodied and bowed, bloodied by crime and bowed in shame. Its reputation is besmirched. Its fame is tarnished for years."[8]

At least one person, however, seemed to have come through the situation with his reputation unscathed. "[Frank] is receiving great commendation for the way in which he is meeting this crisis," Mrs. Lowden preened in her diary on Thursday. And indeed, the sterling performance of the state militia, which was now drawing praise from all quarters, was turning the governor into the hero of the hour. In buoyant public remarks that commended virtually everyone except the mayor of Chicago, Lowden tried to credit the guard troops with dampening the violence even *before* they were deployed. "I shudder to think," he said, "what might have happened Tuesday if the lawless element . . . had not known that 4,000 men armed and equipped to deal with them stood ready to act."[9]

The imminent settlement of the transit strike also promised to burnish Lowden's public image. Union chief Mahon had by afternoon successfully convinced union members to reconsider the governor's hard-won compromise plan. A new vote was to be held on Friday, and early signs indicated that the plan would really be accepted this time, allowing streetcars and elevated trains to start running again by the weekend. Governor Lowden's handling of the entire situation was being praised by no less a figure than former president William Howard Taft, who was just then visiting Chicago to give a speech. For someone preparing to make a run for the presidency, this was very good publicity indeed.[10]

Amid further signs of a reaffirmation of civic authority (including the introduction of a city ban on "promiscuous aviation" and a proposed conference to discuss the creation of "an institution for morons"), Mayor Thompson moved again to reclaim some of the political high ground. That day, he held a signing ceremony in his office for the Chicago Plan ordinances that the city council had passed on the day of the *Wingfoot* crash. In the presence of commission chairman Charles Wacker and other city notables, the mayor was careful to remind his traumatized constituents of the great vision of Chicago's future embodied in the plan—the lakefront parks and boulevards, the electrified train lines, the new railroad terminals, the ultramodern harbor district—and of the leadership role that "Big Bill the Builder" had played, and would continue to play, in its realization. Much of the city may have been burning and in disarray on that July afternoon, but the bright dream of Chicago as "the Metropolis of the World" lived on undimmed.

Or so, at least, the floundering and somewhat desperate-sounding Thompson wanted everyone to believe. The reality of the situation, however, was that the city of Chicago was about to wake from its awful extended nightmare—a nightmare that had bared truths about the city that made a mockery of the high-minded ambitions of the Chicago Plan—and its citizens would soon be looking for someone to blame for it all. True, the rampant violence in the streets would taper off; the transit paralysis would lift; the city would even have the satisfaction of seeing its child predators punished and its downtown heart protected from technological daredevils streaking across the skies. But the horror of those two weeks in July would not soon be forgotten. Someone would have to be held accountable for the profound collapse of civil order that Chicago had just experienced; someone would have to pay. And there were many in the city determined to see that it would be Big Bill Thompson.[11]

PART THREE

From the Ashes

AUGUST 1, 1919, TO LATE 1920

CHAPTER TWENTY

The Morning After

SHORTLY BEFORE MIDNIGHT on Friday, August 1, a single streetcar on the Cottage Grove line left the barns at Eighty-eighth Street and headed northward toward the Loop. Other cars and elevated trains all around the city started soon after, to be met by large cheering crowds who had remained downtown to celebrate the end of the transit strike. As hoped, the unions had voted to accept the Lowden compromise plan, and the companies had acted quickly to get the system running again. By 5 a.m. on Saturday, all lines—except for a few that ran through the worst of the riot zones—would be on a normal schedule. After nearly four days of paralysis, the city of Chicago would finally be moving again.[1]

Down on the South Side, the uneasy peace enforced by the militia had persisted through most of the day on Friday. Scattered shots had been fired, but no one was killed and injuries were few. "There is a quieter feeling in Chicago today," Mrs. Lowden wrote in her diary. "Frank has toured the riot zones several times and has visited the wounded militiamen in the hospital." Even so, city officials were taking no chances. That afternoon, Chief Garrity ordered the temporary closing of all places in the riot district "where men congregate for other than religious purposes"—including poolrooms, cabarets, and (most significantly) athletic clubs. As a further precaution, Friday's issue of the *Chicago Whip*, a radical black weekly, was suppressed when it was found to contain "sensational and alleged incendiary matter." Riot patrols were reinforced, and one thousand new deputy sheriffs—many of them recently demobilized soldiers—were sworn in to assist the militia and police in the Black Belt. "I am greatly impressed with the complete mastery of the situation . . . that the police and military authorities have obtained," Governor Lowden announced late in the day. "I do not mean that the trouble is entirely over, but it appears that the situation is controlled at present."[2]

The governor's caution proved wise, for the violence would still have one last eruption before it was over. In the early-morning hours of Saturday, just when authorities hoped that the worst had passed, a series of fires broke out in a mainly Lithuanian working-class neighborhood in the so-called Back of the Yards district. Sterling Morton's company of militia, now stationed at a school at Fifty-fifth and Morgan about two miles away, got the call at four-fifteen in the morning. Morton had been on watch until four and had just been preparing to go to sleep when the alarm was sounded. "In twelve minutes I had the company loaded on the truck and [the] patrols in, sentries relieved by another company in the neighborhood, and was on the way to the fire," he later wrote to his cousin. They were the first militia on the scene, and what they found was gruesome. Despite the recent rain, the fire had spread rapidly and catastrophically through the blocks of wood-frame houses, leveling a six-block swath of structures, injuring dozens of people, and leaving nearly 950 homeless. "The residents were very excited," Morton wrote. Wild rumors about the cause of the fires were legion, and there was a "considerable amount of looting" going on. By midmorning, however, Morton and the troops had restored order and returned to their barracks at the school.

Fire department investigators immediately determined the cause of the fire as arson. Rioters had apparently doused the small homes with gasoline and set them afire, with their occupants still sleeping inside. By morning, according to the *Post,* "hundreds of scantily clad persons, weeping for terror or grief, sat on the blackened sidewalks among the tumbled belongings they had been able to save." The scenes described were pathetic: "One woman clutched a battered coffeepot. A dazed man wandered about the streets trying to find a cup that would match the nicked saucer he held in his hand. Another walked about holding a derby hat while he wore another [on his head]."[3]

Responsibility for the blaze would never be firmly established, though there was no shortage of suspects. A few witnesses claimed to have seen several groups of black men setting fires with railroad gas torches. Some attributed the fires to labor radicals from the Industrial Workers of the World (IWW), while others thought the culprits might be Poles hostile to their Lithuanian neighbors. The police and the grand jury, on the other hand, decided that the fires were probably the work of the white athletic clubs; the mostly Irish gang members, it was said, blackened their faces before setting the fires in order to incite the eastern European stockyards workers (until now largely uninvolved in the rioting) against their black coworkers.

Whoever the perpetrators were, the fire they set that night did not lead to a reprise of slaughter on the streets, and, in fact, would mark the end of the major outbreak of violence that summer. Though conflicts would continue at the stockyards for several days more, the city's anger seemed to be spent. And so the crisis, which had begun in the Loop on July 21 with a firestorm at the Illinois Trust and Savings Bank, ended in the early hours of August 2 with another firestorm in the Back of the Yards.[4]

Over the next few days, the battered city began—gradually, unsteadily—to recover. Now it was time to make sense of what had occurred, to investigate the causes, punish the offenders, and take measures to ensure that nothing like it would ever happen again. Naturally, everyone had a different theory about what had caused the disorder, and each theory was shaped largely by the interests and obsessions of those doing the theorizing. Organized labor, for instance, insisted on seeing the riot as a manifestation of the ongoing class war, the same war that had caused the transit strike and the other labor unrest of the postwar environment. "The profiteering meat packers of Chicago are responsible for the race riots that have disgraced the city," the Chicago Federation of Labor's (CFL's) *New Majority* maintained. "At every opportunity, the packers and their hirelings fanned the fires of race prejudice between strikebreakers [that is, union-leery black newcomers] and organized workers . . . until the spark came that ignited the tinder." Others blamed wartime Prohibition, attributing the violence to the denial of beer and wine to the working class while "the wealthy have their cellars full." Church groups, on the other hand, found the root of the conflict in the vice and depravity of modern urban life. Citing "desecration of the Holy Sabbath in all kinds of amusements instead of divine worship," one black preacher attributed the violence to "the fact that the masses have forsaken God." One southern judge, visiting Chicago from Mississippi, had a different take: "You Northern folks don't know how to get along with [blacks]," he told listeners on the steps of the Blackstone Hotel. "Down South we don't make any attempt to treat them as equals, and they don't get that idea in their heads. We know how to handle them. And we don't have riots."[5]

The U.S. Department of Justice, which launched an independent investigation of the riot, seemed determined to lay blame on its own villain of the moment—the ubiquitous Reds. "U.S. Seeks Hand of Bolsheviki in Race Riots," the *Tribune* reported in its edition of Sunday, August 3. As their first witness, investigators called Ida Wells-Barnett. The pugnacious Mrs. Barnett—who had been interviewing victims in the Black Belt for days—summarily dismissed all notions that Red agitators had been stirring up black workers. As if explaining an obvious point to a group of children, she informed the investigators that blacks were merely reacting to the poor treatment they'd received since defending their country during the war. "They have been angered by the studied determination of the whites to make the Negro feel inferior," she insisted. "Everything the Negro did in these riots was in self-defense." The *Chicago Defender* agreed: "America is known the world over as the land of the lyncher and of the mobocrat," the paper observed in an August 2 editorial. "[But] the Black worm has turned. A Race that has furnished hundreds of thousands of the best soldiers that the world has ever seen is no longer content to turn the left cheek when smitten upon the right."[6]

This, of course, was not what the Bolshevik-obsessed feds wanted to hear. Nor was it the preferred riot interpretation of certain state and local officials. State's Attorney Hoyne, who impaneled a special grand jury to indict the riot's perpetrators, persisted in seeing blacks as the main instigators, despite the evidence of the final casualty toll (23 blacks versus 15 whites dead; 342 blacks versus 195 whites injured). Hoyne was also rehearsing his blanket condemnation of Mayor Thompson, his city hall associates, and the Black Belt political machine they controlled. "City Hall organization leaders, black and white," he proclaimed, "have catered to the vicious element of the Negro race for the last six years, teaching them that law is a joke and [that] the police car can be ignored if they have political backing."

And now even the local ethnic press was picking up the anti-Thompson refrain. In an editorial under the title "Whose Fault?" *Dziennik Chicagoski*, a Polish Catholic newspaper, fixed responsibility for the riot firmly on the mayor of Chicago, complaining of his long-standing policy of favoring blacks over whites in his Republican organization. According to this increasingly widespread version of events, the Thompson-Lundin machine, by creating an ethos of politically sanctioned lawlessness in the Black Belt, had laid the groundwork for an eruption of violence that, under the circumstances, was all but inevitable.[7]

Governor Lowden, doubtless aware of the dangers of taking on Thompson and Lundin too directly, was letting others pursue this particular line of attack. In his own public statements, he avoided any semblance of petty finger-pointing. Instead he focused (in classic presidential manner) on the grander, big-picture issues behind the city's unrest—the need for ample, high-quality housing for all, the imperative of enforcing laws with "equal impartiality" toward blacks and whites, and the importance of controlling the postwar inflation that was playing havoc with local economies across the nation. Responding to requests from several different citizen groups, he announced the formation of an independent biracial commission to study the causes of the riot, with an eye to making recommendations on avoiding future outbreaks. Called the Chicago Commission on Race Relations, the body represented a typical Progressive Era response to a problem—whenever any trouble arose, public officials were always eager to create a commission to study it—and while the CCRR would for the most part remain admirably above partisan politics, Lowden was careful to name to its board allies including Victor Lawson and Sears president Julius Rosenwald—both of them ardent enemies of Mayor Thompson.[8]

At city hall, meanwhile, the mayor and Fred Lundin were scrambling to find some way to spin the situation in their favor. But for the first few days after the end of the crisis, they seemed uncharacteristically cowed by the criticisms coming at them from all sides. Papers nationwide were taking the opportunity to bash Chicago and its leaders. Southern newspapers in particular seemed almost gleeful about the city's comeuppance. The *Memphis Commercial Appeal,* for instance, claimed that Chicago's leaders would "better understand [the race problem] if they get the viewpoint of the South, which is based on no insane prejudice, but on an experience running through half a century. . . . Mobs in the South vent their revenge only upon the Negro who has been guilty of some foul crime. The innocent seldom if ever suffer." The *Springfield* (MA) *Republican,* in an editorial entitled "Chicago's Shame," made the point most succinctly: "Where a firm hand was needed, none was shown." Even President Wilson, in an article in the *Nation,* was blaming the riot on "a failure of the civic authorities to act promptly and so prevent the loss of life."[9]

In the face of this torrent of criticism, Thompson tried to fall back on his customary tirades against "the greed and arrogance of organized wealth." Acting through the *Republican,* his ever-reliable publicity organ, the mayor tried to lay the blame on the doorstep of his usual enemies. "The recent regrettable disorders in Chicago, [which were] fortunately nipped in the bud by the firm and prompt action of Mayor William Hale Thompson, were largely the logical and inevitable outcome of the encouragement given to violence and mob rule by newspapers like the *Chicago Tribune.* Those who sow dragon's teeth must expect to see armed men spring up, and no faked-up show of injured innocence and virtuous indignation, after the damage has been done, can absolve them from their responsibility." But these familiar broadsides, however colorfully expressed, must have seemed stale even to Thompson's allies by now. The mayor clearly needed a new issue upon which to exercise his demagogic brilliance—something that would enable him to divert attention from the disgrace of the twelve-day crisis and focus criticism somewhere other than the mayor's office.[10]

It wasn't long before the perfect issue arose. Shortly after the end of the transit strike, the mayor and his associates were shocked, *shocked* to learn something that any attentive newspaper reader would have known for days—that is, that a likely consequence of Governor Lowden's compromise wage plan would be a 40 percent hike in transit fares. The higher fares, Thompson "discovered," had been promised to the transit companies in order to offset the cost of employee wage increases. If the state commission approved the increases, then, the governor of Illinois—despite his chiding rhetoric about the spiraling cost of living—would arguably be responsible for raising transit costs by almost half.

The mayor and Lundin quickly went into conference with

corporation counsel Samuel Ettelson to determine what could be done to fight—or at least appear to fight—the fare hike. With the city out of immediate physical danger, pocketbook issues would again become urgent in the public mind. An issue like the fare hike could be just the thing to undermine the governor's rising reputation and make the mayor once again look like the champion of the average, hardworking Chicagoan.[11]

Governor Lowden, seemingly unperturbed by hints of these backstage machinations, decided on Saturday to take advantage of the waning crisis to retreat to Sinnissippi, his country estate outside the city. Praising the people of Chicago for their "admirable patience throughout the entire strike ordeal," and expressing his belief that the riot situation was "under control in the hands of the reserve troops and police," he left the Blackstone Hotel in his chauffeur-driven car at six forty-five on Saturday evening. When he arrived at Sinnissippi four hours later, his wife found him "very tired, of course, but not as worn-out as I had feared." But Lowden's rest would last only a day. After spending most of Sunday in bed, he would drive back to Chicago on Monday morning "to resume his trying duties in these serious times."[12]

It would be an even more trying week in Chicago than the governor or his wife could imagine.

CHAPTER TWENTY-ONE

To the Last Ditch

O N THE MORNING of Monday, August 4—as Governor Lowden was being driven back to the city in the punishing ninety-degree heat—a city hall lawyer named Chester E. Cleveland appeared before the Illinois Public Utilities Commission and made a startling announcement. Mayor William Hale Thompson, Cleveland said, was officially putting the IPUC on notice: If they went ahead and approved transit fare increases in accordance with the Lowden plan, the City of Chicago would be forced to immediately terminate existing traction franchises and seize control of all streetcar and elevated train lines within its boundaries. Cleveland insisted that any fare hike enacted without the consent of city officials would clearly be in violation of a 1907 ordinance limiting fares to five cents a ride for a twenty-year period, making the governor's deal with the traction chiefs both unethical and illegal. If necessary, moreover, the city would call for a full investigation of the process by which the increases were agreed to, and would pursue indictments against all of those responsible on charges of conspiracy.[1]

This was, for all intents and purposes, the equivalent of a municipal insurrection. And it wasn't long before the rebel general himself was on the attack. Firing off a telegram to the governor, Mayor Thompson demanded a full report containing the "secret record" of the commission's closed-door deliberations in the days before the end of the strike. This request, of course, was pure bravado. As one of the commissioners later remarked, "The Mayor could have ascertained that no such written report had been made by the commission if he had seen fit to inquire here." But the move, however disingenuous, did succeed in commandeering the public's attention. And over the next few days—as the commission hearings went on—Big Bill rose to new heights of demagoguery. Calling the fare hike a "vicious public holdup," he loudly insisted that the alleged report would show that "corporate cooties" had set out to rob the poor by breaking "solemn contracts with the people." In alliance with the governor and his commission of "toadies," they had schemed to pick the pockets "of shop girls, washerwomen, and scrub women" to preserve returns on their obscenely overvalued capital shares. "What do the people of Chicago think," he asked, "when they pay their added fares and realize that they are contributing to dividends on over $75,000,000 in watered stock, and to the upkeep of traction officials drawing salaries from $40,000 to $60,000 a year and who hold utter disregard for the public welfare?" This outrage, however, would not be allowed to stand, because Big Bill would not give up on the five-cent fare. "The people of Chicago may rest assured that their mayor will fight to the last ditch this latest attempt to plunder the people. . . . I so promised in my mayoralty campaign, and my word is good."[2]

Blindsided by the vehemence of these attacks, the governor could only respond with dry statistics and expert opinions showing that the fare hikes were both justified and legal. And when, in defiance of the mayor's threats, the commission issued a temporary order allowing fares to rise on August 8, the battle was on. Thompson responded by filing a petition with the Circuit Court to reverse the commission's order and return to the five-cent fare. To the governor's consternation, the petition was granted, but then was almost immediately overturned by the Illinois Supreme Court, which held that the commission was legally entitled to alter the terms of the 1907 ordinance. To this the Thompson forces had an answer, too. If the transit companies had the right to break their long-standing contracts, Cleveland announced, then the court must logically agree that the city had the same right. Therefore, the Corporation of Chicago would scrap all existing transit franchises, legally impound any fares collected above the five-cent limit, and seize control of the lines under a public-ownership scheme to be presented by the mayor at some future date.[3]

This, of course, was a recipe for fiscal disaster, given the state of the city's finances, but the free-for-all was having the desired effect. "When you pay seven cents today for a surface line ride or eight cents for a ride on the 'L,'" the *Daily Journal* advised in an August 8 editorial, "be sure to thank Governor Lowden and his public utilities commission for the 'blessing' thus conferred upon you. They are responsible, and you want to remember it. . . . A grievous wrong has been done to the rights and liberties of the city." Outraged by the size and high-handedness of the fare hike, thousands of commuters began to boycott the transportation lines, walking to work rather than "digging up" the higher fares. "To blazes with your robbing system," one passenger shouted when a streetcar conductor asked for the extra two cents. "Gimme back my nickel. I'll walk."[4]

In early September, Thompson revealed the outlines of his public-ownership plan, proposing the formation of yet another Chicago "government"—yet another independent taxing and bonding entity—to fund and run the transit lines according to the will of the people (that is, at five cents a ride). "It is futile for the people to expect representative government that represents them only through a so-called public utility commission, appointed by a power itself distant from the people immediately concerned [meaning, the governor]," he announced on September 9. "I suggest that a new local government be formed to be known as 'The Transportation District of Chicago'"—said district, of course (with all of its patronage possibilities), to be controlled by the city and not by the state or any privately owned corporation.[5]

To 1919 American ears, this was a radical proposal, an affront to all capitalist notions of free enterprise. Governor Lowden condemned the public-ownership plan as "state socialism." Victor Lawson was nearly apoplectic. "The present proposal is simply a bald-headed fraud," he fumed to one of his editors. "Public ownership is the demagogic politician's meat. . . . It proposes to give people a five-cent fare when everybody knows that, under the present standards of cost of production, transportation in a city like Chicago cannot possibly be produced at five cents a ride. . . . What the country sorely needs is a renaissance of honesty."[6]

But such a renaissance was not in the immediate offing. And although the mayor's grand transportation plan would eventually end up going nowhere—in fact, Chicago would not exercise meaningful control over its own transit system for decades to come, until the creation of the Chicago Transit Authority in 1947—the ultimate outcome of the fare battle was of less interest to Big Bill than was the battle's effects. Win or lose, the mayor was once again able to go on the offensive and play the role of defender of the common man against the greed of big corporations and the politicians in their pockets. After suffering a severe blow for his performance in the July crisis, "the People's David" was now on his way to a comeback.[7]

At the same time, the aftermath of the race riot was also miraculously turning in his favor. Maclay Hoyne's tendentious and one-sided prosecution of the riot cases was actively alienating large sections of the population, redirecting much of the public's ire toward himself. The alleged rioters on the state's attorney's prosecution list, the *Evening Post* noted acidly, were "all the shades of black and chocolate and tan, but . . . no sign of white." Even the all-white grand jury was soon denouncing the prosecutor. After hearing Hoyne present thirty-four consecutive riot cases—all with black defendants—the jurors staged a "strike," refusing to hear any more cases until at least one white defendant was brought in. "What the [hell] is the matter with the State's Attorney?" one juror complained. "Hasn't he got any white cases to present?" Some jury members even vowed to go out into the streets on their own initiative to gather evidence against white rioters.[8]

But Hoyne was defiant. "The State's Attorney will do his duty and does not need any suggestions from anyone regarding the performance of that duty," he lectured the rebellious jurors. In fact, so eager was Hoyne to tie the riots to Black Belt politics that he was soon broadcasting accusations that made even his earlier outrageous claims seem tame. Citing reports of "large quantities of firearms, deadly weapons, and ammunition" cached throughout the neighborhood, he charged that blacks had been "arming themselves for months" before the riot, and that a secret organization with ties to high city officials had been counseling blacks to "obtain what they regard as social equality, by force if necessary." On August 23, while the mayor was conveniently away at Fred Lundin's country house, Hoyne staged a high-profile raid on numerous homes and businesses in the Black Belt, confiscating arms and ammunition and making almost three dozen arrests. "These raids are the beginning of revelations which I believe will stir the City Hall from the roof to the basement," he announced. "Neither the Mayor of Chicago, by his appointed officers, or the police can plead ignorance of these conditions."[9]

Such tactics, of course, were being met with considerable outrage in the city's African American community. "State's Attorney Runs Amok with Flimsy Evidence in Riot Probe," the *Defender* charged in an August 30 headline. The NAACP was incredulous. Eager to elevate the profile of the riot cases, the organization had hoped to hire no less a lawyer than Clarence Darrow to represent the black defendants. Darrow had been eager to get involved—he wanted to make a sociological argument for his notion of "aggressive self-defense"—but ultimately his fee proved too expensive for the financially strapped NAACP and the plan fell through. But now Hoyne's grandstanding was doing more to bring attention to the trials than Darrow's philosophizing ever could have. In a heated public statement, the NAACP was harshly critical of the state's attorney, declaring that "Chicago has outdone even Mississippi in its unjust treatment of colored people."

Local black organizations also united in protest. On the first of September, ten thousand blacks gathered at the Eighth Regiment Armory to protest Hoyne's "vicious methods" and seek his dismissal from the investigation. Ida Wells-Barnett—who had been sending black riot witnesses to the prosecutor for weeks, only to find that he ignored them—was particularly galled by his resort to "storm-trooper" raids on the Black Belt. "[Hoyne] sends his hand-picked confederates to raid gambling houses and homes," she said, "then rushes into print with a 'discovery' which he will not dare to submit to any grand jury in Cook County." Depicting the raids as an act of desperation by a man "either woefully incapable or criminally derelict in his duty," she demanded that he be replaced by a special prosecutor. At the same time, county officials such as Coroner Hoffman and Sheriff Charles W. Peters were also disputing Hoyne's alleged findings, and even Attorney General Brundage admitted that the prosecutor was tracking down black perpetrators "more relentlessly than the equally guilty whites."[10]

The effect of Hoyne's campaign was to widen divisions in an urban population that was already dangerously polarized. More and more references to some kind of "voluntary segregation" of the races began appearing in the press and in the statements of public officials and prominent citizens. "We cannot dodge the fact that whites and blacks will not mix any more than fire and tow," the editors of the *Evening Post* argued in one editorial. "They cannot live peaceably as next-door neighbors, and any solution of the problem . . . must be built upon these basic facts." In an open letter to Mayor Thompson, the Hyde Park–Kenwood Property Owners' Association argued that "the prudent leaders of the Negroes of Chicago make no claim for social equality, but content themselves with asking for the right of opportunity, which should be accorded them. Some of the things that led up to the recent outburst of feeling can be attributed to the promiscuous scattering of Negroes throughout the white residential sections of our city." A letter writer to the *Chicago Daily News,* meanwhile, was more direct: "The sooner the Negro realizes that the two races cannot enjoy the same privileges together, the better it will be for all concerned. The only solution of the colored question in this city, and [in] all other cities where they are in large numbers, is segregation."[11]

Then, at a special city council meeting on August 5, Alderman Terence F. Moran of the Thirty-first Ward introduced a resolution that carried black fears to a new level. "Resolved by the City Council," it read, "that a commission composed of members of both races be formed . . . to ascertain if it is possible to equitably fix a zone or zones which shall be created for the purpose of limiting within its borders the residence of only colored or white persons."

Black alderman Louis B. Anderson immediately objected to the resolution, and Mayor Thompson himself, presiding over the meeting, managed to have it ruled out of order on a technicality. But Moran vowed to reintroduce the measure at the next regular council session. And for the black population of Chicago, the message was clear: A significant number of people in this white-dominated city were determined to deny blacks their basic constitutional rights, and there was apparently only one man powerful enough and sympathetic enough to stop them.[12]

Mayor Thompson did not fail to see the opportunity for redemption in all of this segregation talk. When James G. Cotter, Illinois's black assistant attorney general, began accusing Governor Lowden's riot commission of conspiring to bring about an official system of segregation, Big Bill eagerly took up the cry, accusing the governor himself of "prejudicial conduct against the Negroes." The always-incendiary *Chicago Whip* was even more alarmist. "Segregation measures are in the air," the paper warned. "Lowden's forces are at work. BEWARE, BEWARE, BEWARE!"

Such accusations were not entirely ungrounded; the governor's race attitudes were not impeccable, and when a white Chicago clergyman had suggested that he broker "a common understanding" by which race-specific beaches and parks might be created, Lowden had actually reported the idea to the press with apparent approval. But Big Bill probably didn't care much whether the governor and his commission truly did have a segregation agenda. For the mayor of Chicago, the controversy was another welcome distraction, another exploitable hullabaloo to transform the city's summer crisis from a referendum on his own failed leadership into something quite different. As always, he and Lundin worked best in an environment of divisiveness and confusion. They took advantage of every opportunity to misrepresent facts and use them to attack their enemies and redeem themselves in the eyes of their supporters. And as in any street fight, it was the toughest brawlers, not the fairest fighters, who came out on top.[13]

Meanwhile, amid all of this political jockeying, the last major battlefield of the riot—the stockyards district—had slowly been returning to normal. The passions aroused by the Back of the Yards fire had put off the planned return of black workers to the yards on Monday, August 4. But by the end of that week, things had settled down enough to allow them to go back to work, albeit with "heavy guards about the L stations at 31st and 35th Streets, squads to guard the trains, and large forces of militia, deputy sheriffs, and police within the yards as protection." Thousands of unionized white workers responded by walking off the job, claiming that the soldiers were there not to protect the black workers, but rather to disrupt union activity in the yards. A threatened general strike was averted, however, when city officials agreed to withdraw the militia and the deputy sheriffs, though some police would remain in the district. On Friday, August 8, Mayor Thompson sent a letter to Governor Lowden formally requesting that the troops be demobilized and sent home. Lowden complied, and that night the last of the soldiers left the riot district. No hostilities were reported, and the riot was officially declared at an end.[14]

The next day, Sterling Morton and his company of the Illinois Reserve Militia joined the other troops in a victorious march up Michigan Avenue before being demobilized. By this time, Morton had received a commission as captain (mainly, he thought, for the work his men did on the morning of the big fire) and had been given permanent command of the company. Though he was ready to return to the comforts of home, he was proud of the work he and his men had done. "The whole thing has been a wonderful demonstration of the spirit of the men," he wrote some days later. "I shudder to think of what would have happened to Chicago had there been no reserve militia."

Governor Lowden and General Dickson were on hand to review the departing militiamen as they marched through the Loop. Afterward, the two men were driven to city hall to meet with Mayor Thompson in recognition of the passing of the crisis. An official in the mayor's office informed the two distinguished guests that the mayor was already gone for the weekend, and inquired whether their business was urgent. "No," Lowden replied acidly, "there is no significance in our visit. We just came to see the men with whom we have been cooperating."

Then the governor turned on his heel and marched out of city hall to his waiting automobile.[15]

CHAPTER TWENTY-TWO

"Throw Away Your Hammer and Pick Up a Horn!"

AND SO THE ORDEAL of Chicago's summer of crisis passed. Fall arrived—always welcome after the sweltering prairie August—and with it came the usual sense of renewed possibility, of getting back to normal life, of making changes and starting over again.

Carl Sandburg, for one, decided in September that it was time to upgrade his living situation. Safely reestablished now at the *Daily News,* he felt financially secure enough to move with his wife and daughters from the cramped Maywood cottage to a larger, more expensive house amid the pines and poplars of Elmhurst, Illinois, a few miles farther out of the city. "Why should I be the only poet of misery to be keeping out of debt?" he joked to a friend shortly after the move. Besides, he was making some money in publishing now. Alfred Harcourt had agreed to publish his race riot articles as a free-standing work, the first volume in Harcourt, Brace, and Howe's new pamphlet series. And although work on that book and his reporting duties were interfering somewhat with his poetry production (Sandburg was covering both the riot trials and the continuing labor unrest for the *Daily News*), Harcourt told him not to worry. "We mustn't let our anxiety to have a book of yours on our early list induce either of us to publish [prematurely]," he wrote. "You and Frost, anyway, are the longtime people, and a season more or less mustn't count."[1]

Others were also moving on to new ventures. Ring Lardner, whose contract with the *Tribune* had ended in June, signed a deal with the Bell Syndicate lucrative enough to permit him to take his family east to live in Greenwich, Connecticut. Jane Addams embarked on a speaking tour to raise money for starving German children (much to the outrage of her jingoistic critics). And Clarence Darrow notched up yet another victory in yet another high-profile court case, successfully pleading insanity for an Emma Simpson, a jealous wife who had shot and killed her husband in court during their divorce proceedings. In his final statement to the all-male jury on September 25, Darrow argued that, in a case of this type, more consideration should be shown for a woman than for a man. Why? Because the female of the species doesn't shrug off old loves as easily as her male counterpart does. "You've been asked to treat a man and a woman the same— but you can't," the lawyer maintained. "No manly man can." In the end, the jury apparently agreed; they did the manly thing by saving Mrs. Simpson from the gallows.[2]

Emily Frankenstein, turning to romance again after the violent distractions of midsummer, was also showing some reluctance to shrug off old loves. Despite her stern conviction to part with her soldier-lover (and notwithstanding her parents' explicit command that they stop seeing each other), she and Jerry Lapiner had resumed their secret trysts again amid the chaos of late July. It was the race riot, in fact, that had indirectly brought them back together again. On the third day of the violence, Emily had begun to worry about Jerry: "I heard a rumor of a lot of people being killed downtown," she later wrote in her diary, "[so] I called Jerry up to see how he was." He wasn't at home, so she kept telephoning until she finally reached him after supper, at which time she made him promise to stay in for the rest of the evening. He agreed, and before long they found themselves talking as in the old days. "Well," Emily wrote, "the result was, we didn't part." That Sunday, they met secretly in

Jackson Park. Emily was afraid of being seen by someone they knew, so they retired to the bridle path. "We found a grassy place along the path in the bushes—hidden from even the horseback riders. I sat down prepared to talk and try to reach some decision, but Jerry had suddenly lost his desire to talk—and, well, he never kissed me like that before or since."

By October, their broken engagement was back on—at least in Emily's mind. "It's dreadful and yet wonderful to be secretly engaged to be married and yet not to be able to tell a soul when you're just bubbling over with happiness," Emily wrote in her entry for October 18. "We know our love is not a fleeting fancy. We can't do without each other. . . . It's going to be a dreadful disappointment to the family. They've nothing against Jerry—his character, health, personality, all are O.K., but his lack of education isn't. It doesn't bother me. I love him."

Even the religion issue was no longer a problem. To her delight, Jerry had more or less given up Christian Science, at least as a "medical aid," though he still claimed an interest in the religion. For Emily, this was concession enough. "The Christian Science objection has been removed," she concluded. "I'm sure the other things will turn out all right, too. Besides, I'm happy."[3]

* * *

Chicago's numerous conflicts, of course, did not simply disappear with the passing of the summer crisis. In fact, as autumn set in, the city's labor unrest grew even worse, resulting in a series of railroad strikes and a nationwide steel strike that turned violent in the mills of Gary, Indiana, and South Chicago. The city crime rate also continued to climb, despite numerous "police shakeups" and "neighborhood crackdowns." The passage in October of the Volstead Act, enabling the vigorous enforcement of the Prohibition amendment, did little to improve this situation, setting the stage for the great bootlegging wars that would plague Chicago in the coming 1920s.

Nor was the city's racial strife over, despite the end of the major violence. Bombs continued to go off in buildings occupied by blacks or by realtors who rented to blacks—six more in 1919 and over a dozen in 1920. As for the white athletic clubs, Mayor Thompson eventually revoked their charters, at least temporarily, but incidents of racial antagonism continued in the parks and on the beaches. There would even be rumors of more riots—on Labor Day, on Halloween—but fortunately none of them ever came to pass.[4]

Selective prosecution of the riot cases continued to infuriate the black community, though State's Attorney Hoyne did eventually bring some white perpetrators before the grand jury. Calls from the African American community for the removal of Hoyne came to nothing, and only ended up causing strife among the community's leaders. When the Olivet Protective Association came out in support of Attorney General Brundage as a possible replacement for Hoyne as prosecutor of the riot cases, the organization's cofounder, Ida Wells-Barnett, promptly resigned. Wells-Barnett had never forgiven Brundage for jailing innocent black men during the East St. Louis riot in 1917, and although she had little confidence in Hoyne, she feared that Brundage would be far worse. The association, however, wouldn't listen to her, and so the activist found herself once again rejected by the leadership of her own race. "I rose and laid my membership card on the table and told the men that I would not be guilty of belonging to an organization that would do such a treacherous thing," she later wrote of the episode. "As I passed out of the room, Rev. Williams said, 'Good-bye,' and Rev. Branham said, 'Good riddance.' I walked down South Parkway with tears streaming down my face . . . [and] never went back to a meeting of the so-called Protective Association."

Hoyne proved to be largely ineffectual in any case. Because of a pervasive lack of evidence, the thirty-eight riot deaths ultimately generated just nine formal indictments (six of black rioters and three of whites), resulting in only five successful convictions (of three blacks and two whites). The number of indictments for nonfatal crimes was greater, but even so, the vast majority of rioters ultimately escaped prosecution entirely. Hoyne's attempts to implicate corrupt officials in city hall, moreover, proved just as inconsequential, and so very little justice of any kind was ever meted out.[5]

Besides, there were now other villains for authorities to obsess over. Bolshevism seemed to grow ever more frightening and pervasive, as local and federal officials persisted in seeing Reds wherever they looked. Pacifists like Jane Addams, race activists like Ida Wells-Barnett, labor sympathizers like Carl Sandburg—all were investigated in the era of paranoia that followed the unrest of the summer of 1919. What could the violence of the summer be, after all, if not the product of radical agitation? It was this kind of thinking that would set off, early in 1920, the notorious Palmer raids that resulted in hundreds of specious arrests in Chicago alone.[6]

And even the national pastime would not be immune to the contagion of distrust. At October's World Series, pitting Chicago's own White Sox against the Cincinnati Reds, Ring Lardner would sense something amiss in the dismal performance of the hometown heroes. By the end of the first game, which the heavily favored Sox lost 9 to 1, Ring already had his suspicions; when they lost the second 4 to 2, he was certain. That night, he and three other journalists got together at a roadhouse and composed new lyrics for the popular song "I'm Forever Blowing Bubbles":

> *I'm forever blowing ball games,*
> *Pretty ball games in the air.*
> *I come from Chi.,*
> *I hardly try,*
> *Just go to bat and fade and die. . . .*

It would take months for the story to emerge publicly, but when it did the news was stunning: Seven White Sox players—including Shoeless Joe Jackson, Lefty Williams, and Lardner's good friend Eddie Cicotte—had conspired with a New York gambling syndicate to lose the Series for the sum of $100,000; an eighth player—Buck Weaver—had refused the money, played remarkably well, but failed to reveal his teammates' crime to the authorities. As a result, all eight, though acquitted by a jury, were eventually banned from professional ball by the newly appointed commissioner of baseball, Chicago federal judge Kenesaw Mountain Landis. This so-called Black Sox scandal would cast a pall over the game for many years to come, and it eventually became just another stick with which the city's detractors could bludgeon Chicago's reputation whenever the need arose.[7]

It was not, in sum, a good autumn for Chicago. But with the coming of the colder weather, the city was at least able to step back from the brink of total civic collapse. And the speedy resolution of the Janet Wilkinson case did much to help the city achieve a sense of closure. After pleading not guilty at a preliminary hearing in mid-August, Thomas Fitzgerald came before Judge Robert Crowe on September 22 for trial. Sitting "as in a daze" through the proceedings, he refused to look at any of the witnesses called by prosecutor O'Brien (still conspicuously wearing his red hanging tie). When the defendant changed his plea to guilty, Judge Crowe exclaimed, "If you have any idea the court will not inflict the death penalty, get rid of that notion. . . . If the evidence shows that hanging is proper, there will be no turning aside."

The next day—in a courtroom filled beyond capacity with "morbidly curious men and women"—Fitzgerald quietly repeated the story of the slaying. After the closing pleas were made, Judge Crowe asked the prisoner to stand. Fitzgerald smiled faintly as a bailiff helped him to his feet.

"Have you anything to say before I pronounce sentence upon you for the murder of Janet Wilkinson?" the judge asked.

Fitzgerald's fingers twitched uncontrollably as he muttered, "I'm sorry. I—I ask forgiveness."

"Is that all?"

"I ask God to forgive me."

Judge Crowe did not hesitate: "Thomas R. Fitzgerald," he announced, "I sentence you to be hanged by the neck until you are dead on Monday, October 27, at the Cook County Jail."

Seated at a table opposite the defendant, Mrs. Wilkinson put her face in her hands and wept.[8]

Over the next few weeks, hundreds of requests for tickets to the hanging were received by Chief Deputy Harry Laubenheimer. The date of the execution was moved up to October 17 for technical reasons, but even Fitzgerald himself apparently did not object to this. On October 14, Governor Lowden refused a request by Mrs. Fitzgerald to reprieve her husband. Two days later, the ubiquitous Kenesaw Mountain Landis denied her petition for a stay of execution. And on the morning of October 17—after thanking his jailers and exclaiming, "I have sinned against God and man and I desire to be punished"—Fitzgerald was taken to the platform in the death chamber of the Cook County Jail.

"Fitzgerald," Sheriff Peters asked, "have you anything to say?"

"No, thank you," the prisoner replied.

A shroud was tied over his head. And at 9:24 a.m., Thomas Fitzgerald was hanged before the largest crowd that had ever witnessed an execution in Chicago history.[9]

＊ ＊ ＊

Emerging from the aftermath of his summer struggles—incredibly—more popular than at any time since his first year as mayor, William Hale Thompson spent the waning weeks of 1919 working hard

to burnish his reputation as "Big Bill the Builder." Exhorting the
city's detractors again to "Throw Away Your Hammer and Pick Up
a Horn" (that is, stop knocking Chicago and start celebrating it), he
launched a broad-based public relations campaign to publicize the
Chicago Plan, boom the city as a tourist destination, and promote his
vision of the "City of the Future."[10]

To a great extent, the campaign worked. Helped enormously by
several newspaper supplements extolling the virtues of the plan's goal
of a more beautiful and thus more prosperous Chicago ("Beauty has
always paid better than any other commodity and always will,"
Daniel Burnham once said), Thompson lobbied energetically for
the plan. He urged voters in the November elections to support the
all-important bond issues needed to fund his enormous public works
projects. And by impressive 2-to-1 margins—despite the fact that
the city was virtually bankrupt—they did, opening the door to an
unprecedented wave of city improvements (not to mention kickback
and graft opportunities). For Big Bill, the result was a political triumph, and just the vote of confidence his administration needed to
go forward. As Thompson biographer Douglas Bukowski would
later write, "Concrete, poured in great quantities and with equal fanfare, went a long way in silencing [the mayor's] critics."[11]

Thompson also found other ways of turning attention away from
his summertime failures. He precipitated another school board controversy and made a great show of tackling national issues such as
the punishment of war profiteers, the imposition of an embargo on
food exports, and the rejection of the League of Nations. Why such
issues should concern a city mayor was not entirely clear. But Thompson still had aspirations to national office, and in any case the issues
served him well enough among his local constituents. When Big Bill
railed against the king of England or war profiteers, he was by proxy
railing against bosses, traction barons, and all other representatives
of power and privilege who opposed the common man—a message

that was appreciated by everyone from the city's Irish and blacks to its working-class Poles and its disconsolate middle-class commuters.[12]

The transit issue, too, continued to serve as a convenient vehicle for the mayor's rehabilitation. When Thompson went to the city council in October to ask for money to fund a commission to study his municipal ownership plan, the aldermen voted unanimously to grant it—a legislative victory in and of itself. But then Thompson went on to turn it into a Black Belt coup by naming his assistant corporation counsel, Edward Wright, to the new commission. The move was hailed by the *Defender,* which noted that the appointment elevated Wright to "the highest position . . . ever held in local government by any member of our Race." If any blacks still held the race riot against the mayor, gestures like the elevation of Ed Wright were proof that Big Bill hadn't abandoned them after all.[13]

By the end of December, then, Thompson had once again taken command, all but eliminating the taint of those twelve days when the city he was elected to lead nearly broke down completely. True, the establishment national press still treated him with contempt, and his local enemies certainly had not given up the fight against him. But one thing was definitely clear: Big Bill was back in the saddle, with the Poor Swede sitting right behind him. Having regained his bearings as a political operator, the mayor's Mephistopheles was once again ready to engage the machinery of his far-reaching organization. And his plans were nothing if not ambitious. As one historian put it, Lundin "was going to try to obtain as vise-like a grip on the county and state as he had on the city."

But first, of course, he and the mayor had one piece of unfinished business to attend to. The traitor who had once been their ally would have to be disposed of before they could realize their aspirations to greater power. In other words, Governor Lowden—now training his eye on the White House—would have to be eliminated from the political equation once and for all. It was a fight that Thompson and Lundin both seemed to be relishing.[14]

The Smoke-Filled Room

THE WIDE, ARCHING SKYLIGHTS of the Chicago Coliseum had just begun to darken when delegates of the 1920 Republican National Convention reassembled for a fourth attempt to choose a candidate for president of the United States. Among the fourteen thousand conventioneers packed into the Coliseum's central auditorium, the mood was tense. The day's first three ballots, taken at intervals throughout the afternoon, had been inconclusive. The two frontrunners—General Leonard Wood and Illinois governor Frank O. Lowden—had deadlocked each time at roughly a third of the vote each, with thirteen other candidates trailing far behind. And although Wood and Lowden had each gained some votes on every succeeding ballot, neither seemed to be moving toward the decisive lead required to win the nomination.

It was a dangerous situation. The frontrunners' camps, aware that the convention might resort to backroom tactics to find a compromise candidate if the assembly were to recess for the evening, had agreed to block any motion for an adjournment. But the delegates were growing restless. For one thing, the heat on the convention floor was oppressive. "Crowds enormous and heat stifling," Florence Lowden reported in her diary that day. Edna Ferber, covering the convention for the United Press Association, was more descriptive. As the session wore on, she observed, the delegates' bald heads and "heat-suffused faces" had been turning an alarming shade of pink, and some of the men had even begun to undress: "They shed collars, ties, even shoes in some cases," she wrote. "It was the American male politician reduced to the most common denominator."

H. L. Mencken, also in town to report on the event, found the effects of the heat distressingly olfactory. The Coliseum, he remarked, smelled of nothing so much as a "third-rate circus."[1]

For the Lowden campaign team, the next vote would be crucial. For days they had been telling the press that the governor would steamroll his way past General Wood and take the nomination on the fourth ballot. Wood was still ahead in number of delegates, but he had very little second-choice support; the Lowdenites reasoned that many votes would migrate to the governor once it became clear that Wood had little chance of achieving a majority. And in a wide-open convention like this one, with so many delegates pledged to a candidate for only the first few votes, the numbers could change dramatically from ballot to ballot. Momentum in favor of a second-place candidate, once under way, could be very difficult to stop. But first, of course, that momentum had to be set in motion, and the Lowden forces were finding it very difficult to do so.[2]

It had not been an easy campaign for the governor of Illinois. When the race first started, he'd seemed like a natural choice. With his regal good looks, his solid fiscal record as chief executive of a large and important state, and his general acceptability to both the progressive and old guard wings of the party, he had far fewer negatives than his main competitors—General Wood and California governor Hiram Johnson, both of whom had a talent for making enemies. But Lowden's campaign had been plagued by misfortune and bad publicity throughout the nomination battle. And one of the major causes of that misfortune and bad publicity had been Chicago mayor Big Bill Thompson.

Early in the campaign, Lowden had harbored vague hopes that the mayor might actually be persuaded to support his presidential bid, despite the bad blood between them. Lowden's election to the White

House, after all, would have freed up the governorship of Illinois—a tempting plum for the Thompson-Lundin organization to pluck. And Big Bill had often proved willing to join forces with a bitter enemy if he saw political advantage in the alliance.[3]

But it had become clear almost immediately that the Thompson-Lundin policy toward the governor's bid would be simple—namely, to undermine it wherever and however they could. In the lead-up to the Illinois primary in April, Big Bill had shown no mercy in his bashing of Lowden. At every opportunity, he had railed against his fellow Republican, for everything from his opposition to raises for Chicago's schoolteachers to his numerous ties to big business (being married to George Pullman's daughter was often a political liability for Lowden). Nor was the governor's alleged role in raising Chicago's streetcar fares ignored; Thompson proved amazingly effective at making Lowden look like a hypocritical plutocrat, willing to deny workers their pay increases in the name of controlling inflation but more than ready to allow prices to rise when it meant preserving corporate dividends.[4]

The effect of this constant pummeling had been obvious in the Illinois primary results. Though Lowden had succeeded in winning the overall state advisory vote, he lost Cook County by a significant margin. And in the city of Chicago, the Thompson-Lundin forces had scored an unprecedented victory by winning thirty-four of the thirty-five ward committeeman races. This ultimately meant that Thompson himself would be a delegate-at-large at the convention, with a bloc of seventeen delegates in his control—all of them ostensibly "instructed" to vote for Lowden, but with a very different plan in mind.[5]

By the time the convention assembled on June 8, moreover, the Lowden campaign had given Thompson some extra ammunition. In late May, a Senate investigation into campaign finance had turned up evidence of a scandal: Two $2,500 checks had been given by the

Lowden campaign to a pair of St. Louis politicians who just happened to wind up as members of the Missouri delegation to the Republican convention. The checks had probably been payments for routine campaign expenses, but no one in the Lowden camp seemed able to say what exactly had been done with the money. And although the case was still pending as the convention opened, many people had already drawn their conclusion—that Lowden was guilty of trying to buy delegate votes. As Lowden's biographer later wrote, the governor's enemies "could hardly have concocted a more clever scheme or timed its use at a more effective moment."[6]

Big Bill, of course, didn't hesitate to use the scandal as a weapon for some vigorous character assassination. As unofficial host for the convention, he met delegations from all over the country as they arrived, supposedly to welcome them to Chicago but actually to bad-mouth Lowden wherever he went. "His word's no good," the mayor told his fellow delegates on the eve of the convention. "You can't count on him, believe me. You nominate Lowden and the Republicans'll lose Illinois in the election!"[7]

But Big Bill had saved his coup de grâce for the convention floor itself. After the inconclusive third ballot on the afternoon of June 11, the Lowden campaign had urged Thompson to swing his bloc of seventeen delegates, which had been voting for Hiram Johnson, over to the governor's cause. It was hoped that this would start the momentum needed to push Lowden toward the nomination. But Thompson instead took the opportunity to create a dramatic public scene, abruptly resigning as a delegate-at-large and bolting the convention floor with his fellow delegate Samuel Ettelson. In an open letter to the chairman of the Illinois delegation, Thompson claimed to be resigning because of the "moral issue" of Lowden's campaign expenditures. "It is my opinion," he wrote, "that if the delegates to the Republican State Convention had known of the conditions which were later disclosed by the Senate Investigation Committee, they would not have passed resolutions endorsing Governor Lowden for the nomination for President. . . . I will not knowingly make myself a party to placing the Republican nomination for President on the auction block."[8]

It was a sensational declaration, and within hours the local newspapers—particularly Hearst's *Chicago American,* always friendly to the mayor—were giving Thompson's resignation prominent front-page display in their late-afternoon editions. When Thompson and Lundin saw the headlines, they recognized their opportunity. They ordered a "wagonload" of *Chicago Americans* from the publisher and then hired a beautiful young woman (in a soon-to-be-notorious pink, rose-studded dress) to distribute them free on the convention floor. "Don't let anyone stop you," the mayor instructed her. "Don't ever look back, not even for an instant. There will be men behind you. When you are out of papers, they will hand more to you over your shoulder."

And so, late in the afternoon of June 11, the Lady in Pink entered onto the floor of the Chicago Coliseum with her armful of incendiary newsprint. As one journalist would later describe the scene, "With a dazzling smile, like a vision from a June rose garden, the lady went from delegation to delegation, presenting the men with her newspapers."[9]

The precise effect of this bit of theater would be the subject of much subsequent debate. According to one writer, convention chair Henry Cabot Lodge was given a newspaper just as the roll call on a motion to adjourn was being taken. The fourth ballot had yielded yet another deadlock, and the Lowden and Wood forces were again trying to block the recess motion. But Senator Lodge—allegedly right after reading the headline on his newspaper—slammed down his gavel before the roll call was even half over. The convention was thus adjourned, opening the door to a long night of behind-the-scenes maneuvering to break the deadlock and clear the way for one candidate to win the nomination.[10]

What happened in the early-morning hours of June 12 is still the stuff of legend. The traditional story, as told by Edna Ferber and innumerable popular historians ever since, was that "in a smoke-filled room at the Blackstone Hotel, a little group of shirtsleeved men chose as their candidate a figure stuffed with straw." Less apocryphal accounts hint that the "selection" of dark-horse candidate Warren G. Harding may have had more to do with luck and group psychology than with any sinister conspiracy. What's certain is that many of the powers-that-be at the convention decided to take a closer look at the alternatives to the major candidates. For some, Lowden's baggage in the wake of the finance scandal had become just too onerous. He, Wood, and Johnson, moreover, were perceived by many as too independent, too difficult to control. And so, by the next morning, the fix was allegedly in. Although Lowden led in the early canvasses, by the eighth ballot it was clear that the momentum lay elsewhere. And on the tenth ballot, after Lowden graciously released his delegates, the convention elected as their candidate a man described by the *New York Times* as "a very respectable Ohio politician of the second class"—a man who, according to H. L. Mencken, was "of the intellectual grade of an aging cockroach." He turned out to be the man who would go on to become the twenty-ninth president of the United States.[11]

Lowden and his followers were despondent. "A momentous day for us!" was Mrs. Lowden's complete diary entry for June 12. Her daughter, in her own journal, was more forthcoming: "Everyone said Father was magnificent, but all his friends were very sad, and there were many of them crying quite openly. I'm glad it's all over anyway, for the strain has been awful."[12]

Lowden himself left the convention hall, according to one witness, "with bowed head [and] cries of 'bought delegates' and 'steamroller' in his ears." Later, in a letter to an associate, the governor was philosophical. "Of course, while the contest was on, I wanted to win," he admitted. "Now that the convention is over, however, I feel a deep sense of relief that the responsibility has passed me by." But the fight had taken a physical and emotional toll on him, and after the decisive vote he immediately retired to the farm in Sinnissippi. "We are very tired now that the strain is over," Mrs. Lowden confessed, "and the depression of everyone about us, and the universal signs of disappointment at the outcome. . . . It will take some time, I expect, for us to recover."[13]

For the mayor of Chicago, the victory was sweet. "Bill Thompson exulted," one observer noted. "His vendetta had come to happy fruition." Whether his resignation brouhaha had really been the deciding factor in Lowden's loss is difficult to say, but the cumulative effect of Thompson and Lundin's opposition campaign was undeniably significant. "Had the 17 votes in the Illinois delegation controlled by Mayor Thompson been cast on any ballot for Lowden," the historian and politician Edward F. Dunne would later write, "his nomination would have been practically assured." Sterling Morton, writing about Lowden many decades later, would express the lasting regret of many in the country when he nostalgically exclaimed, "What a great President he would have been!"[14]

And thus did Big Bill and the Poor Swede ultimately triumph in their long-fought war against the governor who had betrayed them. Two weeks after the convention, Lowden announced that he would retire from the governorship and not seek a second term. Though he would continue to be active in local and national politics—and would even make a somewhat halfhearted second try for the nomination in 1928—he would never again hold an elective public office.[15]

As for Thompson and Lundin, this victory only inspired them to become even more ambitious in their aims. Looking ahead to the upcoming November elections, they saw an opportunity to lift their organization to new heights of power. A number of important state, county, and city positions would be up for grabs—the offices of Illinois governor, Illinois attorney general, state's attorney for Cook County, and many more—and the Thompson-Lundin organization wanted all of them. And so they pushed hard to make it happen. Opposition was fierce from the machine's usual enemies, and even Lowden, now headed toward retirement, finally abandoned his reserve and turned uncharacteristically blunt in his attacks on the Thompson-Lundin juggernaut. "Thompson has developed a machine in Chicago to a point where it now holds the business, politics, and education of that great city by the throat," the former beneficiary of that machine announced in July. "Tammany Hall of New York is not so powerful and not less scrupulous. Drunk with power, this new Tammany now seeks to extend its rule over the affairs of the entire state."[16]

But it was to no avail. To the horror of Lowden and the machine's other enemies—Victor Lawson, Robert McCormick, Maclay Hoyne, Ida Wells-Barnett, Jane Addams, and all the rest—the Thompson-Lundin candidates swept the primaries and went on to win in the November elections. Thompson ally Robert E. Crowe (the judge who had sentenced Thomas Fitzgerald to death) replaced Maclay Hoyne as state's attorney, and Thompsonite Len Small defeated Lowden's lieutenant John G. Oglesby for governor, thanks largely to overwhelming voter support in Chicago. "I never did understand the politics of that town," a bitter Lowden grumbled when the results came in. And he had cause to grumble. The election of Small ("a ferret-faced Kankakee banker" who would go on to undo many of his predecessor's achievements in office) made Thompson and Lundin's demolition of Lowden complete. And now, with thirty-eight thousand local, county, and state offices in their control and an annual payroll of $78 million at their disposal, they were in firm command at virtually every level of government in the state. Just a little over a year after nearly self-destructing during the crisis of July 1919, the mayor and his mentor had achieved a reach of power unprecedented in the history of Illinois politics.[17]

"The roof is off!" Big Bill shrieked at his city hall office on election night when the magnitude of their success became apparent. As a cordon of police kept the hundreds of well-wishers in the corridors from mobbing the mayor, he called Lundin on the phone and hooted about their joint triumph. "We ate 'em alive," he cried. "We ate 'em alive with their clothes on!"

At his suite in the Hotel Sherman, Fred Lundin was characteristically more reserved. "Oh, I don't mix in politics," he told some visiting reporters in his still-noticeable Swedish accent. "I'm only a private citizen, y'know."

Then he and the reporters burst into laughter and passed around a bottle of bourbon.[18]

EPILOGUE

The Two Chicagos

MAY 14, 1920

ON THE BRIGHT but chilly afternoon of May 14, 1920—as bands played and choruses sang from parade floats—a line of several thousand festively decorated automobiles crept north through the Chicago streets to mark "the greatest event since the World's Fair in 1893"—the opening of the Michigan Avenue Bridge. The largest double-decker drawbridge in the world, it had cost the fabulous sum of $16 million to build, including the expense of widening the avenue both north and south of the Chicago River. But the result had been worth much more than that. For the first time in the city's history, Chicago's North and South Sides were now linked by something more than narrow, undistinguished bridges. And while this was no small improvement in the city's physical infrastructure, its symbolic meaning was even more important. As the first major part of the Chicago Plan to be completed, the bridge represented the initial step in the transformation of Chicago from a chaotic, makeshift urban conglomeration into a "city beautiful," a rationally planned, optimally efficient, and aesthetically pleasing metropolis worthy of comparison with any other in the world.

At 4 p.m. exactly, a tall, heavyset man rose from his place of honor on the reviewing stand and stepped to the ribbon stretched across the roadway. Mayor William Hale Thompson, with a silk top hat pressed to his heart and an expression of "gravity and pleased emotion" on his face, acknowledged the cheers of the crowds around him. Proclaiming it "the greatest day for our people, the Chicago Plan Commission, and the administration," he proceeded to extol the new bridge and the work of those who had made it possible. But really, what words could be more eloquent than the beautiful, technologically ingenious steel-and-marble structure before him? It had been created only with great effort, requiring the city to buy and condemn no fewer than fifty-one properties (and to fight the resulting court battles) in order to let the boulevard-widening go forward. And, of course, opponents had tried to undermine the effort at every turn, pointing to, among other things, suspiciously numerous "cost overruns," not to mention enormous fees paid to real estate experts for their services. Where, the mayor's enemies persistently asked, had all of the extra money gone?[1]

Admittedly, it was a legitimate question—and one that would be asked again and again over the next decade, about this project and about many others. Big Bill's lakefront parks, his new boulevards and plazas, his glorious museums and stadiums, would continue to rise and change the skyline of Chicago for the better, but at what price? The remarkable triumph of the Thompson-Lundin machine in 1919 would indeed mean a "Greater Chicago" in the 1920s, at least architecturally, but it would mean many other things as well. It would mean a virtually bankrupt Chicago, a Chicago notorious for crime, political corruption, gangland violence, and rampant vice. It would mean a Chicago where city officials and underworld gangsters worked hand in hand to bootleg liquor, run prostitution and protection rackets, and win elections; where a crime lord with a name and reputation known all over the world—Al Capone—would be said to have three pictures hanging on the walls of his office: one of George Washington, one of Abraham Lincoln, and one of William Hale Thompson. In a sense, it can be said that Chicago never really recovered from its descent into violence and lawlessness in July 1919. The so-called Babylon of the 1920s would be just a more controlled version of that chaos.[2]

Of course, that decade would prove to have widely different fates in store for those who had played a role in the events of 1919. Some would go on to achieve great success beyond Chicago and become permanent fixtures in the national culture. Ring Lardner, from his new home base in the East, would rapidly become one of the premier satirists of his time, continuing to skewer the absurdity of virtually everything, though on a much wider stage and for a much larger audience than that afforded by his former Chicago beat. Jane

Addams would survive the anti-pacifist enmity of the wartime years and live to see her reputation rehabilitated in the 1930s, when she would become the first American woman to win the Nobel Peace Prize. And Carl Sandburg, though he would remain on the *Daily News* payroll until 1932, would achieve increasing national prominence as a poet over the next decade. While his later verse would never match the vigor and freshness of the early Chicago poems, and while he would go on to produce much substandard work (including a massive biography of Abraham Lincoln described by Edmund Wilson as "the cruelest thing that has happened to Lincoln since he was shot by Booth"), he would die in 1967 as celebrated as any twentieth-century American poet.[3]

For Ida Wells-Barnett, the 1920s would prove to be a demoralizing time. In November 1920—after months of increasing financial difficulties—she would be forced to close her Negro Fellowship League when the man in charge of the employment office ran off one night, "taking desks, chairs, stove, and most of the equipment of the place" and leaving her with four months of back rent to pay. Within a month she would be in the hospital for a gallstone operation that would nearly kill her. And despite her persistent efforts over the next decade to improve conditions in the Black Belt, the city's African Americans would continue to face widespread hostility and discrimination. True, some would claim that the riots of 1919 actually had some beneficial long-term effects. Many whites, for instance, were forced to confront the city's "Negro problem" for the first time, and the shock would galvanize at least the settlement house progressives to redirect some of their energies from the plight of white immigrants to that of native-born blacks. And for African Americans themselves, the riots would represent something of a psychological turning point. As one veteran of the riot would later put it, "Conditions in the states had not changed, but we Blacks had. We were determined not to take it anymore." But Wells-Barnett knew as well as anyone that this new defiant attitude (which, of course, was hardly new to her) would not do much to change the practical situation of African Americans in Chicago, at least in the area of fair housing and employment. The Black Belt would expand inexorably, absorbing many of the neighborhoods contested in the riot, but Chicago would remain one of the country's most segregated cities for decades to come.

As for Wells-Barnett herself, she would become ever more isolated from mainstream organizations like the Urban League and the NAACP. But she would keep at her independent efforts, running (unsuccessfully) for the presidency of the National Association of Colored Women in 1924, then (again unsuccessfully) for delegate to the Republican National Convention in 1928, and then (yet again unsuccessfully) for a state senate seat in 1930. On March 25, 1931, at the age of sixty-eight, she would die just as she had lived—as an outsider insufficiently recognized for her efforts. Only after the civil rights and women's movements of the 1960s and '70s would her contributions to the rights of blacks and women be given their full due.[4]

* * *

The lesser-known participants in the events of July 1919 also moved on to second acts of varying success in the Jazz Age. After the dismissal of the *Wingfoot* prosecution for lack of any violation of existing law, pilot Jack Boettner returned to Akron to pursue a long and distinguished career as a flying instructor at Goodyear. In 1929, when German aviator Hugo Eckener completed his historic round-the-world flight in the airship *Graf Zeppelin,* it was Boettner, now an admiral, who led the accompanying flotilla of blimps and dirigibles. By then, Goodyear had already made the decision to use nonflammable helium rather than much cheaper hydrogen to fill its airships—largely as a result of the *Wingfoot* debacle.

Tragedy struck Sterling Morton's young family in the spring of 1921, when his daughter Caroline died of cancer at the age of six. This was a terrible blow, but the grieving parents endured, and through the following decade Morton's business ventures continued to thrive. The printing telegraphs manufactured by his Morkrum Company proved to be enormously popular, and when he finally sold the company—then known as the Teletype Corporation—to American Telephone and Telegraph in 1930, the sale brought the Mortons personally the astounding sum of $30 million. Abandoning the progressive Democratic sympathies of his early years, he eventually became a well-known figure in conservative Republican circles, opposing FDR's New Deal and working to keep the United States out of World War II. He also became a great philanthropist in later years. Just before his death in 1961, he donated the funds to build the current Morton Wing of the Art Institute of Chicago. And whatever his politics in later years, he still felt gratified by the role he had played in Chicago's 1919 crisis. "I am indeed proud," he wrote near the end of his life, "to have been a member of the First Infantry, Illinois Reserve Militia."[5]

For Emily Frankenstein, too, the 1920s brought about momentous changes. The life with Jerry Lapiner she had dreamed of for so long did not come to be, after all. Late in 1919, Emily's parents had discovered that she was still meeting secretly with her forbidden beau, and they were furious. For a time—amazing herself with her brazenness—Emily had defiantly continued to date him. But things soon began to change between them. Emily started to chafe at Jerry's bad grammar, his smoking, his reluctance to improve himself, and his little failures of kindness and affection. Meanwhile, her old admirer Albert Chapsky—the more suitable boy whom her parents liked so much—began showing her more attention. On May 21, 1920, just a week after the ceremony at the Michigan Avenue Bridge, Emily went to a surprise party for her friend Marion Leopold. Since Jerry and Albert both attended, she had a chance to compare her two suitors, and she came to a realization: "I felt more tenderly chummy toward

Albert," she wrote, "as well as realizing that Albert far surpassed Jerry."

By the end of the month, she was engaged to Albert. On August 2, she burned her copies of all of the old love letters she had written to Jerry—and she did it in a neighbor's yard, since she didn't want even the ashes on her own property. "It was with a thankful heart that I kept stirring the flames. . . . It was all a mistake. And I'm so happy and thankful things happened as they did."

As for the prospect of life with her new fiancé, Emily was her usual hopeful self: "Albert—oh! He is so wonderful and so good to me," she wrote near the end of her diary. "[He] loves me so with all his being, and, well, I love Albert." That same day, she decided to start a new diary to record her life with Albert. For whatever reason, that document has not survived. But Emily apparently retained her positive attitude to the end. In 1969—exactly fifty years after the summer she documented in her diary—the now-seventy-year-old widow wrote a letter to the *Chicago Tribune* about the Apollo space missions: "The recent moon walks made me too excited to sleep," she wrote. "I didn't want to miss a single part. Every flight is different. When there is an Apollo mission on the moon, it is wonderful just to be alive."[6]

* * *

The arrival of the Jazz Age and the apotheosis of the Thompson-Lundin machine, of course, did not mean the end of all political opposition to the triumphant mayor. True, some enemies—such as Maclay Hoyne and Charles Merriam—did more or less cede the field and move on to other endeavors, Hoyne to a private law practice and Merriam to academia. But the newspapers continued to rage against the Thompson machine. Victor Lawson's *Daily News* launched some of its most heated attacks against the organization's new state's attorney, Robert Crowe. Picking up on one of Big Bill's favorite prevarications, Crowe responded by threatening to buy Lawson "a railroad ticket to the penitentiary at Joliet" for tax evasion. No such prosecution was ever forthcoming, however, and Lawson, after several years of declining health, was permitted to die quietly in his own bed on August 19, 1925. He is remembered today as a seminal figure in the history of American journalism, one of the first major publishers to run his newspaper as a public trust rather than merely as a private business designed to generate profits and propagate a political agenda.[7]

Robert R. McCormick, a much younger man than Lawson, had more time in which to wage his war against the man he despised. Firmly convinced that Thompson must have had some tie to the German secret service during the war, the Colonel spent much of 1920 enlisting the aid of his European and Washington correspondents to find such a connection. When this canard came to nothing, he contented himself with continuing his newspaper's long-standing campaign of resistance to the mayor, stalking him, according to his best biographer, "with the grim tenacity of Ahab chasing his great white whale." Eventually, the feud between Thompson and McCormick assumed absurd proportions, generating numerous suits and countersuits and culminating in 1931 with Big Bill publicly accusing the Colonel of plotting to assassinate him. By that time, however, the city of Chicago was a bit weary of both men. "The people of Illinois have no enthusiasm for Thompsonism, and less for the *Tribune*," one journalist of the day observed. "But they vote for the one, and buy the other. They would shed no tears at the downfall of either. But the fact remains that the *Tribune*, if not the world's greatest paper, certainly is one of them, and Thompsonism does build roads and bridges . . . , even if they cost more than they should."[8]

The ascendancy of the Thompson-Lundin machine, in any case, proved to be a temporary phenomenon. After the zenith year at the beginning of the decade, things began to fall apart in 1921. Overreaching themselves, Thompson and Lundin succeeded in uniting their opposition against them and soon began to lose elections. And before long, the organization was being torn apart by internecine feuding as well. Much to Lundin's annoyance, Thompson began displaying a highly unpleasant independent streak, making political decisions without consulting his mentor. Then State's Attorney Crowe began to show some independence of his own. In an act of brazen rebellion against the machine, Crowe launched a grand jury investigation into a school board scandal that eventually implicated even the Poor Swede himself.

For Lundin, this was to be the end. Indicted for conspiracy to defraud the school board of more than $1 million, he was subjected to a twelve-week trial that brought to light much of the inner workings of the machine he had worked so hard to construct. And although he was ultimately acquitted—mainly because his lawyer was Clarence Darrow, who engineered a brilliant "Who me?" defense that played on Lundin's milquetoast persona—the revelations of the trial severely wounded him as a political force. Mayor Thompson, who loyally testified for Lundin in court, was all but through with him afterward. "My friends have crucified me!" Big Bill complained to all who would listen. Weakened by scandal and reeling from the various lawsuits against him, the mayor recognized that it was time to lower his profile. When he was due to run for a third term, Big Bill Thompson announced that he would not be a candidate for reelection. "What a change in two years," one historian wrote, "the triumphant overwhelming victory in county, state, and nation in 1920, the dregs of defeat in 1922!"[9]

And so the mighty Thompson-Lundin machine collapsed. For Frank Lowden, there was significant satisfaction in seeing the downfall of those who had spoiled his own political prospects. Even so, the sage of Sinnissippi was resolved to remain in retirement, and eventually earned a reputation as a stubborn refuser of nominations and appointments, turning down a post in Harding's cabinet, a U.S. Senate seat, the ambassadorship to the Court of St. James's, and even, in 1924, a nomination by acclamation as Calvin Coolidge's running mate. He claimed to have no regrets, though he would admit late in life that he had sacrificed the presidency largely because he'd failed to heed the advice of "some of my best friends to concede . . . to the worst elements of the party." It was a lesson learned by many who dabbled in Chicago politics, where scruples could be a fatal political liability. Had Lowden been willing to play the game, Fred Lundin might actually have fulfilled his original goal of making "a Mayor, a Governor, a President."[10]

As for Big Bill himself, he would go on to have the most checkered of checkered careers. Having been declared politically dead upon leaving office in 1923, he would watch as his replacement in city hall—William Dever, a well-meaning progressive Democrat of unimpeachable honesty—made a complete hash of his term in office, enforcing Prohibition with such diligence that the city's bootleggers were soon engaged in territorial battles that lifted the crime rate to new heights of bloodiness. Seeing his opportunity, Thompson threw his trademark cowboy hat into the ring for another term in the 1927 election. The *Tribune,* the *Daily News,* and much of the rest of the world were incredulous. But Big Bill knew his city better than they did. The reformers had had their chance and had just made the city worse; so Thompson ran against them as the ultimate antireformer, promising to usher back the wide-open town ("I'm as wet as the Atlantic Ocean," he crowed). By playing to the thirsty, vice-deprived crowds, Big Bill was able to push his way past the incumbent Dever and independent John Dill Robertson (the creature of Thompson's new archenemy, Fred Lundin) to win handily in the April election. Chicago once again had the mayor it wanted—and probably deserved.

The story of Big Bill's third term would fill another full volume. Suffice it to say here that it was not a conspicuous success. Without the guidance of his Mephistopheles, the mayor became increasingly erratic. Under his uncertain leadership (during his third term, he suffered a nervous breakdown that left city hall virtually rudderless for months), Chicago became the gangster city of legend. Al Capone and his ilk had the run of the town while Thompson engaged in quixotic battles against alleged British propaganda in the public schools and turned increasingly ruthless in his efforts to win election for his cronies. When he decided to run for a fourth term in 1931, even some of his staunchest loyalists abandoned him. He lost—to Democrat Anton Cermak—and retreated into political irrelevance. When he finally died on March 19, 1944, investigators discovered that he had left an estate of more than $2 million, more than half of it in bills of large denominations stuffed into secret safe-deposit boxes. Running a great city, it seems, was well-paid work, even if the salary wasn't terribly high.[11]

And yet, as Big Bill was putting his scissors to the ribbon across Michigan Avenue on that sunny day in May 1920 (his fifty-third birthday, by coincidence), it was clear that he would be leaving behind another kind of legacy as well—one represented by that beautiful bridge in front of him, and by the Magnificent Mile of North Michigan Avenue that it would make possible. Granted, much of Daniel Burnham's original grand plan remains unrealized to this day, but the mayor did accomplish much. Would the city have fared better if he had not survived the crisis of 1919, if the Thompson-Lundin machine had been brought down by—or had at least been significantly weakened by—those twelve extraordinary days of civic disorder? The disastrous Dever interregnum of 1923–27 does not inspire confidence that an "honest, scientific administration" would have done a better job of harnessing Chicago's warring factions to the task of building the envisioned great city. For better or worse, the Chicago of the twenty-first century, perhaps the most architecturally distinguished and physically impressive city in the Americas, is in no small part a creation of the Thompson administration—however corrupt, however incompetent, however wasteful its leaders. Big Bill may have been—at times, at least—the buffoonish, crooked demagogue he is remembered as, but he was also more than that. In his coarse, sentimental way, he did love the city and its people, and he wholeheartedly embraced the idea of making them great. The reality of city politics in the early twentieth century was in any case never as simple as the good-government types liked to think. Reform, for all its good intentions, too often put the city's struggling masses in the role of children, wards of the state who had to be cared for and improved through the wise guidance of a privileged, well-educated, native-born white elite. Thompsonism, for all its venality, actually gave them a measure of real representation in government. And while the educated white reformers were by and large the ones who went on to write the history of the era, casting their enemies as the villains, it was the machine politicians who made that history, by being elected again and again.

Big Bill Thompson was not, to be sure, some kind of misunderstood benefactor of the common man. He was a deceitful, intellectually limited opportunist whose first loyalty was to himself and his cronies. But for all his faults and transgressions, he did manage to lead the sixth largest city in the world for well over a decade, keeping it afloat amid the conflicting energies of a vast and deeply divided population at a time of great stress. And when it was all over, the results were hard to dismiss, for Thompson left behind him a city as vigorous, as deeply flawed, and as improbably magnificent as himself.[12]

ACKNOWLEDGMENTS

I FIRST ARRIVED in Chicago—like many a newcomer over the past two hundred years—with no idea of what I was letting myself in for. The city is so much bigger, brasher, subtler, and rifer with wonders, idiosyncrasies, and complexities than anything that can be captured on paper or screen that someone facing it for the first time (or even the hundredth time) is bound to feel overwhelmed. For the narrative historian in particular the city can be hugely daunting. There were times in my research when it seemed that more happened in Chicago in a single week of 1919 than happened in most places over the course of several years.

I was therefore fortunate to find so many people ready and willing to help me make sense of this embarrassment of riches. Much of my research occurred during tough economic times, so a lot of these people were facing the pressures of slashed budgets, curtailed hours, and staff shortages, but never were they anything less than generous with their time and expertise. I owe particular thanks to Lesley Martin of the Chicago History Museum's Research Center, who has been a gracious and informative guide to the museum's vast collections since the very beginning of this project. Lesley, along with Debbie Vaughan, Anne Marie Chase, and everyone else at the center, deserves the gratitude of all who care about the city's varied and fascinating past. I also got plenty of help from the staffs of the University of Chicago's Special Collections Research Center (where the Lowden and Wells-Barnett papers are held), the Newberry Library (which has the Lawson and Lardner archives), the Harold Washington Library Center (especially those in the Newspaper Microfilm

Room and the Municipal Reference Collection), the Vivian G. Harsh Research Collection of Afro-American History and Literature, the library of the University of Illinois at Chicago, and the Spertus Institute of Jewish Studies (with particular thanks to Kathy Bloch). For her regular online doses of Second City lore, and for her enthusiasm about this project, I'd also like to send regards to Sharon Williams, author of the wonderful blog called *Chicago History Journal* (http:// www.chicagohistoryjournal.com).

I received welcome aid outside of Chicago from Eric Gillespie of the Colonel Robert R. McCormick Research Center in Cantigny, Illinois; Chatham Ewing, Dennis Sears, and the staff of Special Collections at the University of Illinois at Champaign-Urbana (where the Sandburg papers are housed); and Christyne Douglas and Beth Howse of Fisk University's Special Collections in Nashville. Closer to home, I'd like to acknowledge the employees of the Library of Congress, the National Archives (Archives II), and the University of Maryland libraries.

And to the people at the Cook County Medical Examiner's Office who tried hard to find the inquest documents I was looking for, I'd like to say "Thanks for trying."

Among the historians who offered me guidance and suggestions along the way, special mention must go to Douglas Bukowski, William Hale Thompson's most insightful biographer. Doug and I don't agree on everything Big Bill, but he has been incredibly generous with his time and his research, once even lending me his copies of some old FBI files that the Bureau itself no longer has. I now consider Doug a friend, and I apologize to him for those suggestions of his that I ended up not taking. I'd also like to express my gratitude to historians Sarah Marcus (now of History Works), Dominick Pacyga of Columbia College in Chicago, and Margaret Garb of Washington University in St. Louis for various comments and advice, and to Carl Smith of Northwestern University, who helped steer me to important sources very early in my research. And, as always, this book is better for having passed before the editorial eye of my pal Lisa Zeidner.

I owe enormous thanks yet again to my astute, erudite, and debonair agent and friend, Eric Simonoff at William Morris Endeavor, and to his assistants Eadie Klemm and Britton Schey. At Crown, I'd like to thank Rachel Klayman, Molly Stern, and especially my editor Sean Desmond and his assistant, Stephanie Chan, for their enthusiasm, insight, and gameness above and beyond the call of duty. And finally, I'd like to express gratitude to my family—Elizabeth Cheng, Anna Chang-Yi Krist, and Lily—for being just about the most wonderful spouse, child, and hound (respectively) I can imagine.

NOTES

All dates are 1919 unless otherwise indicated.

BA = Broad Ax
CA = Chicago American
CD = Chicago Defender
CDJ = Chicago Daily Journal
CDN = Chicago Daily News
CDT = Chicago Daily Tribune
CEP = Chicago Evening Post
CHE = Chicago Herald and Examiner
CSM = Christian Science Monitor
NYT = New York Times

The opening quotations are from Darrow, *Story of My Life*, p. 219, and Haywood, *Black Bolshevik*, p. 1. "Bathhouse John" Coughlin was quoted in Cutler, *Chicago*, p. 62.

PROLOGUE: THE BURNING HIVE

1. Principal details about Carl Otto's morning come from a July 22 article in the *CDT* (in which his wife is interviewed) and from a special July 19 memorial issue of the *Columns*, the house publication of the Illinois Trust and Savings Bank. Weather details are from various local newspaper reports. The death toll from influenza had surpassed that of the war according to the January 9 edition of the *CDN*. Carl Otto's reputation as a conscientious worker and the bank's "all-around utility man" is from the *Columns*, p. 8. The bank's president describes Monday as the bank's busiest day on p. 3 of ibid. (NB: Although the Ottos' son is referred to as "Daniel" in the above-mentioned *CDT* article, later newspaper reports and death notices identify the boy as "Stanley.")

2. The movements of Earl Davenport were reported more widely in the Chicago papers—perhaps because, as a former sportswriter, he was personally known to local journalists. Most details come from the July 22 editions of the *CHE, CEP, CDN,* and *CDT,* the last of which quotes one of White City's owners on Davenport's genial personality. An editorial entitled "Earl Davenport" in the July

22 *CEP* (where Davenport was once a sportswriter) also speaks at length about Davenport's sunny nature. Specifics about the amusement park itself come principally from the "White City" article in "Jazz Age Chicago: Urban Leisure from 1893 to 1945," edited by Scott Newman (http://chicago.urban-history .org). The *Wingfoot Express* and its assembly at the White City aerodrome are described in Hansen, *Goodyear Airships,* pp. 1–3, and in Young, *Chicago Aviation,* pp. 17–20. "Like a kid with his first pair of red-top boots" was reported in the July 22 *CDN* article. Davenport's tennis shoes and his eagerness to fly that day were attested to by blimp pilot Jack Boettner in the July 22 *CHE.*

3. Information about Roger J. Adams comes principally from two newspaper articles—the cited p. 1 interview in the July 21 *CDN* and an article in the July 22 *CDT,* in which Adams describes his movements of the day before. The "Blimpopolis" comment and other quotations in this section were recorded in the *CDN* piece. The *Wingfoot*'s departure time from the aerodrome was reported in a flight log printed in the *CDT* of July 22.

4. Milton Norton, as a *CHE* photographer, was naturally given much attention in that newspaper. The scene in the newsroom and exact quotations ("Have you got a cameraman ready?") were described by Meissner in a July 23 article in the *CHE.* Reports of crowds around town watching the blimp's first flight were reported in the July 21 *CDJ,* an afternoon paper that was hitting the streets just as the blimp was taking its final flight.

5. The account of the *Wingfoot*'s first two flights of the day derive mostly from pilot Boettner's statement to Chicago chief of detectives Mooney, most completely reported in the July 22 *CHE.* (NB: In this statement Boettner refers to the first flight as having taken place "early in the morning," but this is contradicted in other reports and in his later testimony to the state's attorney and the coroner's inquest jury.) In a bylined article in the July 22 *CEP,* writer George Putnam Stone (one of the two *Post* employees on the *Wingfoot*'s second flight) describes Davenport's yielding Stone a place on the second flight but taking a place (with Milton Norton) on the third flight for himself. Boettner frankly admits his unfamiliarity with the experimental rotary engines in his testimony to the state's attorney, most thoroughly reported in the *CDT* of July 22.

6. The *CDJ* of July 21 reported that twelve thousand people watched the *Wingfoot*'s first landing in Grant Park (see also the July 22 *CHE*). Several "experts" were quoted in the papers as having tried to get rides on the blimp (for example, in the *CDT* editions of July 22 and 23). Preston's letter about the publicity value of giving rides on the blimp was first reported in the July 22 *CDT* (which cites Henry Ford's being mentioned as a "desirable" passenger) and was later confirmed by Preston himself in his coroner's inquest testimony, reported in the July 27 *CDT* ("It is desirable to secure prominent men on the first flight"). The

scene between Boettner and Davenport ("a running start would be no good") was recounted by Boettner in the July 23 *CHE*. The preparations for flying, including Weaver's use of a blowtorch to burn off stray oil, were described in the July 22 *CDT*.

7. The angling of Davenport and Norton to get on the flight was reported in the *CEP* and *CDT* of July 22. The exchange between Boettner and the passengers about parachutes comes from Glassman, *Jump!*, p. 3.

8. The most complete existing description of the *Wingfoot*'s final flight is in Glassman, *Jump!*, pp. 31–46. I have also used some scene-setting details from the *CEP* reporter's account of his ride on the blimp's earlier takeoff and flight from Grant Park (*CEP*, July 22), and from the photos reproduced in Hansen, *Goodyear Airships*. The July 22 *CHE* describes the *Wingfoot*'s sailing out over the lake before turning back inland. That day's *CDT* takes note of the day's "faint but steady wind" and the appearance of the blimp from the ground. Other details are from Boettner's inquest testimony, recounted in several papers.

9. For the overall description of Chicago's appearance and geography in 1919, I have relied most heavily on Mayer and Wade, *Chicago;* Cutler, *Chicago;* Condit, *Chicago 1910–29* (NB: the gatefold panoramic photograph on p. 90 was useful); and Duis, *Challenging Chicago*.

10. The citywide excitement caused by the sight of the *Wingfoot* was reported in several papers. Boettner's account of the moments after seeing the fire above him ("Over the top, everybody") was reported in the *CDT* of July 22.

11. The eyewitness accounts by Roger Adams ("I got there just as [the *Wingfoot*] went up again") and Kletzker and Blake ("We went to the window to look again") were reported in the July 22 *CDT*. The scene between Proctor and Lamson ("Exmoor and my Marmon are enough for me") come from the same day's *CHE*. Both the *CDT* and the *CDJ* of July 22 carried stories on the witnessing of the disaster from Comiskey Park (quotation from the *CDJ*).

12. The description of the men abandoning ship is culled from various newspaper accounts, the most complete being the story told by eyewitness R. R. Renisch, an architect in the nearby Insurance Exchange Building ("like a rocket"), which was reported in the July 22 *CDT*. Boettner's fall was described by the pilot himself in his testimony to police chief John J. Garrity (see the same July 22 *CDT*) and in his testimony to the coroner's inquest jury (reprinted in the July 25 *CDN*). Specifics on Davenport's unsuccessful attempt to jump are from the July 23 *CHE*.

13. The scene inside the Illinois Trust and Savings Bank in the moments before the disaster are best described in the *Columns*, pp. 3–5, 16. The July 23 *CHE* (which also mentioned the departure of bank president Mitchell) contains a good description of the bank's interior. Helen Berger is described (with picture) in the

Columns, p. 9; on p. 16 her conversation with Callopy is referred to. Cooper's movements just before the crash were described by him in the July 22 *CDT.*

14. The change in light as the blimp fell toward the skylight was observed by several bank employees, including Harriet Messinger (July 22 *CDT*) and Helen Durland (July 22 *CDN*). The initial ignition of the blimp's fuel suggested a photographer's flash to Maybelle Morey and Maria Hosfield (July 22 *CHE*). Cooper's story ("The body of a man") was reported in the July 22 *CDT.* Joseph Devreaux ("I thought a bomb had been exploded") and A. W. Hiltabel ("The first thing I heard was the breaking of the skylight") were quoted in the July 22 *CDN.*

15. The scene with Carl Otto and Edward Nelson was described by Nelson himself ("an avalanche of shattered window panes and twisted iron") in the July 22 *CDN.* C. C. Hayford's story ("I ran out and an explosion . . . hurled me over") comes from the same day's *CDT.* The scene in the bank's central court ("a well of fire") is from a Mr. Connors quoted in the July 22 *CDN.* The quote from Joseph Dries ("I saw women and men burning") is from the July 22 *CDT.* Hosfield's experience ("I was sitting next to Helen Berger") is from the same day's *CHE,* while William Elliott's ("She was saturated with gasoline") is from that day's *CDT.*

16. The scene on the street (firemen unable to enter, people pouring from windows and wandering the streets) was best described in the July 22 *CDT* (which cited the twenty thousand spectators who had gathered in the southern Loop). Woodward's account ("When I got to the street") is from the same article. The men helping photographer Norton were described in the July 22 *CHE.*

17. Boettner's descent from the Board of Trade Building and his arrest were recounted by him in the July 22 *CDT.* Friends and relatives searching among the charred bodies on the street is from the July 22 *CDN* and *CHE.* Editorials in several papers over the following days, as well as statements from various city officials, raised questions about the audacity of carrying on "experiments in flying" over "the helpless heart of a crowded city" (July 22 *CEP*).

CHAPTER ONE: THE NEW YEAR 1919

1. Glimpses of the New Year's Eve festivities throughout Chicago come from the December 31, 1918, and January 1 editions of the *CHE, CEP, CDN,* and *CDT.* The slushy weather conditions were especially well described in a January 1 *CDT* article ("Slop, Slop, Slop; Six Days of It, More on the Way"). (NB: Thomas G. and Virginia Aylesworth, in their *Chicago,* p. 59, claim that the word "jazz" was coined at the Lamb's Café in Chicago in 1914.) Curly Tim's song about the "lemonade tree" was reported in a *CDT* article of January 1 ("Barrel House Bon Vivants Cheer Year In").

2. "This year, the holiday breathes peace and contentment," from the January 1

CDN. The drop in crime (reported in the *CDN* of December 31, 1918) probably had more to do with the high employment of wartime than with any special effort of the police department. Chicago's experience with the Spanish influenza is documented in "Report of an Epidemic of Influenza in Chicago Occurring During the Fall of 1918" by Robertson in *Report and Handbook of the Department of Health of the City of Chicago for the Years 1911 to 1918 Inclusive,* pp. 40–41. Misguided hopes for the salubrious social effects of Prohibition are described in Behr, *Prohibition,* pp. 82ff.

3. The literature on the Plan of Chicago is extensive. Most useful to me were Smith, *Plan of Chicago;* Bachin, *Building the South Side;* and Whitehead, *Chicago Plan Commission.* "A practical, beautiful piece of fabric out of Chicago's crazy quilt" is a quote from Walter D. Moody cited in Bachin, *Building the South Side,* p. 197. The idealistic hopes of the plan's advocates are best described in Smith, *Plan of Chicago,* pp. 14–15. "The visions that once seemed only heart-breaking mirages" is from the January 1 *CDT.*

4. Two excellent sources for conditions in Chicago as they existed at this precise time are Showalter, "Chicago Today and Tomorrow," and Smith, "The Ugly City," the latter of which is the source of "hurried, greedy, unfastidious folk." Henry Justin Smith also cowrote (with Lloyd Lewis) a very readable history of the city—*Chicago: A History of Its Reputation*—from which other facts and descriptions in these two paragraphs derive (see especially pp. 323–24).

5. Governor Lowden's proclamation—"The new year beholds a new world"— was cited in the January 1 *CDT.* Emily Frankenstein's unpublished diary, covering parts of the years 1918–20, is in the collection of the Chicago History Museum (Emily Frankenstein Papers). Background information about the diary and the Frankenstein family can also be found in Klapper, *Jewish Girls Coming of Age in America,* and Steinberg, *Irma,* the latter about Emily's mother, also a conscientious diarist.

6. Victor Lawson is the subject of a thorough but somewhat tedious biography, *Victor Lawson: His Time and His Work* by Charles H. Dennis. His broken foot is covered in the bio on pp. 433–34, but his New Year's Eve in bed comes from letters he wrote (to Marion K. Bradley and to Mrs. Iver N. Lawson, both on January 6, and to Julius Rosenwald on January 23), which are preserved in the Victor F. Lawson Papers (series 1, box 18) at the University of Chicago. Lilian Sandburg's details are from various sources, including Penelope Niven's biography of her husband, *Carl Sandburg: A Biography,* and *A Great and Glorious Romance: The Story of Carl Sandburg and Lilian Steichen* by their daughter Helga Sandburg; the "lonesome day" on New Year's Eve is described in the latter book, p. 259. For Ring Lardner I have relied principally on Yardley, *Ring.* However, the details and descriptions here ("Two young men were lying on the

floor") come from Lardner's column "In the Wake of the News" in the January 1 *CDT.*

7. "Hundreds of orchestras ushered in the new year" and "shouting and hammering and singing" are from the January 1 *CDT,* which also reported on the two accidents, the car thefts, and John Foll's arrest. Emily's "cold-slippery-tired" ride on the L is from her diary.

8. Events of the first two weeks of January are from various newspapers. Charles Comiskey's announcement and quotes ("The loyal patrons of the White Sox") were covered by the January 1 *NYT* and all of the Chicago dailies. Garrity's one thousand new policemen and the state tax cut were announced in the *CDT* of January 2 and 1, respectively. Chicago's observance of Roosevelt's death was covered widely in all of the local newspapers. The "mighty, roaring, sweltering" description of Chicago comes from Edna Ferber's delightful novel *So Big,* p. 311.

CHAPTER TWO: THE MAYOR ANNOUNCES

1. Accounts of the rally at Arcadia Hall appeared in the January 15 editions of the *CDT, CDN,* and *CHE,* but the most thorough (if not the most objective) report was in the January 18 issue of the *Republican,* a weekly newspaper that served as a mouthpiece for the Thompson-Lundin political machine. The physical description of Arcadia Hall is derived from the building's entry on the Jazz Age Chicago site, http://chicago.urban-history.org/.

2. Specifics of the evening's program of music and speeches are primarily from the *Republican* and other newspaper reports. The campaign song ("Over here we have a leader") was reprinted in its entirety in the *Republican.* "The best administration in its history" was quoted, with some implicit irony, in the *CDT* of September 15.

3. There have been four book-length biographies of William Hale Thompson, ranging in attitude toward their subject from the admiring to the derisive. Two were written by authors who personally witnessed the mayor's first and second terms. John Bright's *Hizzoner Big Bill Thompson: An Idyll of Chicago* is utterly condescending and dismissive, treating the mayor as a quaint political curiosity with few redeeming qualities—a view propounded by many newspapers of the day and all too often adopted uncritically by later Chicago historians. William Stuart's *The 20 Incredible Years,* written by a political columnist for Hearst's *Chicago American,* errs in the other direction, often presenting Thompson and Fred Lundin's propaganda as the unvarnished truth. A more balanced portrait is presented in Lloyd Wendt and Herman Kogan's *Big Bill of Chicago,* though its coauthors, like Bright, give much greater emphasis to the colorful media phenomenon than to the crafty politician. By far the fairest and most serious account is Douglas Bukowski's *Big Bill Thompson, Chicago, and the Politics*

of Image, which is the only biography that does full justice to the mayor's complexities. Specifics about Big Bill's physical appearance and personality in this chapter come mainly from these four biographies and from the Thompson profiles in White, *Masks in a Pageant;* Luthin, *American Demagogues;* and contemporary newspaper and magazine articles. "Loved Chicago like a boy loves his dog" is from Bright, *Hizzoner Big Bill Thompson,* p. 68.

4. Bukowski is particularly insightful on Thompson's appeal to blue-collar Chicago (while not being particularly pro-labor) in 1919; see the introduction to *Big Bill Thompson* as well as the same author's PhD thesis, "According to Image: William Hale Thompson in the Politics of Chicago, 1915–1931," pp. 1–10, and his chapter on Thompson in Green and Holli, *Mayors,* pp. 61–81. "Slangy, vulgar, and alive" is from Bright, *Hizzoner Big Bill Thompson,* p. 3. "I have been requested by petition" is from the *Republican*'s reproduction of the text. "Big, boozy, bellowing" roar is from White, *Masks in a Pageant,* p. 485.

5. In later years—as was common in the early twentieth century—Thompson often lopped two years off his age by citing his birth year as 1869. Some people, including Bright and Stuart, apparently believed him.

6. The State Street Bridge incident is reported in Wendt and Kogan, *Big Bill of Chicago,* pp. 17–18. They are also the best source for details about Thompson's childhood, youth, and early cowboy years.

7. For the account of Thompson's pre-political life, I have relied most heavily on—in addition to the four mentioned biographies—White, *Masks in a Pageant;* Luthin, *American Demagogues;* Leinwand, *Mackerels in the Moonlight;* Thompson's entry in the *Dictionary of American Biography;* and the *CDT*'s premature obituary for Thompson, published in error in 1931 and reprinted by Thompson in the campaign booklet *A Tragedy with a Laugh.*

8. The Jenney incident ("This money says Bill Thompson is scared!") is from Wendt and Kogan, *Big Bill of Chicago,* p. 33.

9. The account of Thompson's announcement speech ("An examination") comes principally from the text as reprinted in the *Republican* of January 18. Much of the text is illegible in the surviving microfilm, however, so I have supplemented it with quotations cited by the other newspaper accounts of the Arcadia Hall speech (particularly that in the *CDT*) and with excerpts from Thompson's standard stump speech for the 1919 campaign as recorded by a stenographer in the employ of Victor Lawson (Victor Lawson Papers, series 4, box 125, folder 828: "Mayor William Hale Thompson—Speeches 1919").

10. The listing of Thompson's achievements comes from the text in the *Republican,* as are the quotations in this section ("with less revenue" and "I know that a vast majority of the people").

11. Bukowski, *Big Bill Thompson,* p. 4, explicitly makes the point that Thompson played politics as an extension of sports. "I'm spending $175 a day" is quoted in Wendt and Kogan, *Big Bill of Chicago,* p. 41.

12. Bukowski, *Big Bill Thompson,* pp. 13–14, has the best account of the politics behind Thompson's aldermanic misadventures. "No one's going to beat Bathhouse" is quoted in Wendt and Kogan, *Big Bill of Chicago,* p. 49.

13. Fred Lundin's history and peculiarities are described in the four Thompson biographies (Bright devotes a whole chapter to him). But some of the best material comes from Zink, *City Bosses in the United States,* and from Eric R. Lund, "Swedish-American Politics and Press Response: The Chicago Mayoral Election of 1915" in Anderson and Blanck, *Swedish-American Life in Chicago: Cultural and Urban Aspects of an Immigrant People, 1850 to 1930.* "Get a tent" is quoted in Wendt and Kogan, *Big Bill of Chicago,* p. 49, as is "He may not be too much on brains," p. 77.

14. "The Five Friends" and their political ambitions are best outlined in Stuart, *20 Incredible Years,* pp. xv, 1–4. The author claimed (in 1935) that the plan had never before been revealed in print. "A thrust for power never before attempted" is from ibid., p. 1.

15. Quotations and paraphrased assertions in this section come from the speech transcripts in the Victor Lawson Papers (box 125, folder 828) and from the text as printed in the *Republican* of September 18.

16. The *Tribune*'s observation about Thompson being the mouthpiece, with Lundin supplying the song, is quoted in Lund, "Swedish-American Politics." The unique symbiotic quality of the Thompson-Lundin relationship, with the Poor Swede controlling his protégé from behind the scenes, is accepted by virtually all writers on the topic, though Stuart and Bukowski give Thompson more credit for being an independent thinker.

17. The scene at the Auditorium Theatre is best described in Bukowski, *Big Bill Thompson,* p. 10, and in Lovett, "'Big Bill' Thompson of Chicago," p. 380. "I could no longer hold out agin 'em" is quoted in an unpublished lecture by Merriam, "Analysis of Some Political Personalities I Have Known," p. 4. The most thorough account of the long odds against Thompson in the 1915 election come from Shottenhamel, "How Big Bill Thompson Won Control of Chicago," p. 33.

18. For newspaper reaction to Thompson's candidacy, see especially O'Reilly, "Colonel Robert Rutherford McCormick," p. 68ff. Lawson's judgment of Thompson as "simply impossible" is from Schmidt, "*Chicago Daily News* and Illinois Politics, 1876–1920," p. 101. "Just who is this Bill Thompson?" is quoted in Wendt and Kogan, *Big Bill of Chicago,* p. 101.

19. Thompson's campaign promises as per Wendt and Kogan, *Big Bill of Chicago,*

pp. 95, 103, and elsewhere. "You're going to build a new Chicago with Bill Thompson!" is from ibid., p. 93.

20. "When in doubt, give a parade" is from Bright, *Hizzoner Big Bill Thompson,* p. 69. Election results as per Stuart, *20 Incredible Years,* p. 16. "Hoorah for Bill!" "Fred, you're a wizard," and other quotations in Thompson headquarters on election night are from Wendt and Kogan, *Big Bill of Chicago,* p. 114. "In six months we'll know" is from ibid., p. 122.

21. "Between the people, on the one hand" is from a Thompson speech quoted in the *CDT* of January 18. "If continued in the office of mayor" is from the text in the *Republican* of January 15. "The audience stood on its feet" is from the same article.

CHAPTER THREE: ENEMIES

1. The Landis demurral ("I would just as soon have you ask me to clean a shit-house") is quoted in Watkins, *Righteous Pilgrim,* p. 177.

2. Merriam's life and work is most completely discussed in Karl, *Charles E. Merriam and the Study of Politics.* For the progressives' preference for middle-class, educated experts over working-class ethnic politicians who might share the same goals, see Lissak, *Pluralism and Progressives,* p. 66. The Jane Addams quotations are from her endorsement in the Charles E. Merriam Papers, section 3, box 75, folder 5. Merriam's attacks on Thompson are from ibid., section 3, box 76, folder 5.

3. The most complete source for details about Olson is Willrich, *City of Courts.* "Thanks to Mayor Thompson" is from the *CDT* of February 10. "They made the school treasury" is from the *CDT* of February 5. The list of scandals outlined by Olson is summarized in Hoffmann, "Big Bill Thompson," p. 18. "Have used the vast public expenditures" is from the *CDT* of February 8.

4. There have been many books devoted to an analysis of urban political machines. Most useful to me were Gosnell, *Machine Politics,* and Allswang, *Bosses, Machines, and Urban Voters.* "Ceaseless devotion" is from Bright, *Hizzoner Big Bill Thompson,* p. xxii. See also Merriam, *Chicago,* p. 137.

5. "No mayor ever entered the City Hall" is quoted in Wendt and Kogan, *Big Bill of Chicago,* p. 120.

6. Thompson's letter about the "fair manner" with which the *Trib* treated him, reproduced in the *CDT* of April 7, 1915, is cited in Bukowski, *Big Bill Thompson,* p. 37. The scene beginning "Victor Lawson listened" is recounted in Dennis, *Lawson,* pp. 318–19.

7. "We're going to drive every crook" is quoted in Luthin, *American Demagogues,* p. 84. "No shadow of corruption" is cited in Wendt and Kogan, *Big Bill of Chicago,* p. 120.

8. "I'm not going to let them leave" and the model boat incident is from Wendt and Kogan, *Big Bill of Chicago,* p. 125. "I am here to emphasize the grief and indignation" is cited in Bukowski, *Big Bill Thompson,* pp. 41–42. The popularity of "Big Bill hats" after the *Eastland* disaster is noted by Stuart, *20 Incredible Years,* p. 19.

9. "Here it is. *You* play with it" is from Wendt and Kogan, *Big Bill of Chicago,* p. 126. "A roster of his nearest and dearest friends" is from Bright, *Hizzoner Big Bill Thompson,* p. 68. The discontent over appointments is best summarized in Chenery, "Fall of a Mayor," p. 37. Chicagoans' mistrust of their hometown papers is cited in Shottenhamel, "How Big Bill Thompson Won Control of Chicago," p. 40.

10. Lundin's early image maneuvering and machine building is recounted in an article on the Poor Swede in the *CDT* of March 31. See also Stuart, *20 Incredible Years,* p. 16. "To the people of Chicago" is quoted by Bukowski, *Big Bill Thompson,* p. 51. "Unscrupulous politicians should be thwarted" is cited in Wendt and Kogan, *Big Bill of Chicago,* p. 143. The suicide note was printed in the *CDT* and *CDN* editions of April 3, 1916.

11. "The people don't want it" is from a diary kept by Max Loeb, quoted in the *CDT* of September 1, 1918.

12. "Chicago is the sixth largest German city" is cited ubiquitously, as in Wendt and Kogan, *Big Bill of Chicago,* p. 151. They also cite "This war is a needless sacrifice" on p. 155.

13. "I think that Mayor Thompson is guilty of treason," "a disgrace to the city," and "a low-down double-crosser" are cited in Wendt and Kogan, *Big Bill of Chicago,* pp. 156–57.

14. Big Bill's response to his attackers is best described in Stuart, *20 Incredible Years,* p. 50ff. The results of the primary vote come from ibid., p. 56. Bright, *Hizzoner Big Bill Thompson,* p. 118, and Luthin, *American Demagogues,* p. 87, discuss the unpopularity of the war among Chicago's ethnic groups. The analogy with Lincoln's loss to Douglas was made in the *Republican* of September 21, 1918.

15. Bukowski, *Big Bill Thompson,* pp. 4, 17ff., has the best discussion of Thompson's shifting image over the course of his first term and his turn away from the increasingly powerless reform element and toward immigrants and workers.

16. "Who are the other two candidates" is from the *Republican* of February 22.

17. Thompson's invitation to debate was reported in the *CDT* of January 25 and 26. The February 11 confrontation was widely covered, with slightly varying details, in most of the papers. I have relied most heavily on the account in the *CDT* of February 12, from which the quotations in this paragraph come.

18. "FIGHT FOR YOUR RIGHTS!" is from a Thompson campaign letter collected in the Charles E. Merriam Papers, series 3, box 75, folder 3.

CHAPTER FOUR: THE FOURTH ESTATE

1. There have been several biographies of Robert R. McCormick, the most complete of which is Smith, *Colonel.* Also useful (and often more sardonic) are Gies, *Colonel of Chicago,* and Morgan and Veysey, *Poor Little Rich Boy.* McCormick's accent as per Gies, *Colonel of Chicago,* p. 8ff. *Tribune* book critic Burton Rascoe's memoir, *Before I Forget,* provides an unforgettable portrait of the Colonel (see pp. 8 and 267 for details on his dogs and his rooftop polo practice). McCormick's height is from his entry in the *Dictionary of American Biography.* "Working for McCormick is a little like working for God" is quoted in O'Reilly, "Colonel Robert Rutherford McCormick," p. 3.

2. The authoritative biography of Lawson is Dennis, *Lawson.* Third-largest-circulation newspaper as per ibid., p. 140. The firing of the pressman is also from ibid., p. 29, as is Lawson's habit of testing advertisers' claims, p. 137. "A man of mental and moral poverty" is quoted in ibid., p. 321.

3. "Some newspapers" is from a Thompson campaign booklet in the Charles E. Merriam Papers, series 3, box 75, folder 3. The two newspaper "scandals" are widely reported in the biographies and elsewhere. Lawson discusses the tax bill issue in correspondence in the Victor F. Lawson Papers, series 4, box 125, folder 827. "Robbing the school children" and "tax dodger" are from Thompson stump speeches transcribed in ibid., folder 828.

4. The two quotations in this paragraph are from a letter from Lawson to Arthur Brisbane dated March 13 (Victor F. Lawson Papers, series 1, box 74).

5. "Mayor's Men Panicky Over Swing to Olson" was in the *CDN* of February 10. "I think 'stocks are up' " is from a letter from Lawson to E. D. Hulbert on February 15 (Victor F. Lawson Papers, series 4, box 117, folder 784).

6. A roundup of the various parades and celebrations for returning soldiers was published in the 1919 *Chicago Daily News Almanac,* p. 804. Emily Frankenstein's reactions to the soldiers are in her diary for January 7 and January 13 (Emily Frankenstein Papers). The *CDN* was particularly concerned about employment prospects for the troops; see two articles in the January 28 edition. The *CDT* carried a story about soldiers hooting at Thompson, for instance, on February 16.

7. "The Case Against Thompson" was in the February 21 edition of the *CDN.* "[Thompson] has failed in everything that could be hoped for him" comes from the *CDT* of February 23.

8. "Actions speak louder than words" and the scene at the Monroe Street Bridge were reported in the *CDN* of February 22. "Bill grabbed the Chicago Plan and raced away with it like a gridiron star" is quoted in Stuart, *20 Incredible Years,* p. 25.

9. The deployment of soldiers by all three candidates was reported in the *CHE*

of February 25. The Thorpe incident is ubiquitously covered (e.g., Wendt and Kogan, *Big Bill of Chicago*, p. 166; Bright, *Hizzoner Big Bill Thompson*, p. 154; and in most of the newspapers); not all accounts are identical, but I have relied most heavily on the report from the *CDN* of February 24 and the *CHE* of February 25.

10. Olson's allegations of a "citywide plot" were reported in the *CA* of February 26. Election vote counts are from Bright, *Hizzoner Big Bill Thompson*, p. 156. Ibid., p. 150, was also the source of the quote about all "who had eyes to see and ears to hear." The February 26 edition of the *CHE* noted Merriam's loss in his own district.

11. "Our cause is crowned with victory" is reprinted in the *CHE* of February 26. "We beat them today and we'll beat them on April 1!" is quoted in Wendt and Kogan, 167.

12. Details of the early-morning bombing on February 28 are from the *CDT* of the same date.

CHAPTER FIVE: A BOMB IN THE NIGHT

1. Most details about the Indiana Avenue bombing are from an article in the *CDT* of February 28. (Significantly, the incident was not covered by most of the other daily papers, although the *CDN* did run a captioned photograph of the damage.) For my description of the interior and exterior damage, I have relied on two photos reprinted in William M. Tuttle Jr.'s excellent *Race Riot: Chicago in the Red Summer of 1919*, p. 177. "The violent result of prejudice against the Negro inhabitants" was quoted in the *CDT* article of February 28.

2. For details about the earlier bombings, see Tuttle, *Race Riot*, pp. 175–6.

3. Tuttle, *Race Riot*, p. 160ff., gives a good background of the early black settlement of Chicago. For information about Chicago's role in the Great Migration, I have also relied heavily on Grossman, *Land of Hope*, and Spear, *Black Chicago*. Two excellent works on the topic appeared in 2010—Berlin, *Making of African America*, and Wilkerson, *Warmth of Other Suns*—though neither focuses on Chicago or on the early stage of the Great Migration relevant here. For the wartime labor shortage and industry's use of labor agents, see Tuttle, *Race Riot*, pp. 82 and 87, respectively. "The land of suffering" is from ibid., p. 91. For other exhortations from the *Chicago Defender*, see Spear, *Black Chicago*, p. 134. "Anywhere north will do" is quoted in Tuttle, *Race Riot*, p. 79.

4. The half-million figure is cited in the exhaustive report by the Chicago Commission on Race Relations (primarily authored by Charles S. Johnson) entitled *The Negro in Chicago: A Study of Race Relations and a Race Riot in 1919* (hereafter cited as *TNIC*), p. 602. Ministers transplanting entire congregations are

cited in Sandburg, *Chicago Race Riots,* pp. 14–15. For the growth of Chicago's black population, see Cohen, *Making a New Deal,* p. 35, and Tuttle, *Race Riot,* p. 66. "Every time a lynching takes place" is quoted in ibid., p. 86.

5. *Chicago Defender* circulation figures as per Tuttle, *Race Riot,* p. 212. For the growth of Chicago's black metropolis, see Spear, *Black Chicago,* as well as Philpott, *Slum and the Ghetto,* and Baldwin, *Chicago's New Negroes.* American Giants attendance as per Baldwin, *Chicago's New Negroes,* p. 213. "The greatest experiment-station" is a quotation from Horace Bridges, president of the Chicago Urban League, cited in the Chicago Urban League's 1920 Annual Report. "Half a Million Darkies" is quoted in *TNIC,* p. 530. "Black Man, Stay South!" and "a huge mistake" are cited in Spear, *Black Chicago,* p. 202. The offer of financial aid is according to ibid., p. 203.

6. For the *Tribune* on banjo-plucking blacks, etc., see Tuttle, *Race Riot,* p. 202. The Stroll is defined and described in Bachin, *Building the South Side,* p. 247, and in Baldwin, *Chicago's New Negroes,* p. 25. For the moving of vice establishments into black neighborhoods, see Spear, *Black Chicago,* p. 25. Ibid., p. 24, also discusses why black housing was plagued by overcrowding and disrepair. For a discussion of the forces creating the downward spiral of black neighborhoods, see Garb, *City of American Dreams,* pp. 182ff. Sandburg, in *Chicago Race Riots,* pp. 12–13, discusses the issue of southern rural ways appearing inappropriate to more established urban dwellers.

7. Spear, *Black Chicago,* p. 36, cites strikebreaking as blacks' only entry into many industries. The equation of the terms "Negro" and "scab" is cited in Tuttle, *Race Riot,* p. 119; see also Sandburg, *Chicago Race Riots,* p. 52. The twelvefold increase in black stockyards workers as per Spinney, *City of Big Shoulders,* p. 169. Blacks' suspicion of unions and the returning soldiers is noted in Tuttle, *Race Riot,* pp. 18, 128. "You pay money and get nothing" is quoted in *TNIC,* p. 177.

8. The lack of residential construction during war is cited in Tuttle, *Race Riot,* p. 168. The Black Belt as home to 90 percent of the city's black population is from Cohen, *Making a New Deal,* p. 34. The factors governing the southward growth of the Black Belt are mentioned in Tuttle, *Race Riot,* pp. 167–68. (NB: Most people moving into white neighborhoods were middle-class, established blacks escaping encroaching vice, as per Spear, *Black Chicago,* p. 150.)

9. For the early peaceful efforts to stop integration, see Spear, *Black Chicago,* p. 211. "Clear of undesirables" is quoted in ibid., p. 210. The efforts to keep neighborhoods "lily white" are discussed in Travis, *Autobiography of Black Politics,* pp. 66–67, and Philpott, *Slum and the Ghetto,* p. 162ff. "Look out; you're next for hell" and "We are going to BLOW these FLATS TO HELL" are quoted in Tuttle, *Race Riot,* pp. 175–76. "Attempted assault and murder" is from the *CD* of June 1, 1918, as quoted in Spear, *Black Chicago,* p. 212.

10. Black vs. white voter registration figures are from Gosnell, *Negro Politicians,* p. 17; see also Spear, *Black Chicago,* p. 192. For Chicago as the first northern city in which blacks made up a significant portion of the population, see Allswang, *Bosses, Machines, and Urban Voters,* p. 92. "The strongest effective unit of political power" is from Sandburg, *Chicago Race Riots,* p. 5. Bright, *Hizzoner Big Bill Thompson,* p. 16, claims that this was the first municipal playground in the country; Wendt and Kogan, *Big Bill of Chicago,* p. 42, says it was the first in the city. "White people from nearby came over" is quoted in Bukowski, *Big Bill Thompson,* p. 14. "My task is not easy" is from Bright, *Hizzoner Big Bill Thompson,* pp. 87–88.

11. "I'll give you people the best opportunities" is quoted in Spear, *Black Chicago,* p. 187. The Second Ward's black voters giving Thompson his winning margins is from Tuttle, *Race Riot,* p. 186.

12. See Stovall, "*Chicago Defender* in the Progressive Era," p. 170, for an assessment of how truly beneficial Thompson's election was for blacks. For De Priest as the first African American alderman, see Spear, *Black Chicago,* p. 187. Other jobs for Wright, Anderson, and Carey is from Spear, *Black Chicago,* p. 124, and Tuttle, *Race Riot,* p. 196. The doubling of the number of black police as per Tuttle, *Race Riot,* p. 232. Thompson's banning of the movie *The Birth of a Nation* is from Spear, *Black Chicago,* p. 124, and Tuttle, *Race Riot,* p. 189.

13. "Uncle Tom's Cabin" and Thompson's backing down on the physician appointment are from Bukowski, *Big Bill Thompson,* p. 49. "The persons appointed were qualified" is from Wendt and Kogan, *Big Bill of Chicago,* p. 168. "Blubbering jungle hippopotamus" reference is quoted in Bergreen, *Capone,* p. 416.

14. "The best friend politically" is from the *CD* of October 2, 1918. "He has treated us fairly" is from ibid., September 7, 1918.

15. The bombing of Jesse Binga's offices and the scene (with quotations) involving the little girl on the street were described in the *CDT* of March 20.

16. The rise in crime and the figures for the first twenty days of March are from the *CA* of March 22.

17. Ida B. Wells-Barnett is the subject of several excellent biographies, the most complete and authoritative being Giddings, *Ida.* Also useful are Schechter, *Ida B. Wells-Barnett and American Reform;* McMurry, *To Keep the Waters Troubled;* and Sterling, *Black Foremothers.* Wells-Barnett herself wrote two revealing autobiographical works, *Memphis Diary of Ida B. Wells* and *Crusade for Justice.* "Mother protector" is quoted in Schechter, *Ida B. Wells-Barnett and American Reform,* p. 141. "A slanderous and nasty mulatress" was quoted in Sterling, *Black Foremothers,* p. 91. The story of the C&O train incident and the quotation ("hooked her feet under the seat") are from Giddings, *Ida,* pp. 62–63. Mob of "leading citizens" and the hanging threat as per Sterling, *Black*

Foremothers, p. 83. "They had destroyed my paper" is from Wells-Barnett, *Crusade for Justice,* pp. 62–63.

18. Working with Jane Addams as per Deegan, *Race, Hull-House, and the University of Chicago,* p. 78. "Mother, if you don't go" is quoted in Sterling, *Black Foremothers,* p. 106. "Lighthouse" and a black version of Hull House is from Wells-Barnett, *Crusade for Justice,* p. 101. Wells-Barnett's appearance is from Giddings, *Ida,* p. 65. "She walked as if she owned the world" is from the very useful supplementary materials in Wells-Barnett, *Memphis Diary of Ida B. Wells,* p. 196. "One spot in this entire broad United States" is from the *Alpha Suffrage Record* of March 18, 1914, as quoted in Wells-Barnett, *Crusade for Justice,* pp. xxviii–xxix.

19. The meeting of the Negro Fellowship League and its subsequent statement ("a willful and malicious libel") were described in the *CDT* of March 25.

CHAPTER SIX: ELECTION

1. Sweitzer's ties to local gas interests as per Bukowski, *Big Bill Thompson,* p. 26ff. "Iron-jawed Irishman" is from Wendt and Kogan, *Big Bill of Chicago,* p. 143. Hoyne's previous lack of interest in the vice issue is asserted in Lindberg, *To Serve and Collect,* p. 145, n. 21. "The fire department will be my special delight" and other Lardner quotes here are from his column in the *CDT* of March 5.

2. "Ruin the Republican Party for years to come" is quoted in the *CDN* of February 4. On the tendency of Chicago Republicans to unite after even the most contentious primaries, see especially Hutchinson, *Lowden of Illinois,* p. 94.

3. "None of the mayoral candidates" is in a letter from Lawson to Arthur Brisbane dated March 24. "Sweitzer cán beat him; Hoyne can't" is in an earlier letter from Lawson to Brisbane dated March 13 (both in the Victor F. Lawson Papers). "The Thompson-Sweitzer issue was fought out four years ago" is from the *CDT* of March 3.

4. Darrow's quote is from an article he wrote for the *CDT* of March 23. "He disgraced Chicago" is from the *CDT* of March 6. Other denunciations of Thompson's antiwar sentiments were cited in, for instance, the *CDT* of March 3, 22, 23, 26, and 27. "A guy was ashamed to acknowledge that he was from Chicago" was quoted in the *CDN* of March 1. "Honestly, I believe if that big fat Bolshevik crook" is from a letter, dated March 2, from First Sergeant Alfred B. Backer of the American Commission to Negotiate Peace to "Dear Folks" (unidentified photocopy in the research files of Douglas Bukowski).

5. For Lundin's focus on the black, Irish, and German vote, see Leinwand, *Mackerels in the Moonlight,* p. 38, and Wendt and Kogan, *Big Bill of Chicago,* p. 168. "Damn him, we know he's no good" is quoted in Davis, "Portrait of

an Elected Person," p. 177. For Thompson's campaigning on national issues, see Wendt and Kogan, *Big Bill of Chicago,* p. 170. For Thompson's appearance before the "Old Eighth," see the *CD* of February 22 ("You have come back decorated"); see also Ovington, *Walls Come Tumbling Down,* pp. 142–43; and Aylesworth and Aylesworth, *Chicago,* p. 11.

6. The background to the Illinois registration law is explained in the *CDT* of January 26.

7. Sweitzer's advocacy of the emergency legislation was reported in the *CDT* of January 26. The passing of the Hughes bill 133–0 as reported in the *CDT* of March 21.

8. For the greatest sins in machine politics, see Allswang, *Bosses, Machines, and Urban Voters,* p. 23. See also George Washington Plunkitt's dissertation on "Ingratitude in Politics" in Riordon, *Plunkitt of Tammany Hall,* pp. 33–36.

9. The details about Lowden's life come principally from his authorized biography, *Lowden of Illinois,* a thorough, generally fair, but perhaps slightly too admiring account by William T. Hutchinson. Garland's characterization of the governor ("the look of an English earl") is cited in ibid., p. 75. Lowden's willingness to accommodate machine politics, when necessary, is conceded in ibid., p. 260. For the colloquy at Eagle Lake, see ibid., p. 265.

10. On the intricacies of Chicago's taxing and bonding limitations and the resulting structure of overlapping "governments," see Merriam, Parratt, and Lepawsky, *Government of the Metropolitan Region of Chicago,* particularly pp. xv and 20.

11. For Lowden's overhaul of the state government's administrative structure, see Hutchinson, *Lowden of Illinois,* p. 314. "An endorsement from Thompson seemed almost equivalent to a blackball" is from ibid., p. 308.

12. "It was a hectic interview" and other quotes from that scene with Lundin come from Stuart, *20 Incredible Years,* p. 31.

13. Lowden's flu was cited in his wife's diary for 1919 in the Pullman-Miller Family Papers at the Chicago History Museum. Lowden's signing of the Hughes bill was reported in the *CHE* of March 27 and the *CDT* of March 28.

14. The *CDN* of March 24 attributed the crime wave to "criminal politics" in city hall. "It is impossible to exaggerate the seriousness of the situation" was quoted in the *CDN* of March 24. The plot whose object was "the overthrow of the government of the United States" was reported in the *CHE* of March 11. For the Bolshevik squad, see Bukowski, "According to Image," p. 146.

15. The election bettors "awaiting next week's developments" as per the *CHE* of March 23. The *Tribune* plea (sometimes mistakenly described in the literature as a countersuit) is discussed in the *CDN* and *CDT* of March 26. The prediction that Sweitzer would run away with the election was reported in the *CDN* of

March 25. Ring Lardner's column about dropping out of the race and running for king appeared in the *CDT* on April 5.

16. The scene at the Pekin Theatre, with quotations, was reported in the *CDT* of March 25.

17. "Never, on the eve of a Chicago mayoralty election" is from the *NYT* of March 30. "Downtown Chicago stood on its head" is from the *CDT* of March 30. The "hurling of stink bombs" was reported in the *CHE* of April 1. "Whenever [Mayor Thompson] drew up at the curb" is from the *CDT* of March 30.

18. The prediction of four hundred thousand total votes and the "general belief that party lines were [being] thrown to the wind" were in the *CDN* of April 1. Schmidt, in "*Chicago Daily News* and Illinois Politics," p. 144, claims that the *CDN* cited Cook County's ballot as the longest in the world. The account of Irma Frankenstein's voting experience is from her diary (Irma Rosenthal Frankenstein Papers, box 3, folder 20).

19. Election figures are from Stuart, *20 Incredible Years,* pp. 16 and 73.

20. "Truth and justice have again prevailed" was quoted in the *CDJ* of April 1.

21. "Chicago's Shame!" as reported in Wendt and Kogan, *Big Bill of Chicago,* p. 171. "It is difficult for outsiders to understand" and other quotes are from the *NYT* of April 3. "He becomes a minority mayor" is from the *CDN* of April 2. "Negroes Elect 'Big Bill'" comes from the *CDJ* of April 1. For white resentment of black voting power as demonstrated in this election, see especially Rudwick, *Race Riot at East St. Louis,* p. 220.

22. "I have been maligned" is quoted in Wendt and Kogan, *Big Bill of Chicago,* p. 171. The lack of a congratulatory note from Lowden is described in Tuttle, *Race Riot,* p. 207.

CHAPTER SEVEN: ON THE WARPATH

1. "Re-Election Starts Mayor on Warpath" and subsequent quotes are from the *CDN* of April 2.

2. "Thompson Men Plan to Extend Rule in State" and the power over Lowden's presidential hopes now held by Thompson are from the *CDT* of April 3. "Mayor Thompson let it be known" is from the *CHE* of April 3.

3. The Wheeler interview with Thompson and all quotes are reported in the *CDT* of April 2.

4. "A constructive program to boom Chicago" was quoted in the *CDT* of April 2. "Be a Chicago booster!" comes from Wendt and Kogan, *Big Bill of Chicago,* pp. 172–73. "A new spirit must control public officials" is from a speech text in the Frank O. Lowden Papers, series 3, box 36, folder 10. "Unless it is one absolutely necessary" was quoted in the *CHE* of April 28.

5. The text of Thompson's address before the legislature was reprinted in the

anonymously published "Catechism: The Truth About Chicago's Financial Condition," pp. 16 and 22. For the success of Thompson's plea and the reference to Lowden's "delayed congratulations," see the *CDJ* of April 29.

6. Baseball results are from the *CHE* of April 24 and 25. Lardner's "I wished you could of [*sic*] seen" was in his column in the *CDT* of April 24. The opening of the White City Amusement Park was reported in the *CEP* of May 14. For the Wartime Prohibition Act, see Allen, *Only Yesterday,* pp. 14–15.

7. "My enemies have recently bored holes in the walls" is from an open letter "To the People of Chicago," dated September 6, 1917, as quoted in Bukowski, *Big Bill Thompson,* p. 66. The actual transcript of an eavesdropped conversation between Thompson and Lundin is in the former's Justice Department file, memo of May 2, 1921 (9–19–1206–3). (NB: Thanks to Douglas Bukowski for lending me his copy of this now-destroyed file.) "Big enough to blow out the entire side" quoted in Allen, *Only Yesterday,* p. 35. For the bomb plot, see also the *CDT* of May 1.

8. The rise in cost of living as per Bachin, *Building the South Side,* p. 290. The most thorough and useful work on Sandburg is Niven, *Carl Sandburg.* Also helpful to me were Helga Sandburg's account of her parents' marriage, *Great and Glorious Romance,* and Yanella, *Other Carl Sandburg,* which is especially good on the poet's early political work. "I believe there are some big, live feature stories" is from a May 31 letter from Sandburg to Smith in the Carl Sandburg Papers at University of Illinois at Champaign-Urbana (Connemara Collection, 3–019–072).

9. "I am with all rebels everywhere" is from an undated (late 1919) letter from Sandburg to Romain Rolland (Carl Sandburg Papers, Sandburgiana Collection, 11–1919). For the best account of the Finnish agent episode, see Yanella, *Other Carl Sandburg,* pp. 123–30. Also see ibid., p. 133, for Sandburg's coverage of the AFL convention.

10. "A sorry world" is quoted in Smith, *Colonel,* p. 218. The protest of twenty-five thousand Jews was reported in the *CDT* of May 22. The June 8 gathering as per Bukowski, *Big Bill Thompson,* p. 96.

11. For the Frankensteins' membership in the city's long-established German-Jewish community, as well as the quotation "in literature, my schoolwork," see Klapper, *Jewish Girls Coming of Age in America,* p. 40. For Emily's visit to the Christian Science lecture and quotations ("So very, very few healthy, robust people"), see her diary for February 2 and 3 (Emily Frankenstein Papers).

12. All quotations in this section are from Emily Frankenstein's diary entries for June 6, 1918; June 12, 1918; and an undated entry on page 198 of the diary (Emily Frankenstein Papers).

13. For the Ellis Avenue bomb, see the *CDT* of April 7. Other bombings are per a

document in the Carl Sandburg Papers, "Interracial Situation in Chicago." For the Harrison bombing, see Giddings, *Ida,* p. 595.

14. "Well, Negroes, you must get guns" is from the *BA* of April 5.
15. For the Barnetts' new home on Grand Boulevard, see Wells-Barnett, *Memphis Diary of Ida B. Wells,* p. 196. For the makeup of the committee and the incident at city hall, see Giddings, *Ida,* p. 595, and the *BA* of June 7. "He could not put all of the police in Chicago on the South Side" is quoted in Giddings, *Ida,* p. 595.
16. "No man is big enough" is from the *NYT* of April 11.
17. "Smiles, tears, hugs, [and] kisses" and "the greatest parade the old town ever saw" are from the *CHE* of May 28. Thompson's absence from other homecoming parades was noted in the *CDT* of May 27.
18. The alleged incident with the boy at the parade ("Gee, he's here!") was reported in the *CDT* of May 28.
19. "I failed to see the Mayor's stand" was quoted in ibid.
20. The Aurora incident and conversation was reported in ibid., June 28.

CHAPTER EIGHT: GOING DRY

1. Scenes from the June 30 debauch come principally from the *CEP* of July 1 ("bowing to the Board of Trade Building"). Garrity's vow of "dire vengeance" on offending proprietors was reported in ibid., June 29. The incident of the stolen whiskey barrel is from ibid., July 1. (NB: Wartime Prohibition did allow consumption of near beer and other very low-alcohol beverages.)
2. "The biggest carnival night in the history of Chicago" was the opinion of the *CHE* of June 29. The $2 million estimate is from the *CEP* of July 1. The smaller crowds in the soft drink emporiums were reported in the *CHE* of July 7. "Slums will soon only be a memory" is quoted in Behr, *Prohibition,* p. 82.
3. The Colonel's ample stash of whiskey as per Morgan and Veysey, *Poor Little Rich Boy,* p. 233. The fifteen thousand doctors and fifty-seven thousand retail druggists applying for licenses are cited in Nelli, *Business of Crime,* p. 151. Lardner's recipe ("Take a glass of sweet cider") is from the *CDT* of July 14. Alternative sources of alcohol as cited in Behr, *Prohibition,* p. 85.
4. The June 17 attack is discussed in Spear, *Black Chicago,* p. 213. The assault on the white principal is from Diamond, "Hoodlums, Rebels, and Vice Lords," pp. 39–40. The fatality report is from the *CHE* of June 23. The Charles W. Jackson incident was reported in the *CEP* of July 1.
5. The Garfield Boulevard signs and the warning to "prepare for the worst" were mentioned in *TNIC,* p. 57. The July 4 upset in the Polish neighborhoods is discussed in Bukowski, *Big Bill Thompson,* p. 96, and in Leinwand, *Mackerels in the Moonlight,* p. 33.

6. Sandburg "interviewing shopkeepers, housewives" is from Niven, *Carl Sandburg,* p. 336. "We made the supreme sacrifice" is quoted in ibid., p. 337.

7. Wells-Barnett's letter ("There had been a half-dozen outbreaks") was printed in the *CDT* of July 7.

8. The 250,000 striking Chicago workers as per Tuttle, *Race Riot,* p. 141. On p. 128, Tuttle describes the expiration of federal employment requirements. Individual strikes in Chicago are per ibid., pp. 138–39, and Taylor, "Epidemic of Strikes in Chicago," pp. 645–46.

9. "The traction volcano" is from the *CEP* of July 15. The 50–1 margin for the strike vote was reported in the *CHE* of July 17.

10. "Frank is much concerned" is from Florence Lowden's diary entry for July 19 (Pullman-Miller Family Papers). The official launch of Lowden's campaign in Washington, D.C., as per the *NYT* of July 14. The admiring profile of Lowden appeared in the July 20 *NYT.*

11. Thompson's citation of legal obstacles was reported in the *CEP* of July 15. The reaction of the president of the elevated railway employees ("That committee arbitrate?") comes from the *CEP* of July 19.

12. "Most important meeting since the world's fair days" is from the *CEP* of July 21. The "dream coming true" quotation is from ibid., July 19. "This bridge'll bring property values around here up by the millions" is quoted in Wendt and Kogan, *Big Bill of Chicago,* p. 172. (NB: Thompson was, of course, right, as Colonel McCormick would build his Tribune Tower a few blocks north of the bridge within a few years.)

13. Baseball details are from the *CDT* of July 20. Emily's tribulations, with quotations, are from her diary, pp. 192–97 (Emily Frankenstein Papers).

14. Davenport's offer of a blimp ride to the mayor, and Thompson's response, as per the *CEP* of July 22. The mayor's two meetings of the day as per the *CEP* of July 21. "The greatest day, barring none, in Chicago's history" is from the *CDT* of July 22. "It marks a new era" is from the *CDN* of July 22.

CHAPTER NINE: TUESDAY, JULY 22

1. Details of the scene around the Illinois Trust and Savings Bank building on the morning after the crash, along with the quotation from John J. Mitchell ("Reports that we lost any money"), are from the *CDN* of July 22.

2. The violation of "all preconceived notions of safety" and the editorial ("That girls working at their desks in the security of a bank building") are from the *CEP* of July 23 and 22, respectively.

3. "The most sensational tragedy" is from the *CDN* of July 22. "There seems little question that the flight was experimental" is from the *CDT* of July 23.

4. Maclay Hoyne's arrest order was reported in the *CDT* of July 22 (the *CDT* of the

next day amended the number of arrests from the seventeen originally reported to fourteen). All quotes in these two paragraphs are from the *CDT* of July 22.

5. Details and quotations from the city council meeting were reported in the *CDT* of July 22.

6. The scene at the Central Undertaking Rooms and the quotation from Mrs. Carl Weaver were recounted in the *CHE* of July 22.

7. The scenes at St. Luke's Hospital involving Marcus Callopy's family and Alice Norton are from the *CDJ* of July 22. Milton Norton's deterioration overnight as per the *CHE* of July 23.

8. Carl Otto's funeral as cited in the *CDJ* of July 22. The scenes with his wife at home and at the hospital, with quotations, were reported in two articles in the *CDT* of July 23.

9. Mrs. Davenport's reaction to the news of her husband's death, with quotations, was recounted in the *CHE* of July 23.

10. "All I can say is, I thought the end of the world had come," was quoted in the *CDT* of July 22. The same edition is the source of the quotation from Maybelle Morey ("I was working in the bond department"). People (including several sportswriters and an alderman) who claimed that they were "almost" passengers on the fatal flight were noted in the *CEP* and *CDT* of July 22 and the *CDJ* of July 23.

11. "While the airship was still burning" is from the *CDJ* of July 22. The coroner's inquest scene was described by columnist Louise Brown in the *CEP* of July 23. Hoffman's somber announcement of Norton's death as per the *CHE* of July 22.

12. For the mayor's reaction to Lowden's "interference" in the traction situation, see the *CDJ* of July 21. The characterization of the closed-door meetings as "star-chamber sessions" was in the *CHE* of July 22. The quotation from the mayor's spokesman is from the *CDJ* of July 21.

13. The 60 percent fare hike as per the *CDN* and *CDJ* of July 22. "If our state constitution were properly constructed" is from the *CHE* of July 22. Thompson's readiness to take the matter to court was cited in the *CDJ* of July 21.

14. The report on the circumstances of Janet Wilkinson's disappearance is from the Chicago Department of Police Daily Bulletin for 1919, first made public on July 26 (in the Chicago Public Library's Municipal Reference Collection, MRC Cc P766). Marjorie Burke's account was reported in the *CEP* and *CDN* of July 23, and later recounted in more detail in the *CDJ* of July 26. Berenice Wilkinson's was in the *CDJ* of July 23.

CHAPTER TEN: WEDNESDAY, JULY 23

1. The search for Janet Wilkinson was described in all of the daily papers, most usefully in the *CDN* of July 23 and the *CHE* of July 24, the latter noting the

fifty volunteer boys and girls. The description of Janet is from the Police Daily Bulletin report cited on the previous page. The first published photo of Janet appeared in the *CEP* of July 23.

2. Marjorie Burke's story as per the *CDT* of July 24. (NB: The *CHE* of July 23 initially misidentified the witness as Marjorie Dee, another of Janet's friends.) The story of the previous incident with Janet and Fitzgerald was reported in the *CDN* and *CEP* of July 23.

3. Fitzgerald's appearance and manner as described in the *CDT* of July 24, which also recounted Fitzgerald's explanation of his movements before his arrest.

4. Fitzgerald's previous arrests on larceny charges as per the *CDJ* of July 23 and the *CDT* of July 24. His earlier arrest for "conspicuous interest" in two girls comes from the *CHE* of July 24. The dropping of the case "for want of prosecution" was cited in the *CDN* of July 23.

5. Fitzgerald's description of the earlier incident with Janet ("It was around Christmastime she came into my home") was quoted in the *CDT* of July 24.

6. The dragging of the lake in response to Fitzgerald's offhand comment was reported in virtually all of the newspapers; see also Lindberg, *Chicago by Gaslight,* pp. 198–99.

7. The Cook County Medical Examiner's Office could not locate the transcript of the coroner's inquest in the *Wingfoot* case, so I have had to rely on descriptions of the proceedings as reported in the newspapers. All of the quotations in these first paragraphs are from the *CEP* of July 23 and the *CDT* of July 24.

8. The various theories about the cause of the fire are from the *CEP* of July 23. Coroner Hoffman's declaration on the requirements for establishing blame and the lack of precedent in Illinois law as per the *CDT* of July 24. "Which did not contemplate airships falling" is from the *CDJ* of July 22.

9. The quotations from Goodyear officials were quoted in the *CEP* of July 23. The rumors of damaging testimony from Wacker were cited in the *CDT* of July 24.

10. The funeral services for Marea Florence were described in the *CDT* of July 24. (NB: The *CDT* identified her as "Maria," but the *Columns,* likely to be more accurate, has her first name repeatedly as "Marea.") "If you ever saw her smile" was quoted in the *Columns,* p. 6. Marcus Callopy's death as per the *CDT* of July 24 and the *Columns,* p. 13.

11. The quotations from W .S. McClenathan are from the *CDJ* of July 23. "Statements by both sides in each meeting today" is from the *CDN* of the same date. The *CEP* of July 24 reported the union leader's reassurances that no strike would take place until the completion of the commission investigation.

12. The mayor's preparations for his trip to Cheyenne were widely reported. "A lariat and a pair of chaps in his valise" comes from the *CDT* of July 24. The committee's invitation "to bring everybody who voted for [the mayor]" was

cited in the *CDJ* of July 23. "Well stocked with ice for lemonades" is from ibid. Ettelson as Samuel Insull's creature as per McDonald, *Insull,* p. 178. The *CEP* of July 23 noted Thompson's assurance that they'd be missing only two and a half working days.

CHAPTER ELEVEN: THURSDAY, JULY 24

1. For the union's intransigence on the eight-hour-day issue, see the *CDN* of July 24. The *CEP* of July 24 reported on the *Wingfoot* funerals. The scene at the Illinois Trust and Savings Bank ("Not a typewriter clicked") was described in the *CDT* of July 25.
2. Goodyear's public apology was printed in the *CEP* of July 24. The formation of the three-man commission as per the *CDT* of July 25. "In justice to our men" is quoted in the *CEP* of July 24.
3. The *CEP* of July 24 describes Senator Sherman's bill and the city council's ongoing work on an aviation bill. "I am going to do everything I can to help establish laws for the regulation of airships" was quoted in the *CDT* of July 25.
4. The interrogation of Fitzgerald, with quotations, was recounted in the *CDN* and *CEP* of July 24.
5. The questioning of Watson and Darby and the phone call to Mrs. Fitzgerald as per the *CDN* of July 24. The *CHE* of the same date reported on Lieutenant Howe's rushing of the photograph to Bangor.
6. Details and quotations from Howe's afternoon interrogation of Fitzgerald are from the *CDN* of July 24.
7. The analysis of the case by Detective Sergeant Powers, with all quotations, are from ibid.
8. Reports of sightings of Janet, as well as the false alarm at the Morrison Hotel, come from the *CDT* of July 25.
9. The scenes with Muriel Fitzgerald come principally from the *CHE* ("The reports about his peculiarities"), the *CDN* ("You did it, you did it"), and the *CDT* ("When I received that telegram"), all of July 25. Mrs. Fitzgerald's appearance as per pictures and descriptions in the *CEP* and *CDJ* of July 25 and the *CDT* of July 26.
10. The finding of the revolver at the Virginia Hotel, as well as Lieutenant Howe's dispatching of a pair of detectives to Michigan, as per the *CDT* of July 25. Wilkinson's offer of a $500 reward was cited in the *CDN* of July 24.
11. The reports of other attacks on children and the calls on Alcock to institutionalize all suspected "morons" come from the *CDT* of July 24 and 25.

CHAPTER TWELVE: FRIDAY, JULY 25

1. The description of the week's weather in Chicago is from reports in the *CDT.* For the scene between Muriel Fitzgerald and John Wilkinson, I have relied

principally on the *CEP* of July 25 ("Oh, Mr. Wilkinson") and the *CDJ* of the same date ("When I [first] received word that my husband was in trouble").

2. Helen Hedin's story as per the *CDT* of July 26. "The Handcuff King" episode as per the *CDN* of July 25. "I'm not the man" was quoted in the *CEP* of July 25.

3. Lieutenant Howe's statement ("In my 25 years of police experience") and the account of the ongoing interrogation ("Look at that picture") are from the *CDN* of July 25.

4. The continuing search for Janet was described in the *CDT* of July 26.

5. "For two days and two nights" is from the *CDJ* of July 24. "I had put [the] baby doll away from her" was quoted in the *CDT* of July 25.

6. The long quotation ("When [Mrs. Fitzgerald] entered the door") is from the *CDJ* of July 25.

7. "I have ordered the arrest of all half-wits" was quoted in the *CEP* of July 25.

8. The aura of mistrust was reported in the *CHE* of July 26; see also the *CDN* of July 25.

9. The scene at the *Wingfoot* inquest was described by several papers, each of which published slightly different accounts of the testimony. "What this man [Lipsner] has to offer is hearsay" was quoted in the *CEP* of July 25. "Wacker told me that he was nervous and scared" is from the *CDJ* of July 25. "He said that the blimp acted up," is from *CDT* of July 26. "Wacker said that Carl Weaver," is from *CDJ* of July 25. "Produce the evidence," is from *CDN* of July 25. Lowery's threat to clear the room as per the *CEP* of July 25.

10. The exchange among Lipsner, Mayer, and Maranville as reported in the *CDT* of July 26.

11. O'Brien's demand that Boettner testify next is from the *CDN* of July 25. Boettner's attire as per a picture in the *CDT* of July 26, in which his manner of testifying was also described. "We had no trouble during our flights on Monday" as quoted in the *CDN* of July 25. The rest of his testimony as reported in that issue of the *CDN* and in the *CDT* of July 26.

12. Conflicting reports on the origin point of the fire as per the *CDT* of July 26.

13. Details and all quotations from the transit talks in these paragraphs come from the *CDJ* of July 25.

14. Lowden's arrival in Chicago and his closed-door meetings as per the *CEP* of July 25 "It is understood that some progress toward reconciliation was made" is from the *CHE* of July 26. "Frank telephones [to say] that the streetcar situation is very bad" is from Florence Lowden's diary entry for July 25 (Pullman-Miller Family Papers).

15. Sandburg's articles for the *CDN* were later reprinted in his pamphlet *The Chicago Race Riots*. "Deplore Unfounded Negro Crime Tales" appeared in the *CDN* of July 25. The *CDT* reported on the two French analyses in its July 25 edition.

16. For the New Negro sensibility and the DuBois quotation, see Boskin, *Urban Racial Violence in the Twentieth Century,* p. 41, and Tuttle, *Race Riot,* p. 209. Claude McKay's poem was published in the *Liberator* 2 (July 1919), cited in Tuttle, *Race Riot,* p. 208.

17. "THE MAYOR SHOULD RETURN" was an editorial in the *CEP* of July 25. Big Bill's cowboy outfit was described in the *CDN* of July 25. The rest of the details and quotations from Cheyenne were reported in the *CDT* of July 26.

CHAPTER THIRTEEN: SATURDAY, JULY 26

1. "All Chicago Seeks Solution of Missing Child Mystery" was the headline in the *CDN* of July 26. The "biggest question" quotation and the four hypotheses are from the *CDJ* of July 26.

2. The additional $2,500 reward was announced in the *CDT* of July 27. The flood of calls, telegrams, and letters, and the Dearborn Station false alarm, were reported in the *CEP* of July 26.

3. The sister superior's admonition and the dragging of the lake as per the *CEP* of July 26.

4. The discovery of bones in the sewer was reported by the *CDT* of July 27.

5. Evidence given by Marie Pearson and William Harris as cited in the *CDT* of July 27. That of W. J. Hogan is from the *CEP* of July 26. The scene with Michael Kezick, with quotations, was described in the *CDT* of July 27.

6. "Ordinarily, the arrest of a suspect" is from the *CEP* of July 26, which also took note of the lack of any formal charges against Fitzgerald and Lieutenant Howe's backup plan.

7. The manner of Fitzgerald's interrogation as per the *CDT* of July 28. The *CEP* of July 26 described the prisoner's fit of weeping. The *CDT* of July 28 noted Fitzgerald's teasing of Captain Mueller about his hat. "He is the most stubborn and one of the shrewdest men I have ever questioned" is from the *CEP* of July 26 and the *CDT* of July 27.

8. The bringing in of five North Side women and their daughters, as well as the order to police to look for "another moron," were reported in the *CDT* of July 27.

9. The questioning of Major York as per the *CEP* of July 26.

10. H. T. Kraft's testimony is from the *CDT* of July 27 ("You know it is possible to test a dirigible on the ground") and the *CDN* of July 26 (the virtual impossibility of leaking hydrogen to ignite).

11. "I have made an effort to see Wacker" was quoted in the *CDT* of July 27. The complaints of the businessmen's jury as per the *CEP* of July 26.

12. The profile of Carl Sandburg appeared in the *CDT* of July 26. The Lowden boom in Washington was reported in the *CHE* of July 27. Emily Frankenstein's

resolution to finally "say goodbye" to Jerry as per her diary for July 26 (Emily Frankenstein Papers).

13. The witnessing of Judge Dolan's fall comes from reports in the *CDJ* and *CDN* of July 26 and the *CDT* and *CHE* of July 27. The quotations from the two witnesses on the seventh floor were from the *CDJ*.

14. The same four papers covered the aftermath of the apparent suicide, but again, all quotations (except "He seemed jolly and carefree," which is from the *CHE* of July 27) come from the *CDJ* of July 26, which had the most complete coverage of the incident. For the Judges vs. Lawyers baseball game, see the *CDT* of June 11.

15. Afternoon temperatures as per the *CDT* of July 27 and Florence Lowden's diary. "Negotiations are over" was quoted in the *CDN* of July 26. "Chicago is in for a streetcar strike" is from the *CEP* of July 26.

16. All of the daily papers had remarkably detailed reports on the culmination of Fitzgerald's interrogation, the most complete being those in the *CDT* and *CHE* of July 28. All quotations in this section are from the former.

CHAPTER FOURTEEN: SUNDAY MORNING, JULY 27

1. The confession scene, with quotations, comes from the reports published in the *CDT* and *CHE* of July 28.

2. The scenes in the Chicago Avenue station and in the basement of the East Superior Street duplex, with quotations, are also as reported in ibid.

3. The *CDT* and *CHE* of July 28 also had the most thorough accounts of the crowds out on East Superior Street, though the shouts ("Lynch him!" "String him up!") are as reported in the same day's *CEP*.

4. All quotations in the taxicab scene are from the *CHE* of July 28, with additional details from the *CDT* and *CEP* of the same date.

5. The *CEP* of July 28 is my principal source for the scene back at the Chicago Avenue station. The reports of "ill-concealed weapons" as per the *CHE* of that date. That day's *CDT* has an account of M. F. Sullivan's interrogation of Fitzgerald. (NB: Among the inconsistencies cleared up was the fact that Marjorie Burke was mistaken about when Fitzgerald and Janet Wilkinson met on the street; it apparently happened before the girls' trip to the playground, not after.) The July 28 *CEP* depicted Fitzgerald as "cool," while the same day's *CDT* described him as "a picture of control." "Don't let them hang me" and Hoyne's appointment of James O'Brien (whose nickname "Ropes" was noted in the *CDN* of July 28) as per the *CDT* of that date.

6. "Acting Chief Alcock already has issued orders" is from the *CEP* of July 26. "This case should cause the people of Chicago to demand a special session of the legislature" was quoted in the *CDT* of July 28.

CHAPTER FIFTEEN: SUNDAY AFTERNOON, JULY 27

1. The story of the five boys' excursion to the Hot and Cold comes from Tuttle, *Race Riot,* pp. 3–10. (NB: Tuttle interviewed John Harris in 1969.)

2. The account of the racial confrontation at the Twenty-ninth Street beach was reported by all of the newspapers, though I have relied most heavily here on the *CEP* of July 28. For this episode of the riot and for those that follow in subsequent chapters, I have relied on numerous other sources. The 1919 race riot has been extraordinarily well documented. The most comprehensive treatment, based on many months of field interviews conducted by a staff of researchers, is *TNIC,* the 650-page report of the Chicago Commission on Race Relations. Other important works on the topic, besides Tuttle, *Race Riot,* include Grossman, *Land of Hope;* Spear, *Black Chicago;* Philpott, *Slum and the Ghetto;* and Sandburg, *Chicago Race Riots;* as well as Grimshaw, *Racial Violence in the United States;* and Waskow: *From Race Riot to Sit-in.* Of the numerous essays and articles on the riot, Pacyga, "Chicago's 1919 Race Riot," collected in Mohl, *Making of Urban America,* deserves special mention for the light it casts on the ethnic and class aspects of the riot, often given short shrift by other works that emphasize the racial aspects exclusively.

3. All of the quotations in this section come from Tuttle, *Race Riot,* pp. 6–7. (NB: According to *TNIC,* p. 4, the coroner later found no contusion or other indication that Eugene Williams had actually been hit by the rock; the coroner therefore concluded that the boy had died by drowning when he couldn't reach shore because of the rock throwing. John Harris may indeed have embroidered the incident in his interview with Tuttle fifty years after the fact [the blood-in-the-water detail, for instance, may be a trick of memory]; however, it should also be noted that coroners at this time typically had little or no medical training [though some on their staff did], and even *TNIC* admits that "rumor had it that [Eugene] had actually been hit by one of the stones and drowned as a result.") Officer Callahan's retreat to a nearby drugstore as per the *CEP* of July 28.

4. The *CDT* of July 28 estimated the crowd at one thousand people. Exaggerated rumors as per Tuttle, *Race Riot,* p. 8. The white bathers who helped search for Eugene Williams were noted in *TNIC,* p. 5.

5. The shooting incidents are most thoroughly described in *TNIC,* pp. 5, 660. The *CEP* of July 28 identified the black policeman as Jesse Igoe. The escalation of the riot ("bubbling cauldrons of action") was best described in the *CDT* of July 28.

6. For the reaction of the athletic clubs to the beach rioting, see Tuttle, *Race Riot,* pp. 32–33. Richard J. Daley's membership in the Hamburg Athletic Club is discussed in Cohen and Taylor, *American Pharaoh,* pp. 27–36. (NB: While there

is no hard evidence that Daley participated in the rioting, as Cohen and Taylor write, "he was, at the very least, extremely close to the violence.")

7. Some individual instances of violence were reported by only one or two newspapers. The locations of the major confrontations as per the *CHE* and *CEP* of July 28. The *CDT* of July 28 reported on the white crowds shooting at streetcars. The tapering off of violence overnight as per Tuttle, *Race Riot*, p. 34. The day's toll of dead and injured as reported in the *CDT* of July 28.

CHAPTER SIXTEEN: MONDAY, JULY 28

1. Mayor Thompson's impromptu press conference at Union Station was covered most completely by the afternoon papers. The dialogue in this section comes from the *CEP* and the *CDJ* of July 28. Thompson's telegram to Alcock, sent while in Cheyenne, was mentioned in the *CDN* of July 28.

2. Details of the car negotiations and the quotation from Governor Lowden come from the *CDT* of July 29. The *CDN*'s praise of Lowden appeared in an editorial in the July 28 edition.

3. Chief Garrity cited the number of police at 3,500; see *TNIC*, p. 36. The quotation from Michael Gallery is from the *CEP* of July 28. (NB: Tuttle, *Race Riot*, p. 34, differs on the exact wording.)

4. Chief Garrity's qualms about the militia as per Tuttle, *Race Riot*, p. 35. For the most complete account of the People's Council incident, see Thurner, "Mayor, the Governor, and the People's Council." "In case rioting should break out" is quoted in ibid., p. 137. "A treasonable conspiracy" and "Freedom of speech will be respected" are quoted in ibid., p. 138. Garrity's announcement ("even if it becomes necessary to fill every jail in Chicago") comes from Tuttle, *Race Riot*, p. 35.

5. Details in this paragraph come from various sources. For Fitzgerald's suicide watch, see the *CDT* of July 29. For the overflowing crowds on the street, see the *CDN* of July 28. "Send him out here and we'll hang him for you!" was quoted in the *CEP* of July 28. "You can never tell what will happen" was cited by the *CDJ* of July 28.

6. Each of the papers had a slightly different account of the very brief coroner's inquest session. I have taken the quotations from the *CEP* of July 28.

7. The quotation from Hoyne and the announcement from Crowe are both from the *CDN* of July 28.

8. The quotations from O'Brien are from the *CEP* of July 28. That day's *CDN* noted that he was wearing his hanging tie. "Fitzgerald may be a moron" is from the *CDT* of the same date.

9. The twenty-five incidents in Chicago that year as per the *CDT* of July 28. The next day's edition of that paper cited the official's estimate of two hundred cases

per year. "There is but one solution to the whole problem" was quoted in the *CDN* of July 28.

10. The scene of Janet's casket being carried into the duplex was described in the *CDJ* of July 28 and in the *CDT* of July 29. The *CDN* of July 29 noted that many mourners remained on the street through the night.

11. For the gangs of white youths waiting just outside the yards, see *TNIC*, p. 6. The attack on Oscar Dozier was described in ibid., p. 656.

12. For the attacks on streetcars, see Tuttle, *Race Riot*, p. 37, and *TNIC*, pp. 656–57. (NB: The latter book describes the weapon used to kill John Mills as a "scantling.")

13. The ineffectiveness of the police was widely remarked upon in the press and later by the coroner's jury. Stories that they "were all fixed and told to lay off on club members" come from *TNIC*, p. 12. The arrest of Joseph Scott as per ibid., p. 659.

14. The unusually aggressive self-defense of blacks in the riot was a recurrent theme in much of the press coverage, particularly in the black weeklies. The *CDN* of July 28 reported the crowd at Thirty-fifth and State as three hundred; Tuttle, *Race Riot*, p. 40, puts it at four thousand (admittedly, the crowds in this location grew throughout the evening). The rumored invasion of the Black Belt by "an army of whites" as per Tuttle, *Race Riot*, p. 40. The killing of Casmere Lazzeroni as described in *TNIC*, p. 663. Eugene Temple's murder as described in ibid., p. 658.

15. The carloads of whites firing at random as per Tuttle, *Race Riot*, p. 40. Edward Dean Sullivan's ordeal was described by him in his book *Rattling the Cup on Chicago Crime*, pp. 1–7.

16. The Angelus incident is most reliably described in *TNIC*, pp. 6, 661–62. The shooting went on for ten minutes according to the *CD* of August 2.

17. That the white gangs seemed to be focusing on the contested neighborhoods with black newcomers is emphasized by Tuttle, *Race Riot*, p. 41; Philpott, *Slum and the Ghetto*, p. 170; and *TNIC*, p. 6.

18. For the aldermen urging suspension of search-and-seizure laws, see the *CEP* of July 28. George Harding's reassuring quotation after his tour of the riot zone was cited in the *CDN* of July 28.

19. The carefully worded text of Thompson's telegram was reprinted in the *CDT* of July 29. *TNIC*, p. 41, breaks down the groups from the Illinois National Guard and those from the state's reserve militia; both groups were typically referred to interchangeably as "the militia."

20. Details about Sterling Morton's experience come principally from two sources—a letter he wrote to his cousin, Wirt Morton, dated August 11, 1919, and a memoir, "The Illinois Reserve During World War I and After," writ-

ten decades later (both in the Sterling Morton Papers at the Chicago History Museum). The quote about the need for the militia being greater after the war is from the memoir, p. 5.

21. Morton's history as per "Illinois Reserve During World War I and After," pp. 5–7, his biography in the Sterling Morton Papers, Joy Sterling Morton's entry in Ingham, *Biographical Dictionary of American Business Leaders,* and the *Fifth Year Record: Class of 1906, Princeton* (Princeton University Press, 1912). The story about choosing the Morton Salt girl comes from an anonymous article in *Kiplinger's Personal Finance* (September 1959), p. 42.

22. The scene in the Loop as described in Morton's letter of August 11 and "Illinois Reserve During World War I and After," pp. 7–9.

23. "Get in my cab" is from Morton, "Illinois Reserve During World War I and After," p. 8. "I saw sights that I never shall forget" is from the letter of August 11. Other details from the memoir, pp. 7–9.

24. "The South Side is a seething cauldron of hate" is from the *CEP* of July 28. The Horace Jennings episode was described in both Tuttle, *Race Riot,* p. 43, and *TNIC,* pp. 38–39.

25. The "grossly unfair" conduct of the police as per *TNIC,* p. 599. See also pp. 34–35. For any white person in uniform as a target, see the *CDT* of July 28.

26. Emily Frankenstein describes her father's close call in her diary, p. 201. The man shot while eating dinner comes from the *CDT* of July 28. Lucius Harper described his harrowing experience in the *CD* of August 2.

27. The number of dead and wounded at the end of the second day of rioting as per Tuttle, *Race Riot,* p. 44. The results of the strike vote and the shutting down of the streetcar and elevated systems were ubiquitously reported.

CHAPTER SEVENTEEN: TUESDAY, JULY 29

1. "I stood up in a truck" and "Oh mother, here comes the lion's cage" are from the *CEP* of July 29. "Never in the history of the city has such a condition prevailed" was quoted in the *CDN* of July 29. All of the other details in these paragraphs come from the same two papers.

2. The *NYT* of July 30 reported that half a million Chicago commuters stayed home. For the stockyards and municipal employees, see Tuttle, *Race Riot,* p. 44. "Snipers, white as well as black" is from the *CEP* of July 29. Edward W. Jackson's death as per *TNIC,* pp. 658–59. The shooting of Parejko and Maminaki is from ibid., pp. 664–65. The absence of larger mobs on Tuesday was noted in the *CDT* of July 30. For the prowling group of twelve black soldiers, see the *CDN* of July 29. "This is the most serious problem that has ever confronted the police department in Chicago" was quoted in the *CDJ* of July 29.

3. Three officers and one sergeant in the Loop as per *TNIC*, pp. 36–38. For the cited incidents in the Loop, see ibid., pp. 19, 666.

4. "The race riots are spreading" is from Florence Lowden's diary for July 29 (Pullman-Miller Family Papers). Calls for martial law as per the *CDN* of July 29.

5. Lowden's abrupt return to Chicago was noted in the *CDT* and *CDJ* of July 29. "I cannot say who is responsible for this situation" was quoted in the *CDN* of July 29.

6. For Dickson's upbeat assessment, see the *CEP* of July 29.

7. The joint news conference of the mayor and the governor was covered by all of the papers. The quotations in this section are as they were reported in the *CDN* and *CDJ* of July 29.

8. For the prison riot, I have relied most heavily on reports in the *CEP* and *CDN* ("Look here, I'm not going to give you more than a minute") of July 29.

9. The sixty armed detectives around city hall as per the *CDT* of July 30. For the far-fetched rumors, see *TNIC*, p. 33, and White, "Causes of the Chicago Race Riot." The *CD* story of the alleged murder of the black woman and her baby appeared in the August 2 edition.

10. For the press distortions, see especially West, "Press Coverage of Urban Violence, 1903–1967." See also Tuttle, *Race Riot,* p. 47, and *TNIC*, p. 26, for discrepancies over the numbers of killed and wounded.

11. For police distortions (seventy-five police dead; "For God's sake, arm [yourselves]"), see Tuttle, *Race Riot,* p. 48. *TNIC*, p. 35, compares the relative number of black and white arrests and casualties. The incident of the arrested and released light-skinned black man ("You'll probably need this before the night is over") is recounted in West, "Press Coverage of Urban Violence, 1903–1967," p. 50.

12. For the North Side gunfight, see the *CDT* of July 30. Threats to household staff are from Tuttle, *Race Riot,* p. 50. *TNIC*, p. 659, reports on the death of Joseph Lovings and the newspapers' exaggeration of it.

13. "While all sensible people" is a quote from Sterling, *Black Foremothers,* pp. 112–13. For Wells-Barnett's other activities during the first days of the riot, see the *CDT* of July 30. Her letter ("Free Chicago stands today humble before the world") appeared on the front page of the *CDJ* of July 29.

14. The *Broad Ax* accusation was reported in the *NYT* of July 30. The quotation from the *CDN* editorial appeared in the July 29 issue.

15. The *CDJ* of July 29 blamed the mayor and police for their failure to protect the city's children. "We have other Fitzgeralds; we have other little Janet Wilkinsons" comes from an editorial in the *CEP* of July 29.

16. "Vast Throng Weeps at Slain Girl's Bier" is from the *CDN* of July 29. Reverend Phelan's and John Wilkinson's quotations were reported in the *CDJ* of July 29.

17. Details of the funeral service and burial in this paragraph come from the *CEP* of July 29.

18. The *CDN* of July 29 wondered aloud how everyone had gotten to the Wilkinson funeral. Denial of strikebreaker rumors as per the *CEP* of July 29. "The fire will have to die out of the men" was quoted in the *CDJ* of July 29. "The compromise was liberal" as reported in the *CDT* of July 29. "The majority of our employees" as per the *NYT* of July 30.

19. The *NYT* of July 30 also reported that the plan was "hooted down." The mayor's quotations in this paragraph are from the *CDT* of July 29.

20. Strikers setting a streetcar on fire as per the *CDN* of July 29. For Hoyne's meeting with Lowden, see Dobbert, "History of the Chicago Race Riot of 1919," p. 62.

21. "Everyone cheered themselves hoarse," "I did my best to put some pep into them," and "For political reasons, we were kept in the armory" are from Morton's August 11 letter to Wirt Morton (Sterling Morton Papers).

22. The spike in nonfatal shootings of police was reported in the *CDT* of July 30. For the shot-out streetlights, see Tuttle, *Race Riot,* p. 50. The *CDT* of July 30 reported on the Provident Hospital incident and the rise in arson.

23. "Our men are all ready" was quoted in the *CEP* of July 29. The late-night conference and the quotations from Thompson ("I am going to go home") and Righeimer ("There are a half-dozen cases on record") are from the *CDT* of July 30.

24. Sandburg's report on the meeting of the Olivet Protective Association and his interview with George C. Hall appeared in that evening's *CDN* of July 29. The text of the poem "Hoodlums" is from Sandburg, *Complete Poems,* p. 201. For Sandburg's composition of this poem, see also Yanella, *Other Carl Sandburg,* p. 144.

CHAPTER EIGHTEEN: WEDNESDAY, JULY 30

1. Excerpts from Emily Frankenstein's diary come from pp. 199–201 (Emily Frankenstein Papers).

2. Death toll by Wednesday morning as per the *CHE* of July 30. "Mayor Refuses Assent to Martial Law" is from the *CDJ* of July 30; "Storm Mayor with Demand for Troops to Quell Race Riots" is from the same day's *CDN.*

3. For the appearance of the South Side, see the *CDN* of July 30. Police cordoning off the Black Belt as per the *NYT* of July 31. The July 30 *CDT* mentions the four hundred crossing guards, while the *CSM* of July 31 reports on the closing of many Loop businesses.

4. "Frank is living through the most anxious days of his life so far" is from Florence Lowden's diary entry for July 30. Hoyne's announcement of his request for martial law as per the *CHE* of July 31. "The troops are to be had for the asking" is quoted in the *CDJ* of July 30. "If we were to order out the militia for riot duty" is as recorded in the *CEP* of July 30.

5. The incident seen from Lowden's window, with quotations, as reported in the *NYT* of July 31.

6. Ed Wright's advice not to call in troops as per "Report on the Chicago Riot by an Eye-Witness," p. 12, published in the *Messenger* of October 1919. The delegation of black leaders is described in the *CDT* of July 31; the second delegation (which included Darrow, Rosenwald, and Sandburg) comes from the *CDJ* of July 30.

7. Details of the city council meeting in these paragraphs, including all dialogue, come from the *CDJ* and *CDN* of July 30. For McDonough as Daley's mentor (and for his prodigious weight), see Cohen and Taylor, *American Pharaoh*, p. 39.

8. Again, all details and dialogue in this section come from the July 30 *CDJ* and *CDN*, except for one exchange ("Don't you believe the militia should supplement the police?"), which is rendered here as reported in the *CHE* of July 31. For the one thousand special policemen, see also Tuttle, *Race Riot*, pp. 51–53.

9. Hoyne's statement about the "secret order of Negroes" as per the *CDN* of July 30. That day's *CDJ* mentioned Brundage's curtailed vacation in Michigan. Brundage's statements in this paragraph as reported in the *CDN* of July 30.

10. The *CDT* editorial appeared in the July 29 edition. "That may be unconstitutional, but we should not waste time over details" was quoted in the *CHE* of July 30.

11. Thompson's first quotation in this paragraph comes from the *CDT* of July 31. His second ("Yes, the situation is better") is from the *CEP* of July 30. The third ("The rookie police are doing wonderfully well") is from the *CDT* of July 31. The arrival of W. D. Mahon as reported in the *CDN* of July 30. Hopes that the cars would be running by Thursday were noted in the *CDJ* of July 30.

12. The coroner's inquest report on the riot deaths was later published as a booklet (see Hoffman, *Biennial Report 1918–1919 and Official Record*, in bibliography). The inquest jurors' trip through the South Side as per the *CEP* of July 30 and the *CHE* of July 31. "My people have no food" is quoted in Tuttle, *Race Riot*, p. 54. The forbidden deliveries as per the *NYT* of July 30. Rumors of a full-scale invasion by Ragen's Colts are mentioned in Tuttle, *Race Riot*, p. 55.

13. "This Is Chicago's Crisis" is from the *CA* of July 30, as cited in *TNIC*, p. 44. General Dickson's assessment ("The condition is very grave") is from the *CHE* of July 31.

14. Location of clashes, and the roaming white mobs, as per the *NYT* of July 31. The 112 fire alarms were reported in the *CDT* of July 31. Philpott, *Slum and the Ghetto*, pp. 173–74, describes the scene on Wells Street. For the late report and Thompson's official request to Dickson, see the *CSM* and *CDT* of July 31, the latter of which printed the full text of the letter.

CHAPTER NINETEEN: THURSDAY, JULY 31

1. For the description of the militiamen heading out into the streets, I have relied on reports in the *CDT* and *CDN* of July 31. The contrast between the police and the militia are discussed in *TNIC*, p. 42. Using guns only as a last resort is as per Tuttle, *Race Riot*, p. 55.

2. For the Sterling Morton episode and all quotes therein, I have relied on the two unpublished documents in the collection of the Chicago History Museum (Sterling Morton Papers).

3. For other confrontations the nights of July 30–31, see the *CDN* of July 31. "You soldiers don't know how glad we all are you are here" was quoted in the *CDJ* of July 31. For the truckloads of food sent into the Black Belt, see the *CDN* of July 31. "Thank God! We can't stand up under this much longer" and "We are tickled to death to see you" were quoted in *TNIC*, p. 42.

4. For the free rein given the athletic clubs, see *TNIC*, p. 42, and Pacyga, "Chicago's 1919 Race Riot," p. 217. For the confrontation at the stockyards, see the *CEP* of July 31 and Tuttle, *Race Riot*, p. 57. Details of Dozier's death are from *TNIC*, p. 667. "Peace has been established" was quoted in the *CEP* of July 31.

5. Thompson's press conference at city hall was covered by all of the newspapers; the quotations in this section are as rendered in the *CDJ* of July 31 and the *CHE* of August 1.

6. The stretched cables across the street as per the *NYT* of August 1. For the pressure from the meatpacking companies, see Tuttle, *Race Riot*, p. 54. See also Pacyga, *Chicago*, p. 211.

7. The emergency city council meeting was also widely covered. I have used the quotations as they appeared in the *CDJ* of July 31 ("More policemen, more vehicle equipment," etc., and "The finance committee has spent many nights"), the *CDN* of July 31 ("The crisis through which our city has passed"), and the *CDT* of August 1 ("It was claimed [that] Prohibition would reduce the need for police").

8. For Hoyne's promise of vigorous prosecution, see the *NYT* of July 31. "Why?" is from the *CDJ* of July 31, while "War in a Great City's Streets" is from the same day's *CDN*. "Chicago is disgraced and dishonored" is (famously) from the *CDT* of July 31.

9. "[Frank] is receiving great commendation" is from Florence Lowden's diary entry for July 31. "I shudder to think what might have happened Tuesday" was quoted in the *CDJ* of July 31.

10. Mahon's arrangement of a second strike vote as per the *CEP* of July 31.

11. For the ban on "promiscuous aviation," see the *CDN* of July 31. The same day's *CDT* reported on a plan to convert the epileptics' hospital into "an institution for morons." For the Chicago Plan ordinance signing, I have relied most heavily on the reports in the *CDN* of July 31 and the *CDT* of August 1.

CHAPTER TWENTY: THE MORNING AFTER

1. The *CEP* of August 2 carried details on the resumption of L and streetcar service.

2. For the sporadic violence on the South Side on Friday, see the *CDN* of August 1. "There is a quieter feeling in Chicago today" is from Florence Lowden's diary for August 1 (Pullman-Miller Family Papers). The closing of gathering places in the riot zone and the suppression of the *Chicago Whip* as per the *NYT* of August 2. The *CDT* of August 3 reported on the thousand new deputy sheriffs. "I am greatly impressed with the complete mastery of the situation" was quoted in the *CDN* of August 1.

3. The Saturday morning fire was ubiquitously reported in the newspapers. Sterling Morton's experience is related in his August 11 letter ("In twelve minutes I had the company loaded") and in his memoir ("The residents were very excited"). (NB: In the memoir, written decades later, Morton puts the time of the alarm at 2:35 a.m., but the time given in his letter is more likely accurate.) Details about the "hundreds of scantily clad persons" are from the *CEP* of August 2.

4. For rumors about groups of black men using railroad torches, see the *CDJ* of August 2. For those about IWW radicals, see the *CDT* of August 3. For Poles hostile to their Lithuanian neighbors, see Bukowski, *Big Bill Thompson,* pp. 99–100. For the ultimate attribution to white athletic clubs, see the *CDN* of August 2; see also Pacyga, "Chicago's 1919 Race Riot," p. 200, about the relative lack of involvement of eastern Europeans in the riot.

5. "The profiteering meat packers of Chicago are responsible" is quoted in Doreski, "Chicago, Race, and the Rhetoric of the 1919 Riot," pp. 295–97. "The wealthy have their cellars full" is from John Fitzpatrick of the CFL, as quoted in Tuttle, *Race Riot,* p. 241. For the quotation about "the fact that the masses have forsaken God," see the *CDJ* of July 31. "You Northern folks don't know how to get along" was quoted in the *CEP* of August 1.

6. "U.S. Seeks Hand of Bolsheviki in Race Riots" was in the *CDT* of August 3. For Wells-Barnett's testimony before the federal investigators, including her quotation, see the *CDT* of August 3 and her own *Crusade for Justice,* p. 406. For deeper background on postwar investigations into black radicalism by the DOJ's Bureau of Investigation (as well as by the army's Military Intelligence Division), see Kornweibel, *Seeing Red.* "America is known the world over as the land of the lyncher" is from the *CD* of August 2.

7. For Hoyne's fulminations ("City Hall organization leaders, black and white, have catered to the vicious element"), see Tuttle, *Race Riot,* p. 252. For the editorial from *Dziennik Chicagoski,* see Pacyga's *Polish Immigrants and Industrial Chicago,* p. 225.

8. Lowden's big-picture analysis is as per articles in the *NYT* of August 3 and the *CEP* of August 4. For the formation of the biracial commission, see the *NYT* of August 2; Hutchinson, *Lowden of Illinois,* pp. 405–6; and Bukowski, *Big Bill Thompson,* p. 99. For the selection of Lawson and Rosenwald, see Tuttle, *Race Riot,* p. 258.

9. The article from the *Memphis Commercial Appeal* is quoted in Bukowski, *Big Bill Thompson,* pp. 101–2. "Chicago's Shame" was reprinted in the *CDT* of August 3. Wilson's quotation ("a failure of the civic authorities") was quoted in Bontemps and Conroy, *Anyplace but Here,* p. 183.

10. "The recent regrettable disorders in Chicago" is from the *Republican* of August 9.

11. For the Thompson administration's outrage at the apparent quid pro quo of the transit compromise, and the conference with Ettelson, see the *CEP* and *CDJ* of August 2.

12. Lowden's praise for Chicago's "admirable patience" was quoted in the *CEP* of August 2. The details of his journey to Sinnissippi ("very tired, of course, but not as worn-out as I had feared") are from Florence Lowden's diary entry for August 2 (Pullman-Miller Family Papers).

CHAPTER TWENTY-ONE: TO THE LAST DITCH

1. Lowden's return to the city as recorded in his wife's diary for August 4. Cleveland's official notice and other details about the Thompson administration's response are from the *CDJ* and *CEP* of August 4, 5, and 6.

2. Thompson's telegram as per the *CDT* of August 6. "Vicious public holdup," "corporate cooties," and "toadies" as quoted in Hutchinson, *Lowden of Illinois,* p. 402. "Solemn contracts with the people" is from the *Republican* of August 16. "The people of Chicago may rest assured" was quoted in the *CDT* of August 8.

3. For Lowden's response to the attacks, and subsequent petitions and court reversals, see Hutchinson, *Lowden of Illinois,* pp. 402–3. Cleveland's announcement as per the *CDT* of August 9. The threat to impound fares and seize control of the lines as per the *CDJ* of August 16.

4. "When you pay seven cents today" and all other quotations in this paragraph are from the *CDJ* of August 8.

5. "It is futile for the people to expect representative government" was quoted in the *CDJ* of August 9.

6. Lowden's condemnation of the plan as "state socialism" as per Hutchinson, *Lowden of Illinois,* p. 403. "The present proposal is simply a bald-headed fraud" is quoted from a letter from Lawson to Charles H. Dennis dated September 20 (Victor F. Lawson Papers, series 1, box 89, folder 166).

7. For the sad history of Chicago's quest to control its own transit system, see especially Young, *Chicago Transit.*

8. "All the shades of black" is from the *CEP* of August 8, as quoted in Waskow, *From Race Riot to Sit-in,* p. 45. For the jury "strike," see Tuttle, *Race Riot,* p. 254 ("What the [hell] is the matter with the State's Attorney?") and the *CDJ* of August 16 (jury members' threat to gather evidence on their own).

9. "The State's Attorney will do his duty" was quoted in the *CDJ* of August 16. For the statements about the "large quantities of firearms, deadly weapons, and ammunition," see the *Literary Digest* of August 9. For Hoyne's raids in the Black Belt, see the *CDN* of August 23. "These raids are the beginning of revelations" was quoted in the *CDJ* of August 23.

10. "State's Attorney Runs Amok" was in the *CD* of September 6. For Darrow and the NAACP, see Waskow, *From Race Riot to Sit-in,* pp. 48–50. The NAACP's statement was quoted in the *Cleveland Advocate* of August 16. For the gathering at the Eighth Regiment Armory, see the *CD* of September 6. For Wells-Barnett's response to the "storm-trooper" raids, see *Crusade for Justice,* p. 407, and Giddings, *Ida,* p. 602 ("[Hoyne] sends his hand-picked confederates"). For Hoffman's and Peters's objections, see the *CDN* of August 25. Brundage's admission as per Hutchinson, *Lowden of Illinois,* p. 405.

11. "We cannot dodge the fact that whites and blacks will not mix" was quoted in the *CEP* of July 31. For the letter from the Hyde Park–Kenwood Property Owners' Association, see the *CDT* of August 6. "The sooner the Negro realizes" was in the *CDN* of August 2.

12. For the special city council meeting, with quoted wording of the resolution, I have relied mostly on the report in the *CDT* of August 6.

13. For Cotter's and Thompson's accusations against the governor, see Hutchinson, *Lowden of Illinois,* p. 405. "Segregation measures are in the air" is from the November 15 issue of the *Chicago Whip,* quoted in Homel, *Down from Equality,* p. 21. Lowden's approving mention of the "common understanding" idea is from the *CDN* of August 1.

14. For events at the stockyards and environs ("heavy guards about the L stations"), see the *CDT* of August 7. The job action by unionized white stockyards workers as per the *CDT* of August 8. For Thompson's official letter and the end of the riot, see the *CDJ* of August 9 and Tuttle, *Race Riot,* p. 64.

15. Morton's new commission and his quote ("I shudder to think") are from his letter of August 11. The scene with Lowden and Dickson at city hall comes from the *CDJ* of August 9 and Tuttle, *Race Riot,* p. 64.

CHAPTER TWENTY-TWO: "THROW AWAY YOUR HAMMER
AND PICK UP A HORN!"

1. For the Sandburgs' new house in Elmhurst, see Sandburg, *Great and Glorious Romance,* p. 276, and Niven, *Carl Sandburg,* pp. 342–45. "Why should I be

the only poet of misery to be keeping out of debt?" is from a September 26 letter to Alice Corbin Henderson (Sandburg Papers). "We mustn't let our anxiety" is quoted in Niven, *Carl Sandburg,* p. 345.

2. Details about the Lardners' moving on come from Yardley, *Ring,* pp. 209, 221. Jane Addams's speaking tour as per Davis, *American Heroine,* p. 260. For the Emma Simpson crime and trial, I have relied on various articles in the *CDT* dating from April 27 to October 3. Darrow's quotation ("You've been asked to treat a man and a woman the same—but you can't") was cited in the *CDT* of September 26.

3. The story of Emily's romance as per her diary (Emily Frankenstein Papers). (NB: Her diary says that she and Jerry reestablished contact on the second day of the riot; however, since she mentions that the streetcar strike was on that day, it was apparently the third day of the riot.)

4. For the subsequent bombings in 1919 and 1920, see Tuttle, *Race Riot,* p. 250. Thompson's (temporary) revocation of the athletic club charters is discussed in Lindberg, *Chicago by Gaslight,* p. 209. Tuttle, *Race Riot,* p. 255, discusses the rumors of more riots.

5. For the Olivet Protective Association incident ("I rose and laid my membership card on the table"), see Wells-Barnett, *Crusade for Justice,* p. 407. Indictments and convictions in the riot cases as per *TNIC,* p. 48; see also Giddings, *Ida,* p. 622.

6. For background on the Red Scare and the Palmer raids, see especially Kornweibel, *Seeing Red,* as well as Murray, *Red Scare.*

7. The most popular work on the Black Sox scandal is Asinof, *Eight Men Out.* For Lardner's role in the episode, I have relied mostly on Yardley, *Ring,* pp. 211–18.

8. Fitzgerald's journey through the criminal justice system as per articles in the *CDT, CDN,* and *CDJ* of August 4, August 18, and September 23 ("as in a daze" and "If you have any idea the court will not inflict the death penalty"). The courtroom filled with "morbidly curious men and women," and the sentencing scene that follows, with quotations, are from the *CDT* of September 24.

9. For the episodes leading up to Fitzgerald's execution, I have relied on reports in the *CDT* of October 5, 14, 17, and 18.

10. For Thompson's peaking popularity, see Stuart, *20 Incredible Years,* pp. 88–91. For the Boom Chicago campaign, see Bukowski, *Big Bill Thompson,* pp. 108–10, and Wendt and Kogan, *Big Bill of Chicago,* pp. 176–77.

11. For one of the special newspaper supplements, see the *CEP* of August 30; see also Stuart, *20 Incredible Years,* pp. 85–88. The Burnham remark ("Beauty has always paid better than any other commodity and always will") was quoted in Bachin, *Building the South Side,* p. 171. For the passing of the bond issues, see Smith, *Plan of Chicago,* p. 124, and Stuart, *20 Incredible Years,* p. 88. The

Bukowski quotation about concrete is from his essay in Green and Holli, *Mayors,* p. 80.

12. For the school board controversy and other distracting issues, see Wendt and Kogan, *Big Bill of Chicago,* p. 175ff, and Bukowski, *Big Bill Thompson,* p. 105ff. Bukowski, ibid., p. 185, is especially good on the real meaning behind Thompson's tirades against King George and the war profiteers.

13. For Thompson's success at getting money for his municipal ownership study, see the Twenty-fifth Annual Preliminary Report (1920) of the Municipal Voters' League (Chicago History Museum). The *Defender's* praise of the elevation of Ed Wright appeared in the *CD* of December 27.

14. For the extent of Thompson's predominance in the fall of 1919, see the *CDT* of September 30. The quotation about Lundin's push for a "vise-like" grip on the county and state is from Bright, *Hizzoner Big Bill Thompson,* p. 166. For the targeting of Lowden, see Stuart, *20 Incredible Years,* p. 92.

CHAPTER TWENTY-THREE: THE SMOKE-FILLED ROOM

1. Much has been written about the 1920 Republican National Convention. In addition to works already cited (especially Hutchinson, *Lowden of Illinois;* Stuart, *20 Incredible Years;* and Wendt and Kogan, *Big Bill of Chicago*), I have relied most heavily on Pietrusza, *1920,* and Sullivan's *Our Times,* along with Dean's respectful *Warren G. Harding* and Anthony's gossipy *Florence Harding.* See Pietrusza, *1920,* pp. 219–21, for the shifting delegate votes. Both the Ferber and the Mencken quotations are from ibid., pp. 205 and 206, respectively.

2. For the Lowden "steamroller," see the *NYT* of June 11, 1920. For General Wood's lack of second-choice support, see Hutchinson, *Lowden of Illinois,* p. 458.

3. For Lowden's early hopes for Thompson's support, see Hutchinson, *Lowden of Illinois,* p. 411.

4. For early hints that Thompson would work against Lowden's nomination, see an interview with the mayor in the *NYT* of December 13. Hutchinson, *Lowden of Illinois,* p. 442, talks about the issues Thompson raised against Lowden, and the latter's liability in being married to the daughter of a great capitalist.

5. For primary results and Thompson's control of seventeen Illinois delegates, see especially Wendt and Kogan, *Big Bill of Chicago,* pp. 179–80.

6. The Lowden finance scandal is most completely discussed in Hutchinson, *Lowden of Illinois,* p. 453ff. The quotation is from ibid., p. 455.

7. Big Bill's bad-mouthing of Lowden ("His word's no good") is from Wendt and Kogan, *Big Bill of Chicago,* pp. 182–83.

8. Thompson's dramatic public scene as per ibid., p. 183. "It is my opinion that if the delegates to the Republican State Convention had known" is quoted in the *NYT* of June 11, 1920.

9. The *CA* story—under the blaring headline "Mayor Bolts Republican Party: Refuses to Aid in Sale of Presidency"—appeared in a June 12, 1920, special extra edition. For the ordering of a "wagonload" of newspapers, the instructions to the woman in the pink dress ("Don't let anyone stop you"), and the "dazzling smile" quotation, see Stuart, *20 Incredible Years*, pp. 100–104.

10. The timing of Henry Cabot Lodge's receipt of the newspaper as per Stuart, *20 Incredible Years*, p. 103.

11. "In a smoke-filled room at the Blackstone Hotel" is from Ferber's memoir, *Peculiar Treasure*, p. 251. Dean, *Warren G. Harding*, and especially Pietrusza, *1920*, p. 226, express doubts about the traditional explanation of the choice of Harding as the result of a conspiracy among a few powerful men. For Lowden's release of his delegates, see the *NYT* of June 13, 1920. Dean, *Warren G. Harding*, p. 67, quotes the same paper's characterization of Harding as "a very respectable Ohio politician of the second class." Mencken's more biting description ("of the intellectual grade of an aging cockroach") is cited in Pietrusza, *1920*, p. 235.

12. Florence Lowden and her daughter Florence Lowden Miller were inveterate diarists. Their many volumes of journals are all in the Pullman-Miller Family Papers at the Chicago History Museum. Quotations here are from the entries of June 12 and 13, 1920.

13. "With bowed head [and] cries of 'bought delegates' and 'steamroller' in his ears" is a quotation from Bright, *Hizzoner Big Bill Thompson*, p. 165. "Of course, while the contest was on, I wanted to win" is from a letter from Lowden to Lucius Teter dated June 24, 1920 (Julius Rosenwald Papers, series 1, box 24, folder 13). "We are very tired" is from Florence Lowden's diary entries for June 13 and 14, 1920.

14. "Bill Thompson exulted" is from Bright, *Hizzoner Big Bill Thompson*, p. 165. For the Edward Dunne quotation, see Stuart, *20 Incredible Years*, p. 107. (NB: It should be mentioned, however, that Mark Sullivan, who was an eyewitness to the convention, does not even name Thompson in his account of the event.) "What a great President he would have been!" is from Morton, "Illinois Reserve During World War I and After," p. 5.

15. Lowden's retirement announcement as per the *CDT* of June 30, 1920. For Lowden's later career and his subsequent failure to hold any other elective office, see Hutchinson, *Lowden of Illinois*, pp. 570–601.

16. For Thompson and Lundin's ambitious agenda in the November 1920 elections, see Wendt and Kogan, *Big Bill of Chicago*, p. 184. Lowden's quotation ("Thompson has developed a machine") was cited in the *NYT* of July 18, 1920.

17. "I never did understand the politics of that town" is quoted in Stuart, *20 Incredible Years*, p. 118. "A ferret-faced Kankakee banker" is from Smith, *Colonel,*

p. 241. For Lundin's control of thirty-eight thousand offices and a $78 million payroll, see a memoir by Robert R. McCormick about Lundin (Robert R. McCormick Papers, I-63, box 20) and Bright, *Hizzoner Big Bill Thompson.*

18. For the victory celebrations on election night, with quotations, see Bright, *Hizzoner Big Bill Thompson,* p. 166, and Wendt and Kogan, *Big Bill of Chicago,* pp. 188–90.

EPILOGUE: THE TWO CHICAGOS

1. The opening of the Michigan Avenue Bridge was covered by all of the newspapers, but my account relies most heavily on an eyewitness account in Williamson, *I Met an American.* "The greatest event since the World's Fair in 1893" is from Bright, *Hizzoner Big Bill Thompson,* pp. 167–68. Thompson's expression of "gravity and pleased emotion" as per Williamson, *I Met an American,* p. 50. Quote from Thompson's speech as per Bukowski, *Big Bill Thompson,* p. 110.

2. Accounts of gangland Chicago in the 1920s—particularly anything having to do with Al Capone—must be regarded with extreme skepticism. A lot of colorful apocrypha has accumulated around those storied years, and much of it gets repeated from book to book as if it were gospel truth. The detail about the three photos on Capone's wall, for instance, was attested to by a single, not-particularly-disinterested witness, but has been uncritically repeated by historians for the better part of a century (which is why I phrase my sentence about that detail with caution). Bergreen, *Capone,* is probably the most reliable account of those years.

3. Information on the later lives of Lardner, Addams, and Sandburg is from Yardley, *Ring*; Davis, *American Heroine*; and Niven, *Carl Sandburg,* respectively. Edmund Wilson's characterization of Sandburg's Lincoln biography ("the cruelest thing that has happened to Lincoln since he was shot by Booth") was cited in Niven, *Carl Sandburg,* p. 635.

4. Wells-Barnett's own account of the closing of the Negro Fellowship League is in her *Crusade for Justice,* p. 414. Drake and Cayton, *Black Metropolis,* p. 69, and Kellogg, *NAACP,* p. 238, both discuss the new awareness of the "Negro problem" among whites. For the settlement house progressives' reaction to the riot, see Philpott, *Slum and the Ghetto,* pp. 273–75. "Conditions in the states had not changed" is from Haywood, *Black Bolshevik,* p. 2. See Philpott, *Slum and the Ghetto,* p. 130, for the city's increasing level of segregation. Other late-life details for Wells-Barnett are from Giddings, *Ida,* pp. 603, 646–47, and 652.

5. Jack Boettner's later career, including the *Graf Zeppelin* episode, comes from Glassman, *Jump!,* pp. 45–46. Goodyear's decision to use helium rather than hydrogen as per Young, *Chicago Aviation,* p. 20. Information about Sterling Morton's later life comes principally from the *CDT* of May 5, 1921 (Caroline's

death) and Morton's obituary in the *NYT* of February 25, 1961. "I am indeed proud" is from "Illinois Reserve During World War I and After," p. 3.

6. Details of the denouement of Emily Frankenstein's romance with Jerry Lapiner are from her diary entries for late 1919 and 1920. Her letter to the *Tribune* about the Apollo moon mission appeared in the *CDT* of December 15, 1969.

7. For Hoyne's misadventures in private life, see the *CDT* of January 21, 1925, and February 19, 1939. Merriam quit trying for elective office, but did later serve as an adviser to Presidents Hoover and Roosevelt. Crowe's threat to buy Lawson "a railroad ticket to the penitentiary at Joliet" is from Wendt and Kogan, *Big Bill of Chicago,* p. 188. Dennis, *Victor Lawson,* pp. 449–50, outlines Lawson's contribution to modern newspaper journalism.

8. For McCormick's quest to tie Big Bill to the German secret service, see his letters to Arthur Henning and to Parke Browne, both dated May 10, 1920 (Robert R. McCormick Papers). The Ahab quote is from Smith, *Colonel,* p. 240. For Thompson's assassination accusation, see O'Reilly, "Colonel Robert Rutherford McCormick, His Tribune, and Mayor William Hale Thompson," p. 89. "The people of Illinois have no enthusiasm for Thompsonism, and less for the *Tribune*" is from O'Brien, "Illinois," p. 118.

9. For the end of Lundin's invincibility, see Bright, *Hizzoner Big Bill Thompson,* p. 179–98, and Wendt and Kogan, *Big Bill of Chicago,* pp. 196–98. "My friends have crucified me!" is quoted in ibid., p. 208. "What a change in two years" is from Stuart, *20 Incredible Years,* p. 177.

10. For Lowden as a refuser of nominations and appointments, see Hutchinson, *Lowden of Illinois,* p. 536ff. The quotation about the "worst elements of the party" is cited in a footnote in ibid., p. 470. Stuart, *20 Incredible Years,* p. 108, believes that Lowden's cooperation would have led to the achievement of Lundin's goals.

11. See the previously cited Thompson biographies for his later career. (NB: Bukowski, *Big Bill Thompson,* p. 149, regards Dever's well-meaning mayoralty as "a disaster.") "I'm as wet as the Atlantic Ocean" is ubiquitously cited. For Big Bill's nervous breakdown, see Wendt and Kogan, *Big Bill of Chicago,* pp. 312–13. I am somewhat skeptical of Thompson's cash-stuffed safe-deposit boxes as definitive proof of his venality. Some writers make much of his more than $2 million estate but seem to forget that he inherited a large fortune upon his father's death. And even some of Thompson's enemies claimed that Big Bill often steered ill-gotten money to his friends but rarely to himself.

12. It is, of course, debatable how much credit Thompson can legitimately be given for the many public works completed during his administrations. In my experience, however, too many historians seem to have no trouble giving credit to leaders they admire, while at the same time being reluctant to give any credit at all to leaders they don't.

BIBLIOGRAPHY

BOOKS

Abbott, Karen. *Sin in the Second City: Madams, Ministers, Playboys, and the Battle for America's Soul.* New York: Random House, 2007.

Addams, Jane. *Peace and Bread in Time of War.* 1922. Reprint, New York: Garland, 1945.

———. *The Second Twenty Years at Hull-House.* New York: Macmillan, 1930.

———. *Twenty Years at Hull-House.* 1910. Reprint, New York: Signet, 1961.

Adler, Jeffrey. *First in Violence, Deepest in Dirt: Homicide in Chicago, 1875 to 1920.* Cambridge, MA: Harvard, 2006.

Algren, Nelson. *Chicago: City on the Make.* Oakland, CA: Angel Island, 1961.

Allen, Frederick Lewis. *Only Yesterday: An Informal History of the 1920s.* 1931. Reprint, New York: Bantam, 1959.

Allswang, John M. *Bosses, Machines, and Urban Voters.* Rev. ed. Baltimore: Johns Hopkins, 1986.

———. *A House for All Peoples: Ethnic Politics in Chicago, 1890–1936.* Lexington, KY: University Press of Kentucky, 1971.

Anderson, Alan B., and George W. Pickering. *Confronting the Color Line: The Broken Promise of the Civil Rights Movement in Chicago.* Athens, GA: University of Georgia, 1986.

Anderson, Margaret. *My 30 Years' War: An Autobiography.* Chicago: Covici, Friede, 1930.

Anderson, Philip J., and Dag Blanck. *Swedish-American Life in Chicago: Cultural and Urban Aspects of an Immigrant People, 1850 to 1930.* Champaign, IL: University of Illinois, 1992.

Anthony, Carl Sferrazza. *Florence Harding: The First Lady, the Jazz Age, and the Death of America's Most Scandalous President.* New York: Morrow, 1998.

Ascoli, Peter M. *Julius Rosenwald: The Man Who Built Sears, Roebuck and Advanced the Cause of Black Education in the American South.* Bloomington, IN: Indiana University, 2006.

Asher, Robert, and Charles Stephenson, eds. *Labor Divided: Race and Ethnicity in United States Labor Struggles, 1835–1960.* Albany: SUNY, 1990.

Asinof, Eliot. *Eight Men Out: The Black Sox and the 1919 World Series*. New York: Holt, 1977.

Aylesworth, Thomas G., and Virginia Aylesworth. *Chicago: The Glamour Years, 1919–1941*. New York: Gallery, 1986.

Bachin, Robin F. *Building the South Side: Urban Space and Civic Culture in Chicago, 1890 to 1919*. Chicago: University of Chicago, 2004.

Baldwin, Davarian L. *Chicago's New Negroes: Modernity, the Great Migration, and Black Urban Life*. Chapel Hill, NC: University of North Carolina, 2007.

Behr, Edward. *Prohibition: Thirteen Years That Changed America*. New York: Arcade, 1996.

Bergreen, Laurence. *Capone: The Man and the Era*. New York: Simon & Schuster, 1994.

Berlin, Ira. *The Making of African America: The Four Great Migrations*. New York: Viking, 2010.

Berry, Brian J. L., et al. *Chicago: Transformations of an Urban System*. Cambridge, MA: Ballinger, 1976.

Bluestone, Daniel. *Constructing Chicago*. New Haven, CT: Yale University, 1991.

Boehm, Lisa Krissoff. *Popular Culture and the Enduring Myth of Chicago, 1871–1968*. New York: Routledge, 2004.

Bontemps, Arna, and Jack Conroy. *Anyplace but Here*. New York: Hill and Wang, 1966.

Boskin, Joseph, ed. *Urban Racial Violence in the Twentieth Century*. Beverly Hills, CA: Glencoe, 1976.

Boyle, Kevin. *Arc of Justice: A Saga of Race, Civil Rights, and Murder in the Jazz Age*. New York: Holt, 2004.

Bradbury, Malcolm, and James McFarland, eds. *Modernism: 1890–1930*. New York: Penguin, 1978.

Bright, John. *Hizzoner Big Bill Thompson: An Idyll of Chicago*. New York: Jonathan Cape/Harrison Smith, 1930.

Bukowski, Douglas. *Big Bill Thompson, Chicago, and the Politics of Image*. Urbana, IL: University of Illinois, 1998.

———. *Pictures of Home: A Memoir of Family and City*. Lanham, MD: Ivan R. Dee, 2004.

Butcher, Fanny. *Many Lives, One Love*. New York: Harper and Row, 1972.

Butler, Rush C., ed. *Chicago: The World's Youngest Great City*. Chicago: Chicago Tribune, 1929.

Caruthers, Clifford M., ed. *Letters from Ring*. Flint, MI: Walden Press, 1979.

Chicago Commission on Race Relations. *The Negro in Chicago: A Study of Race Relations and a Race Riot in 1919*. Chicago: University of Chicago, 1922. Reprint, Arno Press, 1968.

Chicago Daily News. *Chicago Daily News Almanac.* Chicago: Chicago Daily News, 1920, 1921.

Chicago Department of City Planning. *The Chicago Plan Commission: A Historical Sketch, 1909 to 1960.* Chicago: Chicago Department of City Planning, 1960.

Chicago Plan Commission. *Chicago's Greatest Issue: An Official Plan.* City of Chicago, 1911.

Cohen, Adam, and Elizabeth Taylor. *American Pharaoh: Mayor Richard J. Daley: His Battle for Chicago and the Nation.* New York: Little, Brown, 2000.

Cohen, Lizabeth. *Making a New Deal: Industrial Workers in Chicago, 1919–1939.* New York: Cambridge University Press, 1990. Rev. ed., 2008.

Condit, Carl W. *Chicago 1910–29: Building, Planning, and Urban Technology.* Chicago: University of Chicago, 1973.

Cromie, Robert. *A Short History of Chicago.* San Francisco: Lexikos, 1984.

Cutler, Irving. *Chicago: Metropolis of the Mid-Continent.* 4th ed. Carbondale, IL: Southern Illinois University, 2006.

Darrow, Clarence. *The Story of My Life.* New York: Scribner's, 1934.

Davis, Allen F. *American Heroine: The Life and Legend of Jane Addams.* New York: Oxford University, 1973.

Dean, John W. *Warren G. Harding.* New York: Times Books, 2004.

Dedmon, Emmett. *Fabulous Chicago: A Great City's History and People.* 2nd ed. New York: Atheneum, 1981.

Deegan, Mary Jo. *Race, Hull-House, and the University of Chicago: A New Conscience Against Ancient Evils.* Westport, CT: Praeger, 2002.

Demuth, James. *Small Town Chicago: The Comic Perspective of Finley Peter Dunne, George Ade, Ring Lardner.* Port Washington, NY: Kennikat Press, 1980.

Dennis, Charles H. *Victor Lawson: His Time and His Work.* Chicago: University of Chicago, 1935.

Dobyns, Fletcher. *The Underworld of American Politics.* New York: Fletcher Dobyns, 1932.

Drake, St. Clair, and Horace R. Cayton. *Black Metropolis: A Study of Negro Life in a Northern City.* 2 vols. New York: Harcourt, 1945. Rev. ed., 1970.

Dubovsky, Melvyn. *We Shall Be All: A History of the Industrial Workers of the World.* Urbana, IL: University of Illinois, 2000.

Duis, Perry R. *Challenging Chicago: Coping with Everyday Life, 1837–1920.* Urbana, IL: University of Illinois, 1998.

———. *The Saloon: Public Drinking in Chicago and Boston, 1880–1920.* Urbana, IL: University of Illinois, 1983. Reprint, Illini Books, 1999.

Elshtain, Jean Bethke. *Jane Addams and the Dream of American Democracy: A Life.* New York: Basic Books, 2002.

Evans, Elizabeth. *Ring Lardner.* New York: Ungar, 1979.

Falloon, William D. *Market Maker: A Sesquicentennial Look at the Chicago Board of Trade*. Chicago: Chicago Board of Trade, 1998.

Ferber, Edna. *A Peculiar Treasure*. New York: Doubleday, 1939.

———. *So Big*. Garden City, NY: Doubleday, 1924.

Fetherling, Doug. *The Five Lives of Ben Hecht*. Toronto: Lester and Orpin, 1977.

Fiske, Barbara Page, ed. *Key to Government in Chicago and Suburban Cook County*. Chicago: University of Chicago, 1989.

Flanagan, Maureen A. *Charter Reform in Chicago*. Carbondale, IL: Southern Illinois University, 1987.

Garb, Margaret. *City of American Dreams: A History of Home Ownership and Housing Reform in Chicago, 1871–1919*. Chicago: University of Chicago, 2005.

Gardiner, John A., and David J. Olson, eds. *Theft of the City: Readings on Corruption in Urban America*. Bloomington, IN: Indiana University, 1974.

Garland, Hamlin. *Companions on the Trail: A Literary Chronicle*. New York: Macmillan, 1931.

Giddings, Paula J. *Ida: A Sword Among Lions*. New York: Amistad, 2008.

———. *When and Where I Enter: The Impact of Black Women on Race and Sex in America*. New York: Morrow, 1984.

Gies, Joseph. *The Colonel of Chicago: A Biography of the Chicago Tribune's Legendary Publisher, Colonel Robert McCormick*. New York: Dutton, 1979.

Gilpin, Patrick J., and Marybeth Gasman. *Charles S. Johnson: Leadership Beyond the Veil in the Age of Jim Crow*. Albany: SUNY Press, 2003.

Glassman, Don. *Jump! Tales of the Caterpillar Club*. New York: Simon & Schuster, 1930.

Golden, Harry. *Carl Sandburg*. Cleveland: World Publishing, 1961.

Gosnell, Harold F. *Machine Politics: Chicago Model*. Chicago: University of Chicago, 1937. 2nd ed., 1968.

———. *Negro Politicians: The Rise of Negro Politics in Chicago*. Chicago: University of Chicago, 1935.

Gottfried, Alex. *Boss Cermak of Chicago: A Study of Political Leadership*. Seattle: University of Washington, 1962.

Green, Paul, and Melvin Holli, eds. *The Mayors: The Chicago Political Tradition*. Carbondale, IL: Southern Illinois University, 1987.

Grimshaw, Allen D., ed. *Racial Violence in the United States*. Chicago: Aldine Publishing, 1969.

Grossman, James R. *Land of Hope: Chicago, Black Southerners, and the Great Migration*. Chicago: University of Chicago, 1989.

Guglielmo, Thomas A. *White on Arrival: Italians, Race, Color, and Power in Chicago, 1890–1945*. New York: Oxford University, 2003.

Hansen, Zenon. *The Goodyear Airships*. Bloomington, IN: Airship International Press, 1977.

Harrison, Carter H. *Stormy Years: The Autobiography of Carter H. Harrison, Five Times Mayor of Chicago*. Indianapolis: Bobbs-Merrill, 1935.

Haywood, Harry. *Black Bolshevik: Autobiography of an Afro-American Communist*. Chicago: Liberator Press, 1978.

Hecht, Ben. *A Child of the Century*. New York: Simon & Schuster, 1954.

———. *Letters from Bohemia*. New York: Doubleday, 1964.

———. *A Thousand and One Afternoons in Chicago*. Chicago: Covici, Friede, 1922.

Herbst, Alma. *The Negro in the Slaughtering and Meat-Packing Industry in Chicago*. New York: Houghton-Mifflin, 1932. Reprint, Arno/New York Times, 1971.

Heyman, Neil M. *Daily Life During World War I*. Westport, CT: Greenwood Press, 2002.

Hines, Thomas S. *Burnham of Chicago: Architect and Planner*. New York: Oxford University, 1974.

Hoffman, Peter M. *Biennial Report 1918–1919 and Official Record: Report of the Coroner's Jury on the Race Riots*. No publisher, 1919.

Holli, Melvin G. *The American Mayor: The Best and Worst Big-City Leaders*. University Park, PA: Pennsylvania State University, 1999.

Holli, Melvin G., and Peter d'A. Jones, eds. *Ethnic Chicago: A Multicultural Portrait*. Grand Rapids, MI: Eerdmans, 4th edition, 1995.

———. *The Ethnic Frontier: Essays in the History of Group Survival in Chicago and the Midwest*. Grand Rapids, MI: Eerdmans, 1977.

Holt, Glen E., and Dominic A. Pacyga. *Chicago: A Historical Guide to the Neighborhoods: The Loop and South Side*. Chicago: Chicago Historical Society, 1979.

Homel, Michael W. *Down from Equality: Black Chicagoans and the Public Schools, 1920–41*. Urbana, IL: University of Illinois, 1984.

Hough, Emerson. *The Web: The Authorized History of the American Protective League*. Chicago: Reilly, 1919. Reprint, Arno Press/New York Times, 1969.

Hughes, Langston. *The Collected Poems of Langston Hughes*. Edited by Arnold Rampersand. New York: Knopf, 1994.

Hutchinson, William T. *Lowden of Illinois: The Life of Frank O. Lowden*. 2 vols. Chicago: University of Chicago, 1957.

Ickes, Harold. *Autobiography of a Curmudgeon*. New York: Reynal and Hitchcock, 1943.

Ingham, John N. *Biographical Dictionary of American Business Leaders*. Vol. 2. Westport, CT: Greenwood Publishing, 1983.

Jablonsky, Thomas J. *Pride in the Jungle: Community and Everyday Life in Back of the Yards Chicago*. Baltimore: Johns Hopkins, 1993.

Jackson, Kenneth, and Stanley K. Schultz, eds. *Cities in American History*. New York: Knopf, 1972.

Jacob, Mark, and Richard Cahan. *Chicago Under Glass: Early Photographs from the Chicago Daily News*. Chicago: University of Chicago, 2007.

Johnson, Curt, and R. Craig Sautter. *Wicked City Chicago: From Kenna to Capone*. Chicago: December Press, 1994.

Kantowicz, Edward. *Polish-American Politics in Chicago, 1888–1940*. Chicago: University of Chicago, 1975.

Karl, Barry D. *Charles E. Merriam and the Study of Politics*. Chicago: University of Chicago, 1974.

Karlen, Harvey M. *The Governments of Chicago*. Chicago: Courier, 1958.

Kellogg, Charles Flint. *NAACP: A History of the National Association for the Advancement of Colored People*. Baltimore: Johns Hopkins, 1967.

Kennedy, David M. *Over Here: The First World War and American Society*. New York: Oxford University, 1980.

Klapper, Melissa R. *Jewish Girls Coming of Age in America, 1860–1920*. New York: NYU, 2005.

Knupfer, Anne Meis. *Toward a Tenderer Humanity and a Nobler Womanhood: African American Women's Clubs in Turn-of-the-Century Chicago*. New York: NYU, 1996.

Kornweibel, Theodore, Jr. *Seeing Red: Federal Campaigns Against Black Militancy, 1919–1925*. Bloomington, IN: Indiana University, 1998.

Kotlowitz, Alex. *Never a City So Real: A Walk in Chicago*. New York: Crown, 2004.

Lardner, Ring, Jr. *The Lardners: My Family Remembered*. New York: Harper, 1976.

Lardner, Ring, Sr. *The Story of a Wonder Man: Being the Autobiography of Ring Lardner*. New York: Scribner's, 1927.

Leidenberger, Georg. *Chicago's Progressive Alliance: Labor and the Bid for Public Streetcars*. DeKalb, IL: Northern Illinois University, 2006.

Leinwand, Gerald. *Mackerels in the Moonlight: Four Corrupt American Mayors*. Jefferson, NC: McFarland, 2004.

Levin, Meyer. *In Search: The Autobiography*. New York: Horizon, 1950.

Lewis, Lloyd, and Henry Justin Smith. *Chicago: A History of Its Reputation*. Garden City, NY: Blue Ribbon Books, 1933.

Liebling, A. J. *Chicago: The Second City*. New York: Knopf, 1952.

Lindberg, Richard. *Chicago by Gaslight: A History of Chicago's Netherworld, 1880–1920*. Chicago: Academy Chicago, 1996.

———. *To Serve and Collect: Chicago Politics and Police Corruption from the Lager Beer Riot to the Summerdale Scandal*. New York: Praeger, 1991.

Lipsky, Michael, and David J. Olson. *Commission Politics: The Processing of Racial Crisis in America*. New Brunswick, NJ: Transaction Books, 1977.

Lissak, Rivka Shpak. *Pluralism and Progressives: Hull House and the New Immigrants, 1890–1919*. Chicago: University of Chicago, 1989.

Luthin, Reinhard H. *American Demagogues: Twentieth Century*. Boston: Beacon Press, 1954.

MacAdams, William. *Ben Hecht: The Man Behind the Legend*. New York: Scribner's, 1990.

MacArthur, Charles. *A Bugs-Eye View of the War*. Oak Park, IL: Pioneer, 1919.

Mark, Norman. *Mayors, Madams, and Madmen*. Chicago: Chicago Review Press, 1979.

Masters, Edgar Lee. *The Tale of Chicago*. New York: Putnam's, 1933.

Mayer, Harold M., and Richard C. Wade. *Chicago: Growth of a Metropolis*. Chicago: University of Chicago, 1969.

McDonald, Forrest. *Insull: The Rise and Fall of a Billionaire Utility Tycoon*. Chicago: University of Chicago, 1962.

McMurry, Linda O. *To Keep the Waters Troubled: The Life of Ida B. Wells*. New York: Oxford University Press, 1999.

McPhaul, John J. *Deadlines and Monkeyshines: The Fabled World of Chicago Journalism*. Englewood Cliffs, NJ: Prentice Hall, 1962. Reprint, Westport, CT: Greenwood, 1973.

———. *Johnny Torrio: First of the Gang Lords*. New Rochelle, NY: Arlington House, 1970.

Merriam, Charles Edward. *Chicago: A More Intimate View of Urban Politics*. New York: Macmillan, 1929.

Merriam, Charles Edward, Spencer D. Parratt, and Albert Lepawsky. *The Government of the Metropolitan Region of Chicago*. Chicago: University of Chicago, 1933.

Merriner, James L. *Grafters and Goo Goos: Corruption and Reform in Chicago, 1833–2003*. Carbondale, IL: Southern Illinois University, 2004.

Miller, Donald L. *City of the Century: The Epic of Chicago and the Making of America*. New York: Simon & Schuster, 1996.

Miller, William D. *Pretty Bubbles: America in 1919*. Urbana, IL: University of Illinois, 1991.

Mitgang, Herbert, ed. *The Letters of Carl Sandburg*. New York: Harcourt, 1968.

Moody, Walter D. *Wacker's Manual of the Plan of Chicago: Municipal Economy*. Chicago: Chicago Plan Commission, 1911.

———. *What of the City? America's Greatest Issue—City Planning*. Chicago: McClurg, 1919.

Morgan, Gwen, and Arthur Veysey. *Poor Little Rich Boy (And How He Made Good): The Life and Times of Col. Robert R. McCormick*. Carpentersville, IL: Crossroads Communications, 1985.

Murray, Robert K. *Red Scare: A Study of National Hysteria, 1919–20*. Minneapolis: University of Minnesota, 1955.

Nelli, Humbert S. *The Business of Crime: Italians and Syndicate Crime in the United States.* New York: Oxford University, 1976.

———. *Italians in Chicago, 1880–1930: A Study in Ethnic Mobility.* New York: Oxford University Press, 1970.

Newell, Barbara Warne. *Chicago and the Labor Movement: Metropolitan Unionism in the 1930s.* Urbana, IL: University of Illinois, 1961.

Niven, Penelope. *Carl Sandburg: A Biography.* New York: Scribner's, 1991.

Okrent, Daniel. *Last Call: The Rise and Fall of Prohibition.* New York: Scribner, 2010.

Ostewig, Kinnie A. *The Sage of Sinnissippi.* Privately printed, 1907.

Ottley, Roi. *The Lonely Warrior: The Life and Times of Robert S. Abbott.* Chicago: Regnery, 1955.

Ovington, Mary White. *Black and White Sat Down Together: The Reminiscences of an NAACP Founder.* Edited by Ralph E. Luker. New York: Feminist Press, 1995.

———. *Portraits in Color.* New York: Viking, 1927.

———. *The Walls Came Tumbling Down.* New York: Harcourt Brace, 1947.

Pacyga, Dominic A. *Chicago: A Biography.* Chicago: University of Chicago, 2009.

———. *Polish Immigrants and Industrial Chicago: Workers on the South Side, 1880–1922.* Columbus, OH: Ohio State University, 1991.

Pacyga, Dominic A., and Ellen Skerrett. *Chicago: City of Neighborhoods.* Loyola University, 1986.

Philpott, Thomas Lee. *The Slum and the Ghetto: Neighborhood Deterioration and Middle-Class Reform, Chicago, 1880–1930.* New York: Oxford University, 1978.

Pietrusza, David. *1920: The Year of Six Presidents.* New York: Carroll and Graf, 2007.

Platt, Anthony, ed. *The Politics of Riot Commissions, 1917–1970.* New York: Macmillan, 1971.

Rakove, Milton L. *Don't Make No Waves, Don't Back No Losers: An Insider's Analysis of the Daley Machine.* Bloomington, IN: Indiana University, 1975.

———. *We Don't Want Nobody Nobody Sent: An Oral History of the Daley Years.* Bloomington, IN: Indiana University, 1979.

Rascoe, Burton. *Before I Forget.* Garden City, NY: Doubleday, Doran, 1937.

Reckless, Walter C. *Vice in Chicago.* Chicago: University of Chicago, 1933.

Rideout, Walter B. *Sherwood Anderson: A Writer in America.* Madison, WI: University of Wisconsin, 2006.

Riordon, William L. *Plunkitt of Tammany Hall.* 1905. Reprint, New York: Dutton, 1963.

Robertson, John Dill. *Report and Handbook of the Department of Health of the City of Chicago for the Years 1911 to 1918 Inclusive.* City of Chicago, 1919.

Rudwick, Elliott M. *Race Riot at East St. Louis, July 2, 1917*. Carbondale, IL: Southern Illinois University, 1964.

Salwak, Dale. *Carl Sandburg: A Reference Guide*. Boston: G. K. Hall, 1988.

Sandburg, Carl. *Always the Young Strangers*. New York: Harcourt, Brace, and Howe, 1953.

———. *The Chicago Race Riots: July 1919*. New York: Harcourt, Brace, and Howe, 1919. Reprint, Harcourt, Brace, and World, 1969.

———. *The Complete Poems*. Rev. ed. New York: Harcourt Brace Jovanovich, 1969, 1970.

Sandburg, Helga. *A Great and Glorious Romance: The Story of Carl Sandburg and Lilian Steichen*. New York: Harcourt Brace Jovanovich, 1978.

Sawyers, June Skinner. *Chicago Sketches: Urban Tales, Stories, and Legends from Chicago History*. Chicago: Wild Onion Books, 1995.

Schechter, Patricia A. *Ida B. Wells-Barnett and American Reform, 1880–1930*. Chapel Hill, NC: University of North Carolina, 2001.

Simpson, Dick. *Rogues, Rebels, and Rubber Stamps: The Politics of the Chicago City Council from 1863 to the Present*. Boulder, CO: Westview, 2001.

Slayton, Robert A. *Back of the Yards: The Making of a Local Democracy*. Chicago: University of Chicago, 1986.

Smith, Carl. *Chicago and the American Literary Imagination, 1880–1920*. Chicago: University of Chicago, 1984.

———. *The Plan of Chicago: Daniel Burnham and the Remaking of the American City*. Chicago: University of Chicago, 2006.

Smith, Henry Justin. *Chicago: A Portrait*. New York: Century, 1931.

Smith, Richard Norton. *The Colonel: The Life and Legend of Robert R. McCormick*. New York: Houghton Mifflin, 1997.

Spear, Allan H. *Black Chicago: The Making of a Negro Ghetto, 1890–1920*. Chicago: University of Chicago, 1967.

Spinney, Robert G. *City of Big Shoulders: A History of Chicago*. DeKalb, IL: Northern Illinois University, 2000.

Stamper, John W. *Chicago's North Michigan Avenue: Planning and Development, 1900–1930*. Chicago: University of Chicago, 1991.

Starrett, Vincent. *Born in a Bookshop: Chapters from the Chicago Renaissance*. Norman, OK: University of Oklahoma, 1965.

Steevens, G. W. *The Land of the Dollar*. New York: Dodd, Mead, 1898.

Steffens, Lincoln. *The Shame of the Cities*. New York: McClure, Phillips, 1904. Reprint, New York: Hill and Wang, 1957.

Steinberg, Ellen FitzSimmons. *Irma: A Chicago Woman's Story, 1871–1966*. Iowa City: University of Iowa, 2004.

Sterling, Dorothy. *Black Foremothers: Three Lives*. 2nd ed. New York: Feminist Press, 1988.

St. John, Robert. *This Was My World*. Garden City, NY: Doubleday, 1953.

Strickland, Avarh E. *History of the Chicago Urban League*. Columbia, MO: University of Missouri, 2001.

Stuart, William. *The 20 Incredible Years*. Chicago: Donohue, 1935.

Sullivan, Edward D. *Chicago Surrenders*. New York: Vanguard, 1930.

———. *Rattling the Cup on Chicago Crime*. New York: Vanguard, 1929.

Sullivan, Mark. *Our Times: The United States, 1920–1925*. Vol. 6, *The Twenties*. New York: Scribner's, 1935.

Taylor, Graham. *Chicago Commons Through Forty Years*. Chicago: Chicago Commons Association, 1936.

Tebbel, John. *An American Dynasty: The Story of the McCormicks, Medills, and Pattersons*. Garden City, NY: Doubleday, 1947.

Terkel, Studs. *Chicago*. New York: Pantheon, 1986.

———. *Touch and Go: An Autobiography*. New York: New Press, 2007.

Thrasher, Frederic M. *The Gang: A Study of 1,313 Gangs in Chicago*. 2nd ed. Chicago: University of Chicago, 1960.

Travis, Dempsey J. *An Autobiography of Black Chicago*. Chicago: Urban Research, 1981.

———. *An Autobiography of Black Politics*. Chicago: Urban Research, 1987.

Tuttle, William M., Jr. *Race Riot: Chicago in the Red Summer of 1919*. New York: Atheneum, 1974.

Ward, Walker. *The Story of the Metropolitan Sanitary District of Chicago: The Seventh Wonder of America*. No publisher, 1956.

Waskow, Arthur I. *From Race Riot to Sit-in, 1919 and the 1960s: A Study in the Connection Between Conflict and Violence*. Garden City, NY: Doubleday, 1966. Reprint, 1967.

Watkins, T. H. *Righteous Pilgrim: The Life and Times of Harold L. Ickes, 1874–1952*. New York: Holt, 1990.

Wells-Barnett, Ida B. *Crusade for Justice: The Autobiography of Ida B. Wells*. Edited by Alfreda M. Duster. Chicago: University of Chicago, 1970.

———. *The Memphis Diary of Ida B. Wells*. Edited by Miriam DeCosta-Willis. Boston: Beacon Press, 1995.

Wendt, Lloyd. *Chicago Tribune: The Rise of a Great American Newspaper*. Chicago: Rand-McNally, 1979.

Wendt, Lloyd, and Herman Kogan. *Big Bill of Chicago*. Reprint. Evanston, IL: Northwestern, 2005.

———. *Lords of the Levee: The Story of Bathhouse John and Hinky Dink*. Indianapolis: Bobbs-Merrill, 1943.

White, William Allen. *Masks in a Pageant*. New York: Macmillan, 1930.

Whitehead, Helen, et al. *The Chicago Plan Commission: A Historical Sketch: 1909–1960*. City of Chicago, 1960.

Wigmore, John H., ed. *The Illinois Crime Survey*. Chicago: Illinois Association for Criminal Justice, 1929.

Wilkerson, Isabel. *The Warmth of Other Suns: The Epic Story of America's Great Migration*. New York: Random House, 2010.

Williams, Lee E., and Lee E. Williams II. *Anatomy of Four Race Riots: Racial Conflict in Knoxville, Elaine (Arkansas), Tulsa, and Chicago, 1919–1921*. Hattiesburg, MS: University and College Press of Mississippi, 1972.

Williamson, J. H. *I Met an American*. Privately printed, 1951.

Willrich, Michael. *City of Courts: Socializing Justice in Progressive Era Chicago*. New York: Cambridge University, 2003.

Yanella, Philip R. *The Other Carl Sandburg*. Jackson, MS: University of Mississippi Press, 1996.

Yardley, Jonathan. *Ring: A Biography of Ring Lardner*. New York: Random House, 1977.

Young, David M. *Chicago Aviation: An Illustrated History*. DeKalb, IL: Northern Illinois University, 2003.

———. *Chicago Transit: An Illustrated History*. DeKalb, IL: Northern Illinois University, 1998.

Zink, Harold. *City Bosses in the United States: A Study of Twenty Municipal Bosses*. Reprint, New York: AMS Press, 1968.

ESSAYS AND ARTICLES

Chenery, William. "Fall of a Mayor." *New Republic,* May 13, 1916.

———. "Politics in Chicago." *New Republic,* March 15, 1919.

"Crime in Chicago." *New Republic,* November 6, 1915.

Davis, Elmer. "Portrait of an Elected Person." *Harper's Magazine,* July 1927.

Doreski, C. K. "Chicago, Race, and the Rhetoric of the 1919 Riot." *Prospects* 18 (1993).

Fisher, Colin. "African Americans, Outdoor Recreation, and the 1919 Chicago Race Riot." In *To Love the Wind and Rain: African Americans and Environmental History,* edited by Dianne D. Glave and Mark Stoll. University of Pittsburgh, 2006.

Hackett, Francis. "Chicago Marks Time." *New Republic,* February 8, 1919.

Lippmann, Walter. "The Logic of Lowden." *New Republic,* April 14, 1920.

Lovett, Robert Morss. " 'Big Bill' Thompson of Chicago." *Current History,* June 1931.

Merz, Charles. "Tammany in Illinois." *New Republic,* September 29, 1920.

O'Brien, Howard Vincent. "Illinois: First Province of the Middle Kingdom." *Nation,* August 22, 1923.

Pacyga, Dominic A. "Chicago's 1919 Race Riot: Ethnicity, Class, and Urban Violence."

In *The Making of Urban America,* edited by Raymond A. Mohl. 2nd ed. SR Books, 1997.

"A Report on the Chicago Riot by an Eye-Witness." *Messenger,* October 1919.

Shottenhamel, George. "How Big Bill Thompson Won Control of Chicago." *Journal of the Illinois State Historical Society* 45 (1952).

Showalter, William Joseph. "Chicago Today and Tomorrow." *National Geographic Magazine,* January 1919.

Smith, Henry Justin. "The Ugly City." *Atlantic Monthly,* July 1919.

Stovall, Mary E. *"The Chicago Defender* in the Progressive Era." *Illinois Historical Journal* 83, no. 3 (Autumn 1990).

Taylor, Graham. "An Epidemic of Strikes in Chicago." *Survey,* August 2, 1919.

Thurner, Arthur W. "The Mayor, the Governor, and the People's Council: A Chapter in American Wartime Dissent." *Journal of the Illinois State Historical Society,* Summer 1973.

White, Walter. "The Causes of the Chicago Race Riot." *Crisis* 18 (October 1919): p. 25.

UNPUBLISHED AND OTHER MATERIAL

Annual Reports of the Chicago Urban League for 1917–1920. Chicago History Museum.

Bukowski, Douglas. "According to Image: William Hale Thompson in the Politics of Chicago, 1915–1931." PhD diss., University of Illinois at Chicago, 1989.

"Catechism: The Truth About Chicago's Financial Condition." Robert R. McCormick Papers.

Chicago City Club Bulletin 12. Chicago History Museum.

Columns. Illinois Trust and Savings Bank, July 1919.

Diamond, Andrew J. "Hoodlums, Rebels, and Vice Lords: Street Gangs, Youth Subcultures, and Race in Chicago, 1919–1968." PhD diss., University of Michigan, 2004.

Dobbert, Guido. "A History of the Chicago Race Riot of 1919." Master's thesis, University of Chicago, 1957.

Hoffmann, George C. "Big Bill Thompson: His Mayoral Campaigns and Voting Strength." Master's thesis, University of Chicago, 1956.

Jones, Robert Huhn. "The Administration of Governor Frank O. Lowden of Illinois, 1917–1921." Master's thesis, University of Illinois at Champaign-Urbana, 1951.

Merriam, Charles E. "An Analysis of Some Political Personalities I Have Known." Lecture 5 from "Six Walgreen Lectures at the University of Chicago, 1948." Charles E. Merriam Papers.

O'Reilly, Alice M. "Colonel Robert Rutherford McCormick, His Tribune, and Mayor William Hale Thompson." Master's thesis, University of Chicago, 1963.

Papers of Frank O. Lowden, Charles E. Merriam, Ida Wells-Barnett, Julius Rosenwald (all University of Chicago); Pullman-Miller Family, Emily Frankenstein,
Sterling Morton, including his memoir, "The Illinois Reserve During World War I
and After" (all Chicago History Museum); Victor F. Lawson, Ring Lardner Sr.,
Graham R. Taylor (all Newberry Library); Robert R. McCormick, Tribune Company (Cantigny); Carl Sandburg (University of Illinois at Champaign-Urbana);
Charles S. Johnson (Fisk University); Irma Rosenthal Frankenstein (Spertus Institute of Jewish Studies); Aldis Family, Edith T. Ross (both University of Illinois at
Chicago); NAACP (on microfilm).

Perkins, DoLen Marie. "Mob Stories: Race, Nation, and Narratives of Racial Violence." PhD diss., George Washington University, 2003.

Rex, Frederick. "William H. Thompson" from "The Mayors of the City of Chicago
from March 4, 1837, to April 13, 1933." Municipal Reference Library, City of
Chicago, 1934.

Schacht, Sylvia. "Newspaper Riot Coverage in 1966 and in 1919." Master's thesis,
University of Illinois at Chicago, 1969.

Schmidt, Royal J. "The *Chicago Daily News* and Illinois Politics, 1876–1920." PhD
diss., University of Chicago, 1957.

A Tragedy with a Laugh. Pamphlet distributed by the William H. Thompson mayoral campaign of 1931. Robert R. McCormick Papers.

Twenty-fifth Annual Preliminary Report of the Municipal Voters' League (1920).
Chicago History Museum.

West, Patricia Scott. "Press Coverage of Urban Violence, 1903–1967." PhD diss.,
University of Southern Mississippi, 2003.

INDEX